Intersubjective Processes and th

Intersubjective Processes and the Unconscious looks at how the minds of the psychoanalyst/psychotherapist and the patient interact with each other in a profound and unconscious way: a concept first described by Freud.

This book expands Freud's ideas further and examines how these have been greatly elaborated by contributions from the Kleinian School as well as from the work of Bion. It explores how, together, patient and therapist co-create a narrative through these unconscious intersubjective processes. Topics of discussion include:

- the unconscious dimensions of intersubjective processes
- an historical overview of Freudian, Kleinian and Bionian contributions
- an integrated theory of the nature of unconscious intersubjective processes
- the central importance of dreaming in intersubjective processes
- the clinical implications of this intersubjective model

The author offers in-depth clinical examples and case vignettes to illustrate the application of these principles when working with trauma, countertransference dreams and supervision. As such, this book will be invaluable to all psychoanalysts and psychotherapists interested in the topic of intersubjectivity as well as those who want to learn more about the interactional dimensions of Freud, Klein and Bion.

Lawrence J. Brown is a graduate of the Boston Psychoanalytic Society and Institute (BPSI) in both Child and Adult psychoanalysis. He is on the faculty of BPSI as well as the Massachusetts Institute for Psychoanalysis and also a Clinical Instructor in Psychiatry at Harvard Medical School. He has been on the North American Editorial Board of the *International Journal of Psychoanalysis* and is currently on the Editorial Board of *Psychoanalytic Inquiry*. He was also Co-chair of the Bion in Boston 2009 international conference.

THE NEW LIBRARY OF PSYCHOANALYSIS
General Editor Dana Birksted-Breen

The New Library of Psychoanalysis was launched in 1987 in association with the Institute of Psycho-Analysis, London. It took over from the International Psychoanalytical Library, which published many of the early translations of the works of Freud and the writings of most of the leading British and Continental psychoanalysts.

The purpose of the New Library of Psychoanalysis is to facilitate a greater and more widespread appreciation of psychoanalysis and to provide a forum for increasing mutual understanding between psychoanalysts and those working in other disciplines such as the social sciences, medicine, philosophy, history, linguistics, literature and the arts. It aims to represent different trends both in British psychoanalysis and in psychoanalysis generally. The New Library of Psychoanalysis is well placed to make available to the English-speaking world psychoanalytic writings from other European countries and to increase the interchange of ideas between British and American psychoanalysts. Through the *Teaching Series*, the New Library of Psychoanalysis now also publishes books that provide comprehensive, yet accessible, overviews of selected subject areas aimed at those studying psychoanalysis and related fields such as the social sciences, philosophy, literature and the arts.

The Institute, together with the British Psychoanalytical Society, runs a low-fee psychoanalytic clinic, organizes lectures and scientific events concerned with psychoanalysis and publishes the *International Journal of Psychoanalysis*. It also runs the only UK training course in psychoanalysis which leads to membership of the International Psychoanalytic Association – the body which preserves internationally agreed standards of training, of professional entry, and of professional ethics and practice for psychoanalysis as initiated and developed by Sigmund Freud. Distinguished members of the Institute have included Michael Balint, Wilfred Bion, Ronald Fairbairn, Anna Freud, Ernest Jones, Melanie Klein, John Rickman and Donald Winnicott.

Previous General Editors include Dana Birksted-Breen, David Tuckett, Elizabeth Spillius and Susan Budd.

Previous and current Members of the Advisory Board include Christopher Bollas, Ronald Britton, Catalina Bronstein, Donald Campbell, Sara Flanders, Stephen Grosz, John Keene, Eglé Laufer, Alessandra Lemma, Juliet Mitchell, Michael Parsons, Rosine Jozef Perelberg, Mary Target and David Taylor.

The current General Editor of the New Library of Psychoanalysis is Alessandra Lemma, but this book was initiated and edited by Dana Birksted-Breen, former General Editor.

ALSO IN THIS SERIES

TITLES IN THE NEW LIBRARY OF PSYCHOANALYSIS
TEACHING SERIES

NEW LIBRARY OF PSYCHOANALYSIS

General Editor: Dana Birksted-Breen

Intersubjective Processes and the Unconscious

An Integration of Freudian, Kleinian
and Bionian Perspectives

Lawrence J. Brown

Routledge
Taylor & Francis Group

LONDON AND NEW YORK

First published 2011
by Routledge
27 Church Road, Hove, East Sussex BN3 2FA

Simultaneously published in the USA and Canada
by Routledge
270 Madison Avenue, New York, NY 10016

Routledge is an imprint of the Taylor & Francis Group, an Informa Business

Typeset in Times by RefineCatch Limited, Bungay, Suffolk
Printed and bound in Great Britain by TJ International, Padstow, Cornwall
Cover design by Sandra Heath

This publication has been produced with paper manufactured to strict environ-
mental standards and with pulp derived from sustainable forests.

British Library Cataloguing in Publication Data
A catalogue record for this book is available from the British Library

Library of Congress Cataloguing in Publication Data
Brown, Lawrence J., 1946–
Intersubjective processes and the unconscious : an integration of Freudian,
Kleinian, and Bionian perspectives / Lawrence J. Brown.
  p. cm. — (New library of psychoanalysis)
Includes bibliographical references and index.
ISBN 978–0–415–60699–8 (hardback : alk. paper) —
ISBN 978–0–415–60700–1 (pbk. : alk. paper)   1. Psychoanalysis.
2. Subconsciousness.   3. Klein, Melanie.   4. Bion, Wilfred R. (Wilfred
Ruprecht), 1897–1979.   5. Freud, Sigmund, 1856–1939. I. Title.
BF173.B833 2010
150.19′5—dc22

ISBN: 978–0–415–60699–8 (hbk)
ISBN: 978–0–415–60700–1 (pbk)

Dedication

This book is dedicated to:

THE PAST: Pearl and Isie
THE PRESENT: Fran, Tamara, Steve, Ariel, Anne
THE FUTURE: Anya and Leo

Contents

Contents

Foreword

James S. Grotstein

Lawrence Brown's work is a tour de force. It is an invaluable and timely monograph on one of the most important – if not *the* most important – paradigm changes in analytic technique to date. He has chosen to explicate the evolution of countertransference, its ultimate "marriage" to transference, and, together, their virtual absorption by intersubjectivity. His work is quantitatively encyclopedic in its range and is qualitatively pleasingly and eloquently written. He traces the development of the genomes of intersubjectivity and countertransference from their source to their current variegated use by different analytic schools. In the course of his in-depth investigation, Brown takes up the epigenesis of the one-person to the two person model of psychoanalytic technique and, along with it, the history of the development of interest in the countertransference, how the latter ultimately came to be indivisibly attached to the transference, and how the two-person model prevailed and, along with countertransference, came to be embraced within the now-supraordinate concept of intersubjectivity. The real transition in the evolution of technique from the one-person to the two-person mode was the shift in emphasis from the analyst's objectively attributing significance to the hidden meanings within the *text* of the patient's free associations to allowing him/herself to become part of the ongoing *process* as a coparticipant along with the analysand in the analytic "play."

The search for clinical truth in the psychoanalytic session thus shifted from an objective *translation* of the analysand's free associations, which reflected recent or historic reconstructions, to the *here-and-now verdict of living emotional truth* provided by the analyst's recognition of his or her own emotional experience while listening to the analysand. Clinical enactments, whether by analysand or analyst, now became baptized as worthy and legitimate analytic evidence and were considered to be inevitable and even necessary occurrences that offered valuable clues about the analysis. The history behind these developments comes very much alive in Brown's telling of their story.

How this all came about is the subject of Brown's virtually encyclopedic history of the scattered origins of psychoanalysis' step-child. It is wondrous, first of all, that Freud himself had been clearly alert to the communicative value of the countertransference, as had his followers, Abraham, Ferenczi, Reik, and others. Its positive value had been noted but not sufficiently emphasized, largely, perhaps, because of early considerations of ethics and propriety on the one hand and of "objective" scientific acceptance on the other. Ultimately, countertransference achieved widespread acceptance, along with enactments, as valid and useful unconscious communications and revelations.

But what of the relationship between the "transference ↔ countertransference situation" and "intersubjectivity"? This is how Brown helps us to understand the history behind their intertwining involvement. He details the all-but-overlooked emergence of a newly conceived function of the unconscious ego once Freud moved from his first topography of the psychic apparatus to his second topography of the structural model: from Systems *Ucs.*, *Pcs.*, and *Cs.* to id, ego, and superego, in which the former interpenetrated the latter. This change now made the System *Ucs.* more complex – that is, it now contained an id (primary process) and an unconscious ego (secondary process). It allowed for the unconscious ego to be conceived of as a cryptic "thinker" in its own right, one functioning according to the reality – not the pleasure – principle, as did the id.

By attributing reality-principle functions to the unconscious ego, not only did the formation of dreams become more understandable – that is, co-created by the reality principle and the pleasure principle, a change that Bion (1962) was to take advantage of with his concepts of alpha function and dreaming – but room could now be made for the conception of a sentient *unconscious subjectivity* within the analysand who could be cryptically (preconsciously) in contact with its corresponding subjective receptor site in the analyst.[1] This cryptic intersubjective contact had come to be known as "*the transference ↔*

countertransference situation" (meant as an indivisible or irreducible unit); however, analysts from different schools seemed to have noted that transference ↔ countertransference occurs unconsciously between two covert but highly organized sentient as well as emotional *subjectivities*, and thus the concept of "intersubjectivity" emerged as the overarching idea and one that mediated the activities and functioning of the former. We must remember that Freud (1915) believed that the System *Ucs.* lacked subjectivity. His structural theory replaced his belief without his formally acknowledging it, and unconscious sentient and intuitive subjectivity was founded. Let me state the significance of this change in another way. Now that one could conceive of an unconscious ego, the next inescapable step was to conceive of one or more discrete (unconscious) personalities with the inherent capacity to *think* thoughts and to *process* thoughts and emotional experiences. This cryptic subjectivity(ies) constitutes a subpersonality in its own right, one that we do not know but who knows us. Winnicott foretold this unconscious communication in his "Primary Maternal Preoccupation" (1956).

The intersubjective > transference ↔ countertransference models have evolved into even more significant concepts. Brown's research has taken him to the post-Kleinians in London, to the American ego psychologists and interpersonalists, as well as to South America, where interest in countertransference has had a long and distinguished history. He explicates in particular the work of Racker (1968) and of the Barangers (1961–62) ("The River Plate Group"), the latter of whom originated the concept of the "analytic field." My way of understanding the analytic field involves the contributions of Bion (1961) on groups; McDougall (1985), Lothane (2009), and myself (Grotstein, 1979, 2009b) on the concept that the analytic session constitutes a theatrical play ("The play's the thing / wherein I'll catch the conscience of the king"); Ferro's (1999) concept of "narrative"; and Ogden's (1994) "intersubjective (and 'subjugating') third subject of analysis." Because of space limitations, I shall confine my discussion to Bion's theory of groups, to which the Barangers are indebted (Antonino Ferro, personal communication). Bion (1992) states that the human being has two personalities: the "narcissist" (the individual) and the "socialist" (the group personality). He also believes that there is no such thing as group psychology – there is only the psychology of (group) personalities within a group. Conclusion: the psychoanalytic session constitutes individual analysis in a dialectic with group analysis, the two together comprising an analytic field or theater for transference ↔ countertransference, enactments, and the construction of narratives. This new analysis is less interested in historical reconstructions than it is in the current intersubjective co-constructive partnership – that is, in the co-constructed narrative *in* the moment *about* the moment.

In the excitement of the fateful arrival and acceptance of the two-person model, we must not forget the one-person model. In the final analysis, the ultimate arbiter is the analysand's own unconscious – that is, how he or she experiences and "internalizes" the results of the interaction with the analyst. The intersubjective nature of the psychoanalytic process does not free the analysand from the obligation to accept sole responsibility for how he or she views and contributes to the interaction. I term this principle the "psychoanalytic legacy of solitude" (Grotstein, 2009a). It is to Brown's credit that he has not forsaken the one-person model in his enthusiasm to reveal the two-person model.

Note

1   In other contributions I have conceived of "the ineffable subject of the unconscious," which is also known as "the dreamer who dreams the dream" and "the dreamer who understands the dream" (Grotstein, 1979, 1981, 2000).

References

Baranger, M., & Baranger, W. (1961–62). The analytic situation as a dynamic field. *International Journal of Psychoanalysis*, 89 (2008, No. 4): 795–826.

Bion, W. R. (1961). *Experiences in Groups*. London: Routledge/Tavistock Publications.

Bion, W. R. (1962). *Learning from Experience*. London: Heinemann.

Bion, W. R. (1992). *Cogitations*. London: Karnac, 1994.

Ferro, A (1999). *Psychoanalysis as Therapy and Storytelling*. London/New York: Routledge.

Fliess, R. (1942). The metapsychology of the analyst. *Psychoanalytic Quarterly*, 11: 211–227.

Freud, S. (1915). The unconscious. *Standard Edition*, 14: 159–215.

Freud, S. (1923). *The Ego and the Id. Standard Edition*, 19: 3–66.

Grotstein, J. (1979). Who is the dreamer who dreams the dream, and who is the dreamer who understands it? *Contemporary Psychoanalysis*, 15(1): 110–169. Revised version in J. S. Grotstein (Ed.), *Do I Dare Disturb the Universe? A Memorial to Wilfred R. Bion*. Beverly Hills, CA: Caesura Press, 1981, pp. 357–416.

Grotstein, J. (2000). *Who Is the Dreamer Who Dreams the Dream? A Study of Psychic Presences*. Hove: Routledge.

Grotstein, J. (2009a). *". . . But at the Same Time and on Another Level . . . ": Psychoanalytic Theory and Technique in the Kleinian/Bionian Mode, Vol. 1*. London: Karnac.

Grotstein, J. (2009b). "The play's the thing wherein I'll catch the conscience of the king": Psychoanalysis as a passion play. In A. Ferro & R. Basile (Eds.), *The Analytic Field: A Clinical Concept*. London: Karnac.

Lothane, Z. (2009). Dramatology in life, disorder, and psychoanalytic therapy: A further contribution to interpersonal psychoanalysis. *International Forum of Psychoanalysis*, 18: 125–148.

McDougall, J. (1985). *Theatres of the Mind: Illusion and Truth on the Psychoanalytic Stage*. New York: Brunner/Mazel.

Ogden, T. (1994). *Subjects of Analysis*. Northvale, NJ: Jason Aronson.

Racker, H. (1968). *Transference and Countertransference*. London: Hogarth Press.

Winnicott, D. W. (1956). Primary maternal preoccupation. In *Collected Papers: Through Paediatrics to Psycho-Analysis*. New York: Basic Books, 1958, pp. 300–305.

Acknowledgements

I would like to thank the many excellent teachers from whom I have had the good fortune to learn at the Menninger Clinic and at the Boston Psychoanalytic Society and Institute. I am also indebted to the many local Boston, national, and international colleagues who have helped sustain a rich psychoanalytic milieu over the course of my career. A special gratitude goes out to the members of the Klein/Bion Study Group at the Massachusetts Institute for Psychoanalysis: we have nurtured and grown with each other.

Immeasurable thanks also to my wife whose support in this project gave me the freedom and space to think and write.

A thank you as well to Dana Birksted-Breen for her guidance and advice; much appreciation, too, for the Routledge editorial staff, whose friendly emails helped immensely with the tedious details of preparing the manuscript.

I also wish to thank the *International Journal of Psychoanalysis* for permission to use my (2006) paper, "Julie's Museum: The Evolution of Thinking, Dreaming and Historicization in the Treatment of Traumatized Patients," 87: 1569–1585, and the paper I wrote with Dr. Martin Miller (2002), "The Triadic Intersubjective Matrix in Supervision: The Use of Disclosure to Work Through Painful Affects," 83: 811–823.

Finally, thank you to the *Psychoanalytic Quarterly* for permission to use my (2007) paper, "On Dreaming One's Patient: Reflections on an Aspect of Countertransference Dreams," 76: 835–861, my (2009) paper, "The Ego Psychology of Wilfred Bion: Implications for an Intersubjective View of Psychic Structure," 78: 27–55, and some portions of my (2002) paper, "The Early Oedipal situation: Developmental, Theoretical and Clinical Implications," 71: 273–300.

1

Introduction

No one who, like me, conjures up the most evil of those half-tamed demons that inhabit the human breast, and seeks to wrestle with them, can expect to come through the struggle unscathed.

(Freud, 1905a, p. 109)

This book represents an attempt to explore the nature of *intersubjective processes* from a particular theoretical framework – an integration of primarily Freudian, Kleinian, and Bionian perspectives – that typically has not been associated with the terms "intersubjectivity" or "inter-subjective." However, I will argue that embedded in these traditions are theoretical and clinical stances that describe and offer the reader a deep understanding of the nature of intersubjective *processes*, which in their essence are unconscious in nature. These processes are extra-ordinarily complex and, operating under the "radar" of conscious awareness, rapidly engage the psyches of analyst and patient in the creation of a jointly constructed narrative that either removes the cloak of repression from forgotten memories or ascribes meaning to experience for which no language previously existed.

I will begin with a brief, though highly condensed, vignette that quickly came to mind when I sat before my computer and started to gather my thoughts for the project before me. I immediately thought about a poignant session from the analysis of a young boy I treated a few years ago. In addition to the powerful emotions evoked in the analytic hour, I also felt a sense of many disparate thoughts, writings, and personal experiences about intersubjectivity suddenly falling into place as though a kaleidoscope's fragments had unexpectedly taken the form of a stained-glass design. It became clear that, as Beebe, Knoblauch, Rustin, and Sorter (2004) have said, there are many forms of intersubjectivity, and yet it seemed that all these were present in the encounter with Sam.

Sam, 4½ years old, was in analysis for aggressive behavior at home and school. His mother was regularly overwhelmed by his behavior and struggled to set appropriate limits, often feeling like a single parent because her husband was frequently very depressed. Sam's father was a fragile man who had been hospitalized for depression on numerous occasions, and the family tended to walk on eggshells around him. Despite what appeared to be an inability to control his anger, Sam showed a remarkable capacity to rein himself in while with his father. He was often provocative with me, and his play consisted of repetitive variations on aggressive themes.

Sam began the session in a typical manner, dumping all the dinosaurs and action figures onto the analytic couch, which was the arena for battle. Gradually we each gathered an army and then arranged the figures according to fighting skill. As usual, Sam's fighters easily trounced mine, and I was left feeling predictably demoralized. I repeated some of the interpretations of this play that addressed how my men had all the "losing feelings" that felt really bad and made them angry, and that his men were lucky to be so strong and have all the exciting "winning feelings." Sam shrugged his shoulders and said, unimpressed, "yeah, I guess."

At one point I decided to withdraw my men to the desk a few feet away, saying that they needed a break. As I moved my pieces to the desk I noticed that there was an incoming telephone call, and the caller ID indicated that it was from the hospital in New York where my mother was then a patient. I immediately became quite worried, since she was very ill with congestive heart failure. I am not sure what my expression looked like, nor do I know how long I was actively distracted. Nevertheless, I quickly came out of my distraction and said, probably with a somewhat forced exuberance, "Ok, let's get back to the battle!" However, Sam said that he wanted to play something different, and he introduced a theme that had never previously appeared. He said that he was going to be a "mummy," and I heard "mommy." "Mommy?" I asked, and he corrected me, "No, mummy – you know those creepy guys with the bandages wrapped all over them" and pretended to have unraveled, ragged gauze dropping off him. I dismissed

2

my mishearing him as an artifact of worry about my "mommy" and let the play unfold.

Sam said that the mummy had to be buried, lifted up the couch mattress, and began to inter himself between the mattress and the wooden slats it rested on. I was a bit disoriented, in the midst of what felt like an uncanny experience (Freud, 1919). I said something about how dead mummies are buried in a grave just like he was showing me and that's very scary and sad. Sam quickly replied that this mummy "wasn't really dead; it was an alive mummy that used to be dead." I was relieved at hearing this, though I was not aware in the moment why it affected me this way. I said, "when a mummy that used to be dead becomes alive again the people who love that mummy aren't so scared and sad anymore." Now in an excited state, he went over to the desk drawer where the supplies are kept, took out a roll of scotch tape, and asked that I wrap him in it so he could be like a real mummy.

This very brief, but complex, vignette is a multilayered intersubjective precipitate of the interaction between Sam and me that occurred on conscious, preconscious, and unconscious levels. Though this book will explore such intersubjective exchanges on all planes of consciousness, it is my belief that *intersubjectivity is based upon, and is largely comprised of, processes that are a constant unconscious companion to what is occurring on a conscious level*. The session begins with a repetitive game of competition and defeat that left me feeling consciously demoralized, which I interpreted with the comment about the "losing feelings" being in me. However, on this particular day, for reasons of which I was unaware at that moment, I withdrew from the play to my desk. Why on this particular day was I unable to tolerate the demoralized and "losing feelings?" In retrospect, my receptivity to these emotions was most likely curtailed by worries about my mother that were lurking preconsciously and left me closed to "losing" feelings. My telephone emits an almost imperceptible clicking sound when a call is coming in, and, although I was not aware of hearing that, it must have registered an alarm that brought me to my desk rather than stay with Sam. Thus, on this particular afternoon, there was a unique alignment of conscious, preconscious, and unconscious events that defined a singular moment in a fleeting emotional field that Sam and I shared.

I suspect that in my withdrawal I became for Sam his withdrawn and depressed father, a perception of me that was galvanized by the likelihood that he sensed my troubled response to the call from my mother's hospital. Thus, for Sam, the analytic situation had devolved into a familiar conundrum: what to do with a depressed father/ analyst? Although I tried to get us back to the play, it was clear that Sam and I had crossed an emotional Rubicon from which we could not return. Here we can see that Sam was very attuned to my mood and appeared to unconsciously interpret my momentary unavail- ability in the light of experience with his father. Given his propensity to be carefully attuned to his father's emotional states, it is not surpris- ing that he sensed my distress at the telephone message. He picked up this distress signal and worked on it unconsciously to transform it into a play theme that was meant to comfort his sad father/analyst as well as himself.

I should add that this book is not a volume on technique, and I am aware that there are alternative points of view regarding the technical handling of this interaction with Sam. My purpose with this vignette is to convey the nearly instantaneous ways in which Sam and I are cueing each other that in the moment remain preconscious at best. It was this kind of exchange that, subsequent to unraveling what was being expressed in the session, permitted me later to interpret to Sam how worried he was about his father and how the feelings felt too big for him when his mother got overwhelmed (as well as how these affects were manifest in the transference). These kinds of rapid-fire encounters were frequent in the earlier parts of his analysis and were necessary preliminary steps before I could offer an interpretation aimed at helping Sam become consciously aware of his powerful emotions.

Sam's introduction of the *mummy* character[1] signaled the start of a process of mutual regulation of affects, which was accomplished through the shared narrative that we unconsciously spun together. The fascinating question is, how did Sam's unconscious, through its collaboration with my mine, choose the mummy out of a myriad of potential characters? The mummy figure seems to be a condensation of my worry about my *mommy* and his worry, in the moment, about his distressed analyst/father. If he had been solely focused on my emotional state, then he might have conjured a story about bringing back to life a dying mother. I thought he was doing just that when I heard *mommy*, but then he made it clear that he referred to a *mummy*, which is a masculine figure. I believe that Sam's description of the ragged mummy must have conveyed his unconscious perception of me as his somewhat emotionally disheveled father/analyst. But what about the maternal implications of the *mummy* character, and did Sam sense, through some ill-defined channel of unconscious communication, my dread of losing my mother?

It is uncanny that Sam's attunement was so refined as to pick up the "signals" of being anxious about one's mother. Is there a designated unconscious "wavelength" along which concerns about one's mother are transmitted? Or, to use another metaphor, are there specific pheromones that are emitted by one's mind when that psyche is disquieted by possible maternal loss? Are such messages encoded in the panoply of *wild thoughts* (Bion, 1997) that include rhythmic and other apparently extraneous experiences, which actually may be carriers of vital meaning? It is also likely that Sam's well-honed attunement was a necessary adaptation (Hartmann, 1958) developed to keep aware of his mother's overwhelmed states in order to help regulate his and her emotional world. In this regard, Sam was probably well acquainted with the "signals" associated with worry about one's mother, and his unconscious quickly identified such signals emanating from me.

Thus, the *mummy* was a highly condensed character that was born out of the analytic intercourse of the transmitting and receptive unconscious work we were doing together. Owing to the unique adaptations that Sam had to make to his father's depression and his mother's tendency to be overcome with emotion, he brought to the analytic encounter a finely sharpened sensitivity to my emotional states. Regardless of the means by which he sensed my anxiety about maternal loss, he transformed this affect into something less scary for me: a masculine *mummy* rather than a feminine *mommy*. Simultaneously, the mummy appeared to represent Sam's perception of my tattered emotional state that was linked with his experience of his father.

At this point in the hour, I was feeling somewhat disoriented and grew concerned that the sadness in the room was too much to bear for Sam (probably my projection) when he said he was going to bury the mummy. However, my interpretation that "dead mummies are buried in a grave just like he was showing me and that's very scary and sad" was clearly off, because he responded with "this mummy wasn't really dead; it was an alive mummy that used to be dead." I felt relieved at hearing this, or, put another way, Sam's response to the interpretation transformed my pain into something more hopeful.

Additionally, on another level, he had restored his transferential father's mood while simultaneously diminishing his mother/analyst's overwhelmed state. However, all this "magical" alchemy of transmuting his analyst/father/mother, and rescuing himself from a fate of being without any parental figures to regulate his emotional world, appeared to have triggered an excited manic state. Thus, he took out the scotch tape and asked me to wrap him up – that is, it was now my turn, having been restored by Sam to my analytic competence, to contain him. His mummy play was partly aimed at restoring his analyst's emotional equilibrium, but it was also expressive of his being a small boy burdened by very big feelings without the parental support he required to contain and transform his emotions.

So, what do we learn about the nature of intersubjectivity from this brief, but richly complex, vignette? In simplest terms, it refers to how the minds of the analyst and patient interact with, and affect, each other. In addition, the encounter with Sam showed that intersubjectivity refers to an exchange between the conscious, preconscious, and unconscious systems of each participant in the analytic dyad. There is a continuous streaming communication between these three levels of awareness in the analyst and those in the patient. For example, while Sam and I were engaged in conscious conversation ("my men need a break," as I moved to the desk) there was a simultaneous unconscious dialogue (analyst: "I am not in the mood for any more 'losing feelings'"; patient: "That's ok, I'll talk about *mummy*, not ,").

In addition, a shared emotional field is created through a unique blending of conscious, preconscious and unconscious experiences in the analyst and patient. Sam began the session in a typical manner by defeating my soldiers and projecting "losing feelings" into me that, on that particular day, I was unable to tolerate. I was unable to bear them because of fears about my mother's health percolating preconsciously and likely magnified by subliminally hearing the telephone click. Sensing my dysphoria, I was equated in Sam's unconscious with his depressed father, thereby repeating a familiar loss for him. Thus, a shared emotional field arose defined by anxiety about parental loss.

Intersubjectivity also consists of a process of mutual affective attunement and regulation that is a means of unconsciously working on the shared emotional field through the co-creation of a narrative. Sam's unconscious quickly went to work to modify the shared experience of anxiety about parental loss by bringing the mummy character on the conscious stage. This seemed to be an effort to regulate his analyst's troubled mood by offering me a *mummy* who "wasn't really dead; it was an alive mummy that used to be dead," a statement that I found reassuring. The masculine nature of the mummy also seemed to represent a maneuver to comfort himself at the temporary loss of his disheveled (depressed) analyst/father. In my statement that "when a mummy that used to be dead becomes alive again the people who love that mummy aren't so scared and sad anymore," I was consciously elaborating our collective story further with an interpretation meant to soothe Sam, but I was unconscious of also consoling myself.

Furthermore, intersubjectivity is a process of unconscious communication, receptivity, and meaning making within each member of the dyad to bring idiosyncratic signification to the shared emotional field that interacts with an analogous function in the partner. I have been emphasizing that intersubjective exchanges occur on a mostly unconscious level and that Sam and I were engaged in collaborative unconscious work to create meaning out of our collective emotional field. This transaction begins first with our individual constructions of the field – mine primarily of maternal loss and his of paternal absence – that are conveyed verbally and nonverbally to each other. Having received these messages, a process begins of mutual attunement and regulation that is accomplished through the rapid back-and-forth threading of a conjoint story made up from emotional themes contributed by each member of the analytic dyad. In my view, this is accomplished through the cooperative efforts of an aspect of our unconscious egos working in tandem.

This unconscious communication between analysand and analyst travels along many pathways including linguistic, pictographic, "extraneous" experiences (random thoughts, unbidden tunes), bodily sensations, and other yet to be understood channels that, from a mystical point of view, may be called telepathic. In the intersubjective domain, words uttered deliberately may carry disparate meanings for each member of the dyad – that is, Sam's use of *mummy* that registered with me as "mommy." The significance of what Sam intended did not reach me until he described the ragged mummy, a graphic pictogram that transmitted his unconscious view of me as his emotionally disarrayed analyst. It remains a mystery how he was attuned to signals emanating from me of apprehension about my mother and also how, and by which channels, such signals were broadcast. One is tempted to attribute such phenomena to telepathy, which Freud (1922) attempted to discuss without confirming or denying its existence. He asserted that if it did exist, the "laws of unconscious mental life may then be taken for granted as applying to telepathy" (p. 220) and that there is an "incontestable fact that sleep creates favorable conditions for telepathy" (p. 220). I leave aside the riddle of whether telepathy is a fact and emphasize that *what is enigmatic in the intersubjective encounter has mainly to do with the qualities of the unconscious in general, and specifically the characteristics of dreaming.*

The co-created narrative, ideally weighted more heavily in the direction of the patient's difficulties, not only owes its lineage to the psychic issues of each partner activated at the moment, but also contains, in part, a highly distilled historical record of each individual's family history. In the session with Sam, my receptivity to "losing feelings" was diminished by my distress that put him into a familiar situation of being with a depressed father whose emotional state required revitalizing. In addition, and on another level (Grotstein, 2009a, 2009b), I had likely become his emotionally overcome transferential mother. If there were a camera that recorded emotional emanations, and not those of light, we would have a snapshot of a moment in our analytic history together colored by the deep hues of melancholy, loss, and aloneness, with bursts of excited flashes of dreams of magical reparation. Thus, aspects of Sam's and my history concatenated at this point of interaction (Brown, 2004). However, both of us came into this world in the context of unique family histories stretching generations into the past; histories that formed around factual kernels, like a dream around a day residue, passed from parent to child through projective and introjective identifications and retold, reconfigured, and re-imagined in the mind's workshops – histories constantly in the making that come for a temporary rest and reappraisal in the analytic relationship.[2]

The intersubjective encounter, therefore, entails growth in both partners of the analytic dyad by virtue of the influence they have upon each other, an influence that is achieved through the reorganization of aspects of their respective psyches that occurs as unconscious work that is constantly renarrating the story of the analytic hour. Growth in analysis is achieved in small increments consisting of momentary shifts in the intersubjective field (Bion, 1967; Stern, 2004; Stern et al., 1998), which is defined by the unique ways each of the analytic couple is engaged in spinning a joint narrative that flows from the conscious, preconscious, and unconscious engagement they share.

Even when the analytic interaction is focused primarily on the patient's analysis (or the analyst's state of mind, as it was with Sam), the analyst's (or patient's) mind is perpetually undergoing some degree of reorganization as he is receptive to, and affected by, the analysand's (or analyst's) unconscious communications that are processed through the receiving mind. In the session presented, Sam was subliminally aware that his gloomy analyst/father was temporarily out of commission and "decided" to cheer me up with the mummy story that, in fact, did make me feel relieved. It was a well-practiced job at which he was skilled from many similar experiences with his father. Just like the play with the nearly interred mummy, he brought me back to life in the hour, thereby enabling me to interpret that things were less sad and scary when a mummy who appeared dead was really alive. Thus, our story about the mummy, initiated by Sam and elaborated by me, became the agent of change by which each of us was able to come to terms with our respective experience of the emotional field of loss through our cooperative "production" of the play sequence.

★   ★   ★

Although the term intersubjectivity tends to be associated with the American relational school, first used by Stolorow, Atwood, and Ross (1978), *intersubjective processes* have been described since the beginnings of psychoanalysis: witness Freud's (1905a) observation, cited at the head of this chapter, that analyst and patient are both deeply affected by the analytic endeavor. Indeed, Levine and Friedman (2000) assert that no analytic school can lay claim to intersubjectivity since it refers to an essential aspect of human relatedness. So while it is true that no analytic school has a "patent" on the term, it is also true that intersubjective concepts have been present in most of the major psychoanalytic frameworks of the clinical encounter. And just as the session with Sam was comprised of several kinds of interactions that fall under the heading of "intersubjective," various analytic teachings emphasize different aspects of this phenomenon.

I have several purposes in writing this book. My primary objective is to consider intersubjective experiences from the perspective of unconscious processes, namely unconscious phantasy, dreaming, and the formation of a jointly constructed narrative that emerges organically in the analytic hour after its creation unconsciously. I am aware that such an approach may leave out consideration of phenomena often associated with intersubjectivity by other authors, such as mutual recognition and authenticity (Benjamin, 2002, 2009), the authority of the analyst (Mitchell, 1998), the "myth" of free association (Hoffman, 2006), critiques of "neutrality" (Renik, 1995), to name just a few, but my intent is to stay focused on the unconscious dimensions. The primary theoretical orientation in this book is one that combines classical Freudian, ego psychological, Kleinian, and Bionian points of view. While clustering these analysts together may seem like creating strange bedfellows to some, these viewpoints have been areas of interest in my professional career; therefore, a second aim of this book is to explore the implicit intersubjective framework inherent in these theories and to bring them into bold relief. I do not intend to be one of "those defending the classical approach . . . that the new [intersubjective] school's major tenets have been there all along" (Friedman, 2009, p. 1207); however, I firmly believe that a concentrated look at intersubjectivity from the vertex of unconscious processes can broaden our understanding of such phenomena.

A third purpose is to explore the history of *intersubjective processes* and to try to trace the lineage of these ideas from their inception in Freud's work through the present. This is a journey that will take us from Victorian Vienna to a less buttoned-down Berlin of the 1920s, to Kleinian London, to the safe havens from the Nazi terror in North and South America, and including some brief stops in contemporary Italy and France. A fourth purpose is to offer an integrated theory of intersubjectivity that takes into account each of these psychoanalytic perspectives. Finally, since intersubjectivity essentially refers to the clinical interaction, I will, for the most part, stay close to analytic experience with patients as the primary data upon which our theories are built and by which they are tested. Thus, most chapters will feature extensive analytic material on which the ideas are based in order to illustrate the thing (intersubjectivity) itself as it appears in the analyst's consulting room.

This book is organized into ten chapters. Chapters 2, 3, and 4 explore the contributions from the Freudian, Kleinian, and Bionian schools, respectively. This is a somewhat artificial division since there is considerable mutual influence between the schools. Nevertheless, despite the overlap between these points of view, it is useful for didactic purposes to keep them separate. Special attention is paid to the origin of certain ideas and how these are expanded upon from one generation to the next (Kancyper, 2005). For example, Freud's theory of dreaming was productively widened by some European analysts of the 1930s and 1940s by the study of ego factors in dreaming and of dream-like ego states, which led to the investigation of preconscious phenomena that are akin to what Bionians today call *reverie*. However, for complicated reasons (see Chapter 2), contemporary ego psychologists of the 1950s and 1960s were dismissive of these earlier explorations of the analyst's subjectivity; hence, traditional American analysis took a turn in the direction of examining the work of the unconscious ego in defense. The study of unconscious processes (other than the unconscious part of the ego) was largely left to Kleinian writers in the United Kingdom and South America. It was only much later with Bion's enlargement of Freud's theory of dreaming that analysts were drawn back to a sustained focus on the legitimacy of the analyst's subjectivity as worthy of consideration in the psychoanalytic situation.

Chapter 2 explores Freud's ideas about unconscious communication between the analyst and patient. Many of his ideas about the unconscious collaboration between the analytic couple are remarkably contemporary. Karl Abraham, a member of Freud's inner circle from Berlin, also plays an important role in the genesis of concepts that evolved into the idea of intersubjectivity. Several of his analysands (Robert Fliess, Melanie Klein, and Theodore Reik) have significantly extended our understanding of how the analyst and patient affect each other. Chapter 3 addresses the legacy of Melanie Klein and her followers. Though she did not reject Freud's drive theory, her emphasis on the importance of phantasy offered a view of the unconscious populated by various interpersonal presences (Brown, 1996), and, by introducing projective identification, she opened the door to understanding how the minds of analyst and patient affect each other. Though she was loath (Spillius, 2007) to use countertransference as an aid to understanding the analysand, her successors – from Money-Kyrle to Racker to Bion – have been instrumental in crafting our modern views on the subject.

In Chapter 4, I discuss Bion's theory of *alpha* (α) *function* and argue that it is an aspect of the unconscious ego that accounts for unconscious communication. It is that aspect of the ego that receives unconscious signals, processes these through the analyst's (or patient's) *reverie*, and transforms unprocessed affects into pictograms that are suitable for secondary-process thinking. I assert that the intersubjective exchange depends on the link between the communicating and receiving α functions of patient and analyst. Detailed clinical material from the analysis of an adolescent female is offered for illustration.

Chapter 5 weaves together these various perspectives on intersubjectivity into an integrated theory. As a starting point, I see Freud's ideas about unconscious communication and his recommendation that the analyst use his unconscious "as an instrument of the analysis" (Freud, 1912) as essential bedrock. However, Freud never instructed the analyst how this is to be done or what the mechanisms of unconscious communication are. Klein's (1946) concept of projective identification, and especially Bion's (1958) delineation of its communicative aspects, provides us with a means of understanding how one unconscious communicates with another. Thus, the analyst's subjectivity becomes increasingly important, an emphasis that we see implicit in Kleinian writings and made more explicit by American relational and Bionian writers. In addition, I explore the role of the analyst's mind in the transformation of concrete emotional experience into abstract thoughts that may then be woven into meaningful narratives. Analytic material from the analysis of an adolescent male is offered to demonstrate growth in his capacity for representation as evidenced in his drawings. Chapter 6 explores intersubjectivity from a three-person, Oedipal point of view implicit in the work of Kleinian and Bionian authors as well as in some recent American relational contributions by Benjamin and Aron. These theories are compared, discussed, and integrated into a composite viewpoint.

In Chapters 7, 8, 9, and 10, I apply the integrated theory of intersubjectivity to different clinical situations. Chapter 7 focuses on severely traumatized patients who have seemingly lost the capacity for symbolic thought, including the inability to dream dreams that foster emotional growth. As a result, the patient is unable to historicize the trauma and requires the mind of the analyst to assist the analysand in recovering the capacity for thinking and dreaming. An extended clinical example is offered to demonstrate how these concepts are applied in the analysis of a severely traumatized woman. Chapter 8 deals with supervision and the ways in which a shared emotional field may develop that is unconsciously constituted by individual conflicts that the patient, analyst, and supervisor may share around an issue in the treatment that leads to a collective resistance. A clinical vignette is given to illustrate this phenomenon. Chapter 9 investigates the intersubjective dimensions of the countertransference dream. In addition to the possibility that such dreams indicate problems in the analytic relationship, I say that these dreams may also indicate the ways in which the analyst comes to know the analysand on a deep unconscious level by processing the communicative projective identifications. Two examples of countertransference dreams are presented to elucidate these points.

The book concludes with Chapter 10, which focuses on the central role dreaming plays in historicizing past experiences into a personal narrative. Under optimal conditions, a child has within him/herself an intersubjectively constructed internalized thinking/dreaming couple (Grotstein) that dreams and digests potentially traumatizing experiences. I discuss the analysis of a latency-age girl who revealed a repetitive dream of dangerous parental neglect during treatment and how this dream was lived out in her play and in the transference. The young analysand and I became a thinking couple who *dreamed* (in the ways described by Bion and Ogden) what previously she, on her own, was unable to emotionally process. I propose that this kind of dreaming is necessary for the operation of *Nachträglichkeit* and *après coup*, without which there cannot be any reworking of the past and there is little hope for a fresh future.

★   ★   ★

The mapping of the various branches of human history through the genome project offers a complex network of intersecting and diverging "highways" over which our ancestors traveled from their cradle in Africa to their ultimate homes across the earth:

> a small population of humans moved out of the [African] continent, then grew in size in a new home until another subgroup of "founders" broke off and moved away – a process that was repeated until the entire world was settled
>
> (Stix, 2008, p. 60)

This ancient pilgrimage we have all traversed may now be traced though each individual's genetic road map etched into his or her DNA material. The maternally inherited line of this trail is revealed through the DNA encoded in the mitochondria (energy-producing aspect) of the cells, while the male transmitted DNA is engraved in the Y-chromosomes. Interestingly, genetic diversity decreases the farther in its odyssey from African ancestral roots:

13

each time a smaller group split off, it carried only a subset of the genetic diversity originally present in the African population.

(Stix, 2008, p. 60)

Thus, as man's inexorable spread across the globe ultimately peopled even the remotest corners of the world, our original passage "out of Africa" was forgotten, though still registered in the strange hieroglyphics of our genetic language.

And so it was with the seeds of intersubjectivity that were initially sown at 19 Berggasse in Vienna, pollinating from there to the emerging psychoanalytic centers around the world. In instance after instance, "the 'founders' broke off and moved away," perhaps forgetting or actively denying their connection to roots that always wound back to Austria. Regardless of the tenacity with which new "founders" broke from their progenitor, Freud was present deep within their invisible psychoanalytic DNA, like a stem cell from which other manifestations develop. In addition to exploring the meaning of intersubjectivity, this book will attempt to trace the origins of *intersubjective processes* within and across varying psychoanalytic communities. I review the development of the concept of intersubjectivity as having evolved over successive psychoanalytic generations through a process of "inheritance" transmitted by identifications within each analytic tradition – and between those heritages as well – that has constantly refined our understanding of intersubjectivity through a kind of *Nachträglichkeit*, or *après coup*, of ideas.

Why has the intersubjective model become what appears to be the predominant approach of thinking about the psychoanalytic interchange? One way of looking at this question is to consider the relationship between our understanding of the transference/countertransference interplay and the emergence of intersubjectivity. The term "intersubjectivity," first used by Stolorow, Atwood, and Ross in 1978, referred to the link between transference and countertransference feelings, which Stolorow (1994) later characterized as the "reciprocal mutual interaction between the patient's transference and the analyst's transference" (p. 38). Grotstein (1999) states that "Countertransference has thankfully been transformed into intersubjectivity" (p. 191), an assertion that views intersubjectivity as an evolved version of the transference/countertransference linkage. Frie and Reis (2001) also see intersubjectivity as the wider concept and state

14

that "Intersubjectivity broadens for inclusion the analyst's subjective bodily states, reveries, and historical experiences in a way that does not reductively treat these as countertransference phenomena" (p. 324). Thus, Grotstein (a Kleinian/Bionian) and Frie and Reis (relational analysts) come to similar conclusions by viewing inter-subjectivity as having developed out of analytic exploration of the transference/countertransference dialogue.

It seems reasonable to hypothesize that intersubjectivity is a natural outgrowth of our investigation into countertransference that became a topic of earnest study beginning in the late 1940s with many published papers, but especially with Winnicott's (1949) "Hate in the Countertransference." He argued that the analyst's experience of hatred toward the analysand was frequently an expected – even necessary – part of the treatment, thus normalizing such feelings. More relevant to our consideration of intersubjectivity, Winnicott alludes indirectly to, but does not expand upon, the psychotic patient's subtle experience of the analyst's subjectivity: "a psychotic patient in analysis cannot be expected to tolerate his hate unless the analyst can hate him" (p. 74). In normalizing one's countertransference, he was reaping new knowledge that was gained from analytic work with psychotic patients, largely in the United Kingdom, that seemed to give the clinician "permission" to feel such previously taboo emotions toward his or her patient. Indeed, this pioneering work on the beneficial use of countertransference was always open to the criticism that it was a problem to be dealt with either in the analyst's analysis or through his or her self-analysis. In this regard, the concept of intersubjectivity does not carry with it the long history of stigma that has dogged the term countertransference.

But are some valuable psychoanalytic insights lost when we jettison the traditional understanding of countertransference as an impediment to the analysis in favor of the more inclusive view of an intersubjective approach? I hope to avoid the "straw man" of declaring as extinct psychoanalytic teachings that may seem outmoded when, in fact, these principles are our ancestral background. Rangell (2002) expressed concern about the tendency of intersubjective analysts (he was discussing Renik) to engage in self-disclosures that could be intrusive to the patient and bemoaned the diminished appreciation for the importance of the analyst's neutrality, which is "a frequent subject of caricature" (p. 1123). In Chapter 10, I discuss the usefulness of redefining the concept of *infantile neurosis* as a living and breathing entity in the here-and-now that is a preconception of one possible future, but which itself is constantly being redefined and reworked through a process of dreaming that underpins *après coup*. It is tempting to dismiss the view of countertransference as negative, neutrality as anachronistic, and the infantile neurosis as Victorian or, put another way, as "your father's Oldsmobile." Whatever one's opinion of these precepts, they nevertheless reside in every analyst's DNA, and though they may be on the endangered list of psychoanalytic ideas, their presence is palpable through their "negation" (Freud, 1925) by subsequent generations of analysts. My intention is for us to gain a thorough-going understanding of the essence of intersubjectivity, "the thing-itself" (Bion, 1965) – its history, its current status, and its clinical application. We may paraphrase Stix's (2008) statement, "Each time a smaller group split off, it carried only a subset of the genetic diversity originally present in the African population" with "Each time an analytic school split off, it carried with it, consciously or not, psychoanalytic ideas that originated in a consulting room at 19 Berggasse."

In addition to transcending some of the negative connotations of countertransference and *intersubjectivity* being "neutral" in the sense of not belonging to any one analytic persuasion, advances in infant observation bolster the wide acceptance of intersubjectivity as a model for analytic interaction. In contrast to Mahler, Pine, and Bergman's (1975) observations of separation–individuation in infancy, which did not emphasize the baby's role in shaping its interpersonal environment, contemporary researchers (Beebe et al., 2004; Salomonnson, 2007; Stern, 1985; Tronick, 2007) highlight the infant's mutual activity with its mother in initiating interactions of subtle cues that regulate each other affectively. These findings have added evidence to support a view of the analytic enterprise as an encounter between two psyches that are closely attuned to one another to co-create a shared emotional field to which each partner contributes. The kind of jointly constructed narrative that Sam and I established, in which both of us unconsciously conferred, is built upon successful early experiences of mother and infant regulating each other and making meaning together.

On a more speculative level, we may consider intersubjectivity in psychoanalysis as an analogue of changes in the broader social milieu. The cultures in Western democracies have grown more egalitarian, and there is a greater freedom to question authority than existed in previous generations. This shift on a societal level is matched by a parallel movement in psychoanalysis that questions the analyst as being the authority of what is "true" and replaces it with a vision of "truth"[3] as being mutually cobbled together by analyst and analysand. Indeed, in the wider culture the nature of what constitutes "truth" has also been challenged, and the concept of an "absolute truth" has largely been supplanted by the idea that supposed verities are relative and ever-changing. In psychoanalysis, the loss of the comfort of believing that there is one correct analytic technique is a source of anxiety for many candidates and for many graduate analysts as well (Wallerstein, 2005). And just as some cultures regress to forms of fundamentalism in response to a vacuum of absolutes, so psychoanalytic institutions are similarly prone to developing rigid systems in the face of evolving changes in theory and technique (Kernberg, 2006; Reeder, 2004). Addressing the profound global effects of the internet, Thomas Friedman (2005) writes in *The World Is Flat*:

> It created a global platform that allowed more people to plug and play, collaborate and compete, share knowledge and share work, than anything we have ever seen in the history of the world.
>
> (p. 158)

Similarly, an intersubjective orientation holds that knowledge is shared, that analyst and patient plug into their respective transmitting and receiving unconscious processes, and that they playfully engage in subliminal collaboration.

★   ★   ★

As I mentioned at the start of this chapter, the session with Sam had the effect of bringing together a variety of my observations, clinical experiences, and theoretical ideas about what constitutes intersubjectivity. Over the course of my training I have been fortunate to have been exposed to different theoretical schools taught by some outstanding teachers. I was a Postdoctoral Fellow in Clinical Psychology in the mid-1970s at the Menninger Clinic, an experience that has had a profound and lasting impact. The Fellows were privileged to benefit from a long line of outstanding thinkers and a rich heritage of psychological testing developed by David Rapaport, Roy Schafer, Martin Mayman, just to name a few. Ego psychology was the coin of that realm, coins adorned with the cameos of Hartmann, Kris, and

Loewenstein. Otto Kernberg, who had been the Chief of the C. F. Menninger Hospital, had moved to New York from Topeka a year before I arrived, and he left in his wake a very significant contribution to American psychoanalysis. Having been trained in Chile from a largely Kleinian perspective, he creatively integrated many aspects of ego psychology with elements of Klein, especially her observations of "primitive" defense mechanisms. These contributions opened the door to new treatment approaches to patients with "borderline personality organization" (Kernberg, 1967), a diagnosis that was formulated by integrating Kleinian object relations theory with Freudian structural concepts. This comparative and integrative methodology impressed me greatly and fit naturally with a current in my personality that aims at bringing things together. Though Kernberg left before I arrived in Topeka, he had brought many Kleinian colleagues from South America who remained in Kansas and became my teachers.

I moved to Boston to pursue psychoanalytic training at the Boston Psychoanalytic Society and Institute (BPSI) in adult and child psychoanalysis. The predominant orientation was ego–psychological in the early 1980s, and I received an excellent education in this tradition. However, my interest in the Kleinian school remained active, and upon graduating from the institute I began to teach Klein at BPSI, which, like many other institutes, had grown increasingly open to systems of thought that were not exclusively ego-psychological. My good friend and colleague, Jim Grotstein, encouraged me to read Bion, and I found myself immediately taken with his clunky sort of logic and brilliant insights into the nature of thinking. BPSI recently recruited me to teach ego psychology, which brought me back to my Menninger and early analytic-training roots, thereby permitting me to see some of Bion's ideas in a different light. It struck me that his theories of thinking were partly elaborations of some of Freud's ideas about the ego, so I wrote about Bion as an ego psychologist (Chapter 4), and it was rewarding to bring my comparative predilection to the paper.

Boston is fortunate to have three excellent psychoanalytic institutes: in addition to BPSI, there is the Psychoanalytic Institute of New England East (PINE); both of these are affiliated with the American and the International Psychoanalytic Associations. The third – the Massachusetts Institute for Psychoanalysis (MIP) – is an independent institute that defines itself as "comparative." I have also had the privilege to teach and supervise there, and the comparative atmosphere has engendered the founding of a Klein/Bion Study Group, which has now been meeting for over a dozen years. This group has been an important meeting place for its members, including myself, and has fostered a rich intellectual tradition coupled with a consistent focus on clinical psychoanalysis as well. In addition, MIP has a strong component of relational analysts, and this has been an opportunity to learn how clinicians in this tradition think about and treat patients.

In conclusion, this book represents my effort to explore the nature of intersubjectivity from multiple analytic perspectives that emphasize unconscious processes. I cannot cover every viewpoint on this subject, but a significant part of that territory is subsumed by the contributions from Freudian, Kleinian, and Bionian analysts. I hope that these efforts at developing an integrated theory of intersubjectivity do justice to the topic and that the chapters dealing with the clinical application of the model I propose are helpful illustrations. And now, in the spirit of the Chinese proverb, "Every journey begins with a first step," we turn our sights to Vienna, circa 1900.

Notes

1 Ferro (2002, 2005) discusses at length the spontaneous emergence of characters as signifying the collaborative unconscious transformation of affects in the analytic field into narrative themes. This is a central component of *intersubjective processes* and will be explored further in this book.

2 The question of how the personal history of the patient is reworked through *Nachträglichkeit* or *aprés coup* is addressed in depth by Davoine and Gaudilliere (2004) as well as by Faimberg (2005). I would add that the intersubjective exchange between analyst and patient may often involve a reconfiguring of aspects of the analyst's inner world. This is one of the main themes of the book and is discussed in much greater detail, especially in Chapters 2 and 8–10.

3 We will be revisiting the concept of "truth" in several of the chapters. "Truth" is used throughout the book to indicate *emotional truth*, i.e., what is felt to be true in the analytic hour. This may be experienced by the patient and/or by the analyst individually, and a shared (intersubjective) emotional truth may also exist, which was the case with Sam when we each unconsciously elaborated the shared emotional truth about parental absence and loss.

2

The analyzing instrument: unconscious communication and classical psychoanalysis

> ...he [the analyst] must turn his own unconscious like a receptive organ towards the transmitting unconscious of the patient. He must adjust himself to the patient as a telephone receiver is adjusted to the transmitting microphone. Just as the receiver converts back into sound waves the electrical oscillations in the telephone line which were set up by sound waves, so the doctor's unconscious is able, from the derivatives of the unconscious which are communicated to him, to reconstruct that unconscious, which has determined the patient's free associations.
>
> (Freud, 1912, pp. 115–116)

If there is a "big bang" statement from which the universe of intersubjectivity has emanated, it is the quote above from Freud's paper, "Recommendations to Physicians Practising Psycho-Analysis." It contains within it the basic elements from which the various factors that comprise the intersubjective exchange (see Chapter 1) have been constructed as they have evolved over the last century. This quote is sandwiched between Freud's discussion of how the analyst's "evenly suspended attention" is a correlate of the patient's "free associations" and his proposal that the analyst "use his unconscious . . . as an instrument in the analysis" (1912, p. 116). There is an implicit assumption that the "evenly suspended attention" of the analyst and the analysand's "free associations" are linked, though this linkage remains unexamined. Similarly, Freud leaves us tantalized by the notion of an unconscious that can be both "transmitting" as well as a "receptive organ." Furthermore, it is the analyst's unconscious that "is able . . . to reconstruct that unconscious, which has determined that patient's free associations" (p. 116). How does the unconscious achieve this understanding, and are we to assume that the patient's unconscious is similarly tuned into that of the analyst? And, finally, what did Freud have in mind when he said that the analyst "must adjust himself to the patient," advice that seems to counsel against a rigid one-size-fits-all approach to technique?

Note that Freud attributes these complex processes to an unconscious that is capable of encoding, transmitting, receiving, interpreting, and working collaboratively with another unconscious. In discussing the relationship between the unconscious and consciousness, Freud (1915c) states

> It is a very remarkable thing that the *Ucs.* of one human being can react upon that of another, without passing through the *Cs.*
>
> (p. 194)

Freud continues by saying that "This deserves closer investigation" (p. 194), but he proceeds to elaborate the interactions between the conscious, preconscious, and unconscious while leaving aside the question of how one mind unconsciously communicates with another. Indeed, Freud never returns to this topic, and it does not receive analytic attention again until the early 1940s. Instead, his writings, like those of other analysts of the period, are concerned with the intersystemic relations between the three levels of consciousness. Later, with the introduction of the structural theory (Freud, 1923a), he becomes largely focused in his metapsychological works on id, ego, and superego as well as concerned with the question of anxiety (Freud, 1926). Although Freud (1923a) located some part of the ego as unconscious, he did not deal with the possibility that this portion of the ego was involved in unconscious communication (see Chapters 4 and 5).

Before continuing with our inquiry into unconscious communication and the analyzing instrument, we must take a lateral detour to pick up some concepts from two of Freud's contemporaries that we will need as we move forward. Sándor Ferenczi, a member of

Freud's inner circle, was a close confidant and sometimes ambivalent friend; their quarter-century relationship is a poignant story of allegiances, conflict, and feelings of betrayal for both men. From the outset of their relationship, Ferenczi had wished for a greater "mutuality" between them and was frustrated by Freud's reluctance to engage in a reciprocal analysis. Indeed, the question of mutuality, which blurred the distinction between patient and analyst, dogged their friendship until Ferenczi's death in 1933. A major source of friction between Freud and Ferenczi was the latter's involvement with patients that experimented with shared disclosures, culminating, at the end of his career, with a technical innovation he called *mutual analysis* in which analyst and analysand took turns analyzing each other (Berman, 2004). While this approach was highly criticized by the analytic community, it was Ferenczi who broke new ground in elevating the important role of the analyst's mind as a factor in the analytic interaction and also exploring analyst disclosure.

However, Ferenczi also introduced concepts that were not controversial and have become accepted into the psychoanalytic canon. He (Ferenczi, 1909) coined the term *introjection* to describe a psychological mechanism that accounted for some of the dynamics of neurotic patients. Freud (1894) had already introduced the notion of *projection* in his analysis of the mechanisms of paranoia, and Ferenczi thought that

> Whereas the paranoic *expels from his ego* the impulses that have become unpleasant, the neurotic helps himself *by taking into the ego* as large as possible a part of the world. . . . One might give to this process, in contrast to projection, the name of Introjection.
>
> (Ferenczi, 1909, p. 47, italics added)

For Freud, projection was a means of unburdening the psyche of unwanted impulses, with no consideration given to the effect upon the object. Ferenczi, on the other hand, adds an object-relational component to his understanding of introjection:

> The neurotic is constantly seeking for objects with whom he can identify himself, to whom he can transfer feelings, whom he can thus draw into his circle of interest, i.e., introject.
>
> (pp. 47–48)

Projection and introjection later will be employed by subsequent generations of analysts as the means by which the individual psyche (including that of the analyst) relates to another mind and also how unconscious communication transmits and receives unconscious dispatches.

Ferenczi also pioneered the idea that countertransference may be put to a positive use. Freud (1910b) had admonished his followers to be wary of feelings toward the analysand and to suppress these:

> While the patient attaches himself to the physician, the physician is subject to a similar process, that of countertransference. This countertransference must be completely overcome by the analyst; only this will make him master of the psychoanalytic situation; it makes him the perfectly cool object who the other person must lovingly woo.
>
> (p. 447)

These comments to the Vienna Society are in apparent conflict with his statement two years later recommending that the analyst use his unconscious as an instrument of the analysis, and they reflect Freud's ambivalence about the analyst's subjective reactions, perhaps accounting for his lack of pursuing further a study of unconscious communication. Ferenczi had obviously been reflecting on Freud's proscription regarding countertransference when he wrote to Freud in 1911:

> Besides monitoring the countertransference, one must also pay heed to this "*being induced*" by the patients.
>
> (Ferenczi, 1911, p. 253, italics added)

The belief that countertransference is induced by the patient suggests a purposive aspect to this induction, though Ferenczi does not expand on this idea. Thus, Ferenczi gives us several important tools that will be vital in our understanding of intersubjectivity: his prompting us to consider issues of mutual influence between patient and analyst, introjection, the positive use of countertransference, and the notion that the patient may unconsciously seek to induce these countertransference feelings in the analyst.

Karl Abraham, a Berlin analyst and also one of Freud's inner circle, has significantly contributed to the conceptual foundation of intersubjectivity through his writings and, perhaps even more, through his

influential analysands. He was in the vanguard of analysts who under-
took the analytic treatment of schizophrenic and manic–depressive
patients, and he described the central role that processes of introjection and projection play in these disorders. Abraham referred to a
psychosexual metabolism in speaking of the dynamics of mania:

> in his manic phase he . . . proclaims his power of assimilating all his
> objects into himself. But it is characteristic that this pleasurable act
> of taking in new impressions is correlated to an equally pleasurable
> act of ejecting them as soon as they have been received.
>
> (Abraham, 1924, p. 472)

In outlining this rapid alternation between introjection and projection, Abraham was laying the groundwork for an understanding of
how two minds transmit and receive unconscious communications.
Furthermore, his application of Freud's and Ferenczi's concepts of
projection and introjection to describe the manic patient's style
of relating to his objects introduces to psychoanalysis the idea of
"metabolism." To return to Freud's (1912) telephone analogy of
unconscious communication: if projection and introjection are
viewed as the mechanisms underlying transmission and reception,
then metabolism may be seen as the means by which "the doctor's
unconscious is able from the derivatives of the unconscious which are
communicated to him, to reconstruct that unconscious, which has
determined the patient's free associations" (pp. 115–116).

We know little of Abraham's clinical technique, and the Berlin
School of psychoanalysis was criticized for being "too theoretical"
(Grubrich-Simitis, 1986). However, it seems safe to presume that his
emphasis upon projection, introjection, and metabolism found its way
into his practice of analysis and, by extension, into the thinking of his
analysands. Indeed, several of his patients – Melanie Klein, Robert
Fliess, and Theodore Reik – developed ideas that built upon the
contributions of Freud, Ferenczi, and Abraham to offer a further
scaffolding for our contemporary views on intersubjectivity. Melanie
Klein, of course, placed projective and introjective processes at the
center of her view of object relations. It is interesting to note that her
first analyst was Ferenczi; however, we know little of that analysis
during the time she lived in Budapest (Aguayo, 1997; Grosskurth,
1986). We will examine in greater depth the contributions of the
Kleinian school in Chapter 3. Fliess and Reik have greatly extended

our appreciation of the role that the analyst's mind plays in the thera-peutic encounter, and we now turn to their work, having detoured through Ferenczi and Abraham.

Robert Fliess's 1942 paper, "The Metapsychology of the Analyst," is a psychoanalytic classic that was reprinted in 2007 in the *Psycho-analytic Quarterly* along with commentaries by Roy Schafer and Theodore Jacobs. Fliess examines the analyst's "work ego" that has at its core a capacity for *trial identification*, which is commonly referred to as empathy. This requires the analyst's ability

> to step into his [patient's] shoes and obtain in this way an inside knowledge that is almost first hand . . . a person who uses empathy on an object *introjects this object transiently, and projects the introject again onto the object.*
>
> (1942, p. 212, italics added)

Here we have a direct clinical application of the concepts of projec-tion and introjection, promoted by Freud, Ferenczi, and Abraham, as the essential process by which one mind comes to know another. Fliess, however, goes further in his exploration of what is entailed in the analyst's trial identification by describing the "psychic *working metabolism* of the analyst" (p. 215, italics added), a term he acknowledges was developed by Abraham (1924). This "working metabolism" is comprised of four steps:

> (1) The analyst is the object of the [transference] striving; (2) he identifies with the subject, the patient; (3) he becomes this subject himself; (4) he projects the striving, after he has "tasted" it, back onto the patient and so finds himself in the possession of the inside knowledge of its nature, having thereby acquired the emotional basis for his interpretation.
>
> (Fliess, 1942, p. 215)

Fliess's description of the "working metabolism" in the analyst's metapsychology is a remarkably prescient observation that anticipates many of the themes that future authors will elaborate in the develop-ment of the concept of intersubjectivity.[1] Like Ferenczi before him, he sees a countertransference *induced* in the analyst in the first two phases, which, in Phase 3, raises some potential dangers for him because "the patient's striving has been transformed into a narcissistic one in the analyst, who by now has become its subject as well as its object" (Fliess, 1942, p. 216). This internal state of affairs may shake the analyst's equilibrium and "potentially threatens his mental health" (p. 216) because the necessity of introjecting, even transiently, difficult transference strivings such as aggression may cause internal conflict. Having managed to "taste" the analysand's transference, the analyst must reproject back to the patient his emotional understanding in the form of an interpretation; however, here too another possible complication challenges the analyst

> to guarantee that no instinctual additions of our own distort the picture after the reprojection of the striving onto the patient.
>
> (p. 219)

Fliess's detailed adumbration of the stages of "working metabolism" represents a significant elaboration of Abraham's original concept and underscores the difficulties for the analyst inherent in doing analytic work. There is a de-emphasis on the conscious activity of deciphering the analysand's free associations and a greater importance accorded to the analyst's receptivity to the patient's unconscious transmissions. Regarding the analyst's openness to his patient, instead of "free-floating attention" he prefers

> the term *conditioned daydreaming* . . . . The analyst certainly does not indulge in ordinary "free" daydreaming, where the stimuli come largely from within, for his daydreaming is almost certainly stimulated from without, and by one particular source: the patient's reactions.
>
> (p. 219)

Though Fliess does not use the term "analyzing instrument," he is essentially offering us an insider's look at the process occurring in the analyst's mind. Thus, by introducing trial identification, the work ego, working metabolism, and conditioned daydreaming into our lexicon, contributions that Schafer (2007) states "helps launch psychoanalysis towards its contemporary form" (p. 698), Fliess has expanded the range of conceptual tools to apply to our understanding of intersubjectivity beyond those bequeathed by Freud (projection), Ferenczi (introjection and induced countertransference), and Abraham (introjective/projective mechanisms and psychic metabolism). Schafer also notes that Fliess gives no consideration to the impact of the analyst's personality on the analytic dyad, a point with which Jacobs (2007) is in agreement. Regardless, Jacobs notes that

> rarely do we find in the contemporary literature an effort such as Fliess made to deconstruct the concept of subjectivity and to demonstrate just how it functions to affect both the interpretive process and the analytic work as a whole.
>
> (pp. 720–721)

Fliess's lack of "any acknowledgement that mutual influences are at work in analysis" (Jacobs, 2007, p. 716) is surely an accurate statement, but we must also take it in its historical context. Beginning in the 1930s, classical analysis bifurcated into two different paths: one, which eventually emerged as *ego psychology*, turned its focus to exploring the ramifications of Freud's (1923a) introduction of the structural theory. The ego psychologists offered valuable insights into the nature of defense (A. Freud, 1936), resistance, and the theory of anxiety (Freud, 1926), but in doing so they tended to shift attention away from a sustained study of unconscious processes, other than the role of the unconscious portion of the ego in defense. The former *topographical model*, which divided the mind into unconscious, preconscious, and conscious realms, was folded into the structural theory and tended to be seen as outmoded. However, there was a second branch of classical analysts who, while acknowledging the importance of structural theory, continued their investigations into unconscious processes in general and, specifically, into unconscious communication. This divide between the two offshoots of classical analysis was most evident in the attitude toward countertransference – the ego psychologists tending to develop techniques that sought to "cleanse" a patient's material from being alloyed with countertransference, while the other group viewed countertransference as a pathway to the analyst's empathic understanding. In my opinion, we can see in Fliess the tension between these two perspectives: on the one hand, his open advocacy of the relevance of the analyst's subjective experience, and, on the other, his wish to be "able to guarantee that no instinctual additions of our own distort the picture after the reprojection of the striving onto the patient" (p. 219). Jacobs (2007) comments:

One suspects that issues of loyalty to Freud, as well as fears of

Ferenczi's influence and of wild, undisciplined behavior on the part of colleagues, influenced Fliess and others who held this idealized and sanitized view of the analyst's functioning

(p. 717)

Theodore Reik, another of Abraham's analysands, was less concerned about the analyst keeping his or her "instinctual additions" separate from those of the internalized patient, and he even saw a benefit to both parties who grew through a process of

reciprocal illumination of unconscious happenings . . . the analytic investigation of the other person continued one's own analysis, penetrating to profounder depths.

(Reik, 1948, p. 397)

Reik's personal style was somewhat effusive and matched his analytic emphasis upon the analyst's spontaneity and intuitions, attitudes that permeated his 1937 book, *Surprise and the Analyst*. He borrowed the term *third ear* from Nietzsche (Lothane, 2006) to describe the analyst's attunement to his or her unconscious processes and underscored that the analytic couple equally entered a dreamy ego state in which the "analyst shares with the patient this realm between reality and fantasy" (Reik, 1948, p. 109). Here, Reik was furthering the role of a shared ego state linking the patient and analyst in order to create "an unconscious sharing of emotion" (Reik, 1937, p. 198). Like Fliess, he emphasized that the analyst temporarily *became* the patient through an empathic trial identification, but additionally he highlighted the importance of a joint *regression in the service of the ego* (Kris, 1936) that promoted an analytic mood of dreamy reflection. Finally, though other authors had warned of the danger inherent for the analyst's "mental health" (Fliess, 1942) that "conjures up the evils of those half-tamed demons that inhabit the human breast" (Freud, 1905a), Reik appears to be the first analyst to speak to the possibilities for emotional growth in both partners of the analytic dyad.

Otto Isakower, a Viennese analyst who eventually settled in New York via London, is an unsung pioneer in the evolution of an intersubjective perspective on the analytic dyad. He trained in Austria and was analyzed by Paul Federn, a close devotee of Freud and an early ego psychologist, who was interested in the role of the ego in dreaming and was the first analyst to speak of various kinds of "ego feelings" (Federn, 1926, 1932). We can see Federn's influence in Isakower's early work, especially his classic 1938 paper, "A Contribution to the Psycho-Pathology of Phenomena Associated with Falling Asleep," in which he introduced what later would be called the *Isakower phenomenon*, which was characterized by a regressive experience akin to an infantile state in which internal and external boundaries are blurred, a similar loss of distinction between different regions of the body occurs, and there is a general "regressive revival of ego-attitudes" (p. 345). In his later work, Isakower, like Reik, applied his interest in regressive ego states to the analytic relationship and gave a series of lectures at the New York Psychoanalytic Institute in the late 1950s to early 1960s on the *analyzing instrument*. These presentations had analytic supervision as their primary topic, and Isakower argued that the central goal of supervision is to teach about and strengthen the candidate's analyzing instrument. Unfortunately, Isakower, who "was known for his perfectionism" (Wyman & Rittenberg, 1992, p. 173), never published the lectures because he did not feel they were quite suitable for a journal; thus, his thoughts about the analyzing instrument remained relatively unknown except for a small circle of authors who later published papers inspired by his ideas (Balter, Lothane & Spencer, 1980; Jacobs, 1992; Lothane, 2006; Spencer, Balter & Lothane, 1992). The lectures were finally published in 1992 in the *Journal of Clinical Psychoanalysis*.

Freud (1912) said the analyst should use his unconscious as an instrument of the analysis, and Isakower (1957) redefined the *analyzing instrument* as the reciprocal working together of the analyst's evenly hovering attention with the patient's free associations: "this so-called analytical instrument is the same when it works in the analysand as in the analyst" (p. 189). Unlike Ferenczi's "mutual analysis" (Berman, 2003), Isakower was much more circumscribed as to the extent that the analyst revealed himself:

> ideas or images that come spontaneously to the analyst's mind during the session should be taken seriously as data *for understanding the patient* and perhaps even presented to the patient as a means of furthering such understanding.[2]
>
> (Spencer, Balter, & Lothane, 1992, pp. 248–249, italics added)

Furthermore, probably rooted in his earlier study of dream processes,

Isakower placed great importance on the *visual images* that enter the analyst's psyche while in the dream-like and regressed ego state of listening. Though he does not use the contemporary term *analytic field*, Isakower (1963a) does regard these visual images as arising from the interplay between the analyst's and analysand's minds:

> The phrase "evenly hovering attention" ... hovering between what comes from the outside, from the patient, and what is approaching from inside, from the analyst. One could think of both ultimately coinciding ... *within an area where visual images take part in representing a given conflict.*
>
> (p. 198, italics added)

Isakower takes great pains to describe the interface between patient and analyst and unambiguously states his elaboration of Freud's original concept:

> In describing the analytic instrument, it is useful not to think of it as a permanently integrated, unitary system within the psychic structure of one person, the analyst. It seems more adequate to regard it, in its activated state, as being in rapport with its counterpart in the patient; or, better perhaps, to see it as a composite consisting of two complementary halves. It will be remembered that in Freud's description both halves function together as one unit in continuous communication.
>
> (Isakower, 1963b, p. 201)

Isakower views the analyzing instrument, that "composite consisting of two complementary halves," as an intimate liaison and he waxes poetically when portraying the end of the session:

> The session is broken off, the patient is leaving the room; you, the analyst, are in the process of emerging out of the 'analytic situation' – that near dream-like state of hovering attention; the patient is being separated from you and you are left alone. In this short moment of the severance of the "team" you are left in midair and you become aware of the denuded raw surface of your half of the analyzing instrument, the surface of which is opposite the patient's half.
>
> (p. 202)

30

In the wake of this wistful separation, the analyst may experience both visual images and auditory representations of nonverbalized content from the session that are percolating on the edge of conscious awareness. Isakower says that the patient and analyst share a "state of consciousness" (1963c, p. 207) that is more than an identification, "Rather, there prevails a near identity in the quality of wakefulness in both the analyst and the analysand" (p. 207). In this regard, he is suggesting a merger between patient and analyst on the level of ego state that is in parallel with Fliess's observation that the analyst fleetingly *becomes* the patient's transference striving through a *trial identification*.

For Isakower, the emergence of preconscious visual images during, or immediately after, the session in either the patient or analyst was a sign that the *analyzing instrument* – a product of their intersecting psyches – was unconsciously at work. He presented a supervisory hour with one of his students in which the candidate reported a visual image of the Mona Lisa that he revealed to the patient. The supervisee was apologetic and worried that introducing this took the patient off track from his stream of associations and therefore was an analytic miscue. Isakower noted that, to the contrary, the spontaneous image of the famous painting actually was evidence that the analyst's unconscious was responding to the analysand, which stimulated the appearance of a visual image in the candidate, and that "This [image of the Mona Lisa] could be regarded as rudimentary form of a communicable formulation" (1963d, p. 215). In addition, Isakower said that the sharing of the preconscious pictogram fostered a greater openness in the patient to previously blocked-off material:

> This formation [image of Mona Lisa], emerging from the preconscious of the analyst, then had proved its usefulness – in retrospect. It made it possible for the patient to communicate something that was *made to emerge* within him. The tentative offering from the analyst had the effect of a shift of cathexis within the preconscious of the patient toward the visual mode of representation . . .
>
> (p. 215, italics in original)

It is important to note Isakower's qualifying "in retrospect" that underscores the interplay of visual images in the analyst and analysand occurring preconsciously – that is, this process may only be grasped after the fact. Moreover, it was the analyst's revelation of his preconsciously formed visual image that prompted ("made to emerge") a transformation ("shift of cathexis") in the patient of something from his unconscious to be represented visually.

Arlow (1969a, 1969b) also emphasized the importance of the visual images occurring for both the analyst and the patient, attributed these to an "unconscious fantasy function" (1969b, p. 5), and stated that

> Unconscious daydreaming is a constant feature of mental life. It is an ever-present accompaniment of conscious experience. What is consciously apperceived and experienced is the result of the interaction between the data of experience and unconscious fantasying as mediated by *various functions of the ego.*
>
> (1969b, p. 23, italics added)

Shapiro (2008) notes that Arlow's introduction of "unconscious daydreaming" was instrumental in raising its importance for psychoanalytic practice to a near-equal level of unconscious fantasy. Arlow (1969a) states that both analyst and analysand are engaged in unconscious daydreaming,[3] which is the basis for the development of what we would today call a "co-created narrative":

> In a sense, we dream along with our patients, supplying at first data from our own store of images in order to objectify the patient's memory into some sort of picture. We then furnish this picture to the analysand who responds with further memories, associations and fantasies; that is, we stimulate him to respond with a picture of his own.
>
> (p. 49)

His notion of "dream(ing) along with our patients" highlights the role that dreaming plays in the intersubjective analyzing instrument and would seem to anticipate later elaborations of the central place *reverie* holds in the analytic dialogue as described by Ogden, Ferro, Grotstein, and others. However, these theorists take their inspiration from Bion's (1962a) ideas about the importance of dreaming for the psyche. Why is this, and why did the concepts formulated by Fliess – but especially by Isakower, Arlow, and Reik – fall into disfavor and near obscurity in ego-psychological circles?

Returning for a moment to Isakower's lectures at the New York Psychoanalytic Institute, it is informative to examine the discussion that followed his presentations. There was a tension in the room as to whether the candidate's sharing his image of the Mona Lisa was a sign of what Martin Stein worried could be "the student going astray" (Wyman & Rittenberg, 1992, p. 216) or, perhaps, a useful intervention. Victor Rosen raised the concern as to whether the candidate would assume "that his associations should always be taken as part of the optimal functioning of the analyzing instrument" (Wyman & Rittenberg, 1992, p. 219). Isakower dismissed this concern on the basis that it would represent a misunderstanding of what he proposed in his conceptualization of the analyzing instrument. Later in the discussion, Martin Stein questioned whether the supervisee's disclosure of the visual image

> has to do with some unanalyzed personal problem? To use an analogy from medieval times – when a person had a vision to tell, was the vision sent by God or the Devil?
>
> (Wyman & Rittenberg, 1992, p. 221)

While many of the other comments were positive, or at least skeptical, the main vexation centered on the possible bedeviling misuse of countertransference by the candidate. This was still an era in classical analysis when countertransference was largely considered an impediment to be dealt with in one's personal or self-analysis. The long shadow of Freud's controversy with Ferenczi about the analyst's use of his personal reactions clouded the American analytic scene, which, in most corners, still sought the Holy Grail of a "sanitized view of the analyst's functioning" (Jacobs, 2007, p. 717). One unfortunate consequence of this attitude was to lump together all of the analyst's private experiences; thus, Fliess's idea of the analyst temporarily *becoming* the patient, Reik's concept of listening with the *third ear*, and Isakower's expanded definition of the *analyzing instrument* were generally viewed as too susceptible to countertransference influences and not considered as innovative advances of Freud's encouraging the analyst to use his unconscious as an instrument of the analysis.

As mentioned above (p. 27), the ascendancy of the structural model was another factor in the diminished interest in the study of the unconscious and its properties, except for the attention paid to the role of the unconscious ego in defense and resistance. It is also likely that political forces played a part in actively suppressing analytic perspectives at variance with the hegemony of ego psychology as promoted by Hartmann, Kris, and Loewenstein (H. Smith, personal communication in 2007). Lothane (2006) puts it succinctly:

> Since defenses appeared somehow to be more real and substantial, while images were dream-like, unreal, merely transference, resistance analysis came to be regarded as the more hard-nosed, cerebral, and scientific, while content analysis was relegated to the domain of the introspective, artistic, and mystical.
>
> (p. 713)

Consequently, the mainstream point of view proffered by institutes under the umbrella of the American Psychoanalytic Association tended to de-emphasize the notion of unconscious communication as well as the analyzing instrument, and these interactional phenomena were left to lie fallow. Theoretical positions considered at odds with the predominance of ego psychology were often expunged:[4]

> Following the arrival of the ego psychologists in the late 1930's and early 1940's, internal purges within the United States, beginning with Horney's expulsion from the New York Psychoanalytic Institute, ensured ego psychology's triumph and the marginalization of the homegrown interpersonal-cultural school
>
> (Chodorow, 2004, p. 214)

This sharp divide between the ego psychologists and those classically trained analysts interested in studying the unconscious aspects of the analytic dyad began to recede somewhat in the mid-1970s. A group of analysts (Paul Gray and his adherents) stayed true to the tradition of seeking a clinical approach that removed the analyst's subjectivity as a factor in the therapeutic relationship.[5] However, there emerged another circle that Chodorow (2004) has termed *intersubjective ego psychology*:

> Intersubjective ego psychologists use the ego psychological language of interpretation, individuality, autonomy, and insight, analytic neutrality, and other similar concepts, and also the language of enactment, transference-countertransference, the contribution of the analyst's mind and subjectivity, and other similar concepts that arose initially from interpersonal psychoanalysis.
>
> (p. 210)

34

This nascent shift of emphasis has also been described as a movement from a "one-person" to a "two-person" psychology – implied, according to Michael Balint (1969), in Ferenczi's work. The term "two-person psychology" is first mentioned in a paper by John Rickman[6] in 1951, who defined it as "the psychological region of reciprocal relationships" (Rickman, 1951, p. 219). It is instructive in our efforts to trace the lineage of the concept of intersubjectivity to note that Rickman was first analyzed by Freud; later, like Balint, by Ferenczi, and then with Melanie Klein in London.[7] Thus, we can see "tracings" of Ferenczi's "DNA" across several analytic generations, its markings more apparent the closer we look, though his work is rarely cited by the so-called intersubjective ego psychologists.

The evolution in classical analysis toward "the psychological region of reciprocal relationships" begins with a change in view of countertransference from an impediment of the analysis to an aid in understanding the inner world of the patient. The literature on countertransference is extensive, and I will limit myself to the issue of the "psychological region of reciprocal relationships." In his classic 1976 paper, "Countertransference and Role Responsiveness," Joseph Sandler introduced[8] the idea that the transference has an intended purpose of *actualizing* an internal object relationship of the analysand in the analytic relationship. The patient assumes a certain role in accord with an internal phantasy and also deliberately, though unconsciously, acts to evoke in the analyst a complementary role of that fantasy. Sandler emphasizes that this *role responsiveness* is not just a phantasy existing in the patient's psyche, but is an actual state of emotional affairs that permeates the subjective experiences of the analyst and analysand. In this brief paper, Sandler is offering a widened view of transference to include what the analyst feels:

> The patient's transference would thus represent an attempt by him to impose an interaction, an *interrelationship* (in the broadest sense of the word) between himself and the analyst.
>
> (p. 44, italics added)

Accordingly, he adds to the analyst's task of maintaining free-floating attention the necessity of holding *free-floating behavioral responsiveness* – that is, a receptive capacity to being placed in a variety of roles that pull him in the direction of specific actions delimited by the nature of the role he has been pushed to assume. The analyst may find himself placed into a role which causes some distress, and Sandler cautions him not to simply view this upset as a mere "blind spot," but to consider his reaction as a "compromise-formation" between his own proclivities and his reaction to the nature of the role forced upon him.

> Johnny, a 9-year-old boy in analysis for encopresis, began a session by announcing, "Dr. Brown, today we're going to kill women!" He motioned to the wall, said that there was a lineup of women whom I was supposed to shoot, and placed an imaginary gun in my hand. I was taken aback by this command and hesitated, offering that I did not know how to fire a weapon, but Johnny barked like an angry sergeant "Do it!" Still I hedged and said I didn't feel right killing these women, but my delaying was quickly remedied when Johnny turned me into an emotionless robot. His impatience with me grew until he held a rifle to my head and said "It's them or you!" Reluctantly I gave in, followed orders, and shot all the women. Returning to my human form, I said I felt badly about the murders, at which point Johnny gave me a puzzled look and said "Dr. Brown, we were only playing."

Johnny needed me to adopt the role of a murderer of women, but my anxiety about assuming that position caused my resistance. This resistance arose from a "compromise formation" between the role Johnny needed me to step into and my conflicts over matricidal feelings (I knew the women represented his mother). In drawing our attention to this blending of the analyst's psychology with the inner dynamics of the analysand, Sandler moved the classical analytic understanding of countertransference forward to include the patient's pressure on us to take on a role in his inner world and the effect upon the analyst in acquiescing. However, it is through the experience of that "role responsiveness" that we are able to gain knowledge of the patient's inner workings.

Thus, when Johnny said, "Dr. Brown, we were only playing," it was as though he implicitly understood Sandler's technical suggestion that the analyst *become* one of the patient's inner objects. This task runs parallel with Fliess's idea of a "trial identification" but is different in two ways. First, for Fliess, the trial identification was with a "transference striving" of the analysand, not a representation of the patient's inner object world. And second, Sandler was underscoring the importance of action, that transference involved a pressure on the analyst to take a specific action vis-à-vis the particular fantasy that was *actualized* in the here-and-now of the session. Finally, I want to note for future reference that Johnny, like Sam in the previous chapter, was quite tuned into my subjective reactions to the role he needed me to take. We will return to the topic of the patient's experience of the analyst's subjectivity in Chapter 3.

The emphasis in Sandler's paper on the patient's pressure for us to assume a role and act it out provides a central theoretical grounding for the focus upon *enactments*[9] beginning in the analytic literature in the 1980s. In Sandler's concept of role responsiveness, it was the patient's inner world, and its externalization into the analytic situation, that spurred the analyst's involvement – that is, that the analyst's psyche was viewed as reactive rather than an active participant in initiating the interaction. Theodore Jacobs (1991) has written extensively about the actualizing component of enactments, adding a two-person dimension that was essentially absent in Sandler's discussion, bringing us closer to the "region of reciprocal relationships." The patient and analyst may engage in an unconscious mutual enactment that serves resistance:

> ... the enactments carried out by both patient and analyst ... [may be seen as having] opened the way, not only to uncovering an essential piece of history that had not yet surfaced, but to bringing to the fore certain crucial aspects of the interaction between patient and analyst that, arousing anxiety in each and strongly defended by both, had until then been insufficiently explored.
>
> (p. 40)

For Jacobs, the analyst is typically drawn into an enactment because of his or her unconscious resonance with an aspect of the unconscious conflict that the patient is manifesting. Not uncommonly, the analyst identifies with an internal object of the patient who may represent a figure in the analyst's inner world or a split-off piece of him/herself (Jacobs, 1983). In this situation, personages from the analysand's representational world (Sandler & Rosenblatt, 1962) may become unknowingly linked with presences in the analyst's mind. Invariably, however, for Jacobs an enactment and its successful analysis allows for the emergence and clarification of unconscious conflicts in the patient; thus, *an enactment is considered within the framework of the classically established goal of making the unconscious conscious.*

Other "intersubjective ego psychologists" similarly draw our attention to the mutuality involved in analytic enactments. Boesky (1990) suggests that, in addition to helping to foster the conscious awareness of previously unconscious elements, another benefit to the analyst's being drawn into an enactment is that the analysand senses the analyst's engagement with him or her:

> If the analyst does not get emotionally involved sooner or later in a manner that he had not intended, the analysis will not proceed to a successful conclusion.

(p. 573)

Similarly, Ellman (1998) states that development of *analytic trust* is bidirectional, and the patient's awareness that he or she has had such an impact on the analyst is an important factor in its formation:

> the patient must penetrate the analyst's psychological world, and the analyst must allow this penetration to be gradually perceptible to the patient. This process is at the heart of analytic trust.

(p. 187)

Here Boesky and Ellman are beginning to introduce the notion of the patient's awareness of the analyst's subjectivity; however, this is a matter that intersubjective ego psychologists had largely left unexamined until very recently.

Renik broke new ground in his 1993 paper, "Analytic Interaction: Conceptualizing Technique in Light of the Analyst's Irreducible Subjectivity," which emphasized an aspect of the literature on enactments that he believed was underappreciated. Renik argued that enactments tended be seen as useful because they represented

> the skillful recovery of an error . . . [embedded in a] theory of technique [that] directs the analyst to eliminate personally motivated action as much as he or she can.

(p. 555)

Our technique, as Sandler (1976) suggests, must allow for the inevitability of being drawn into an enactment, and Renik underscores the value of the analyst's self-analysis in order to grab hold of his or her "irreducible subjectivity" activated in the clinical engagement. In later contributions, Renik (2004, 2007) enlarges upon the perspective that successful analysis of an enactment is aimed at making the unconscious conscious by stating that insight is *"co-created by the analyst and patient as much as it is something discovered by the analyst and patient"* (2004, p. 1054, italics added). This comment marks a significant elaboration of the traditional analytic take on enactments as resistance to the emergence of repressed – and therefore pre-formed – memories, fantasies, and analogous phenomena in the patient and/or the analyst. Instead, Renik puts it quite simply:

> that analytic truths are co-created by analyst and patient, rather than unveiled by means of the analyst's objective observations of the patient's projections.
>
> (2004, p. 1056)

Thus, Renik is moving the focus of the intersubjective encounter in the analytic dyad away from the discovery of buried hidden "truths" (i.e., repressed facts to be dispassionately unearthed, described, and examined) to the co-creation of new constructions (i.e., a developing sense of the "truth" as a shared emotional construct) that bear the personal stamp of each participant, thereby putting to rest the quixotic quest for a technique to "guarantee that no instinctual additions of our own distort the picture" (Fliess, 1942, p. 219).

It has been axiomatic from early psychoanalytic days that the analyst's emotional equilibrium is susceptible to being shaken, sometimes quite severely, by the demands of doing analysis. Though it was never stated explicitly, the obverse of this danger is that the potential disruption of the analyst might also result in emotional growth. Theodore Reik (1948) may have been the first to identify what he termed the *"reciprocal* illumination of unconscious happenings" (p. 397) by which analyzing another allowed the possibility of the analyst "penetrating to profounder depths" (p. 397) in his or her associated self-analytic work, an idea hinted at by Freud (1910a) when he stated that "no psycho-analyst goes further than his own complexes and internal resistances permit" (p. 145). I italicized the word "reciprocal" in order to highlight the interconnection between the analytic work each member of the dyad undertakes. Blum (1980), in discussing the topic of reconstruction, states that when the analyst offers a reconstruction of the patient's childhood, this may be useful to the analyst as well because "reconstruction of the analyst's childhood and reconstruction of the patient's childhood are quite separate if *at times reciprocal processes"* (p. 49, italics added). Jacobs (1991) delineates the process of this reciprocal growth: it is through the analyst's associations in his or her own life with the analysand's narrative that he or she is able to truly understand the patient's troubles; therefore, any reworking of the patient's inner world is inevitably linked with analogous reorganizing in the analyst's psyche.

The so-called intersubjective ego psychologists have significantly broadened our knowledge of how two minds may work reciprocally to create behavioral enactments of unconscious forces. These interactions are initiated by some inner conflict of the patient that is *actualized* in the session and has an animating effect upon related conflicts in the analyst. Through his self-analysis, the analyst detects his identification with some aspect of the analysand's unrecognized conflict – information that the analyst employs to gain some sense of an unconscious problem in the patient that can now be made conscious through an interpretation that is partly based on the analyst's knowledge gleaned from his countertransference. Ellman (1998) has importantly accentuated the need for a *bidirectional* analytic trust, but the intersubjective ego psychologists do not explore the bidirectional nature of mutual influence between analyst and patient. Boesky and Ellman hint at it, but typically these analysts do not address the impact on the analysand of having an analyst drawn into a particular enacted role. In addition, the text of the enacted narrative is viewed as scripted by an actualized internal fantasy (Sandler) of the patient or by a previously camouflaged memory of the analysand (Jacobs) that has been unconsciously expressed in the enactment. Finally, though Chodorow (2004) calls these analysts "ego psychologists," they do not discuss the role of the ego as a structure of either patient or analyst in this intersubjective encounter. A notable exception is Jacob's (1986) paper that dealt with the analyzing instrument in which he referred to the shared regressed ego states of the analytic dyad that may result in the appearance of visual images.

We have now come to the end of this review of how classical analysis and its closely related offshoots have contributed to our understanding of intersubjective processes. Like a cluttered garage with an entire toolchest of implements scattered haphazardly around waiting to be gathered together and organized, *we have within the classical tradition most of the instruments necessary to fashion a comprehensive theory of intersubjectivity.* The following summary delineates these elements of intersubjectivity that are implicit in traditional analytic theory and practice and how the contributions of each author shed light on the components of a tacit intersubjective point of view.

In Chapter 1, it was stated that intersubjectivity refers to an exchange between the conscious, unconscious, and preconscious systems of each participant in the analytic dyad. This facet is central to Freud's ideas of a "transmitting" and "receptive" unconscious as well as his concept of projection; Ferenczi's description of introjection and the inductive aspect of countertransference; Abraham's delineation of the rapid oscillation between projection and introjection; Fliess's concept of the "work ego," trial identification, and conditioned daydreaming; Reik's "reciprocal illumination of unconscious happenings," the third ear, the dreamy ego state shared by analyst and patient, and unconscious shared emotion; Isakower's widened definition of the analyzing instrument, the "regressive revival of ego–attitudes," and how visual images assist in the process of making the unconscious conscious; Arlow's emphasis upon "unconscious daydreaming" in analyst and analysand and that we "dream along with our patients"; and, finally, Sandler's and Jacobs' description of how actualization "calls out" for a partner in the analyst's psyche. All these concepts capture from different angles the various components of the exchange within, and between, the patient and analyst on an unconscious, preconscious, and conscious basis. It is noteworthy that only Isakower and Arlow directly addressed the *preconscious processes* that were responsible for the creation of visual images that are a way-station on the "royal road" from the domain of the unconscious to the conscious. Preconscious mentation, in general, is a neglected topic in analytic writings (Busch, 2006a), and we shall see in Chapter 5 how André Green (1974, 2000) links preconscious thinking with intersubjectivity.

We can also see embedded within the classical tradition an inchoate intersubjective viewpoint that combines a unique blending of conscious, preconscious, and unconscious events to create a shared emotional field. Fliess's concept of trial identification is a component of the "psychic working metabolism" of the analyst by which he transiently *becomes* the patient's "transference strivings." From a somewhat different vertex, Reik refers to the analyst and analysand engaged in "an unconscious sharing of emotion" (Reik, 1937, p. 198), while Isakower and Arlow emphasize that the analytic pair share a near identical ego state of dreaminess. In each case, the emotional field is colored by the patient's affective states with which the analyst temporarily identifies, and the analyst's role is to follow the analysand's lead. This does not take into account any input from the analyst in creating the emotional field. However, Isakower comes closest when he related the incident from supervision in which the supervisee told the patient of his visual image of the Mona Lisa, a somewhat controversial intervention that nevertheless fostered the emergence in the patient of a resonant visual experience. This brings us to the threshold of the next intersubjective factor, that of the co-creation of a narrative.

We have also discussed that intersubjectivity consists of a process of mutual affective attunement and regulation, which is a means of unconsciously working on the shared emotional field through the co-creation of a narrative. Classical analysts until very recently have not dealt with this aspect of intersubjectivity except obliquely, in the idea that a resistance may be co-created (Ellman, Jacobs) because the emotional situation in the consulting room stirs sufficient anxiety in patient and analyst that they unconsciously collude to avoid the painful issue. In this regard, it is as though the analytic couple have co-created a narrative that reads, "Let's not talk, or let's talk about the weather, because this is too distressing to face." However, Renik's recent publications have increasingly stressed the view that the developing narrative of analysis is co-created by the interpenetration of the analyst's and patient's psyches. While descriptively rich, Renik leaves the reader wondering about the nature of the process by which the joint narrative is formed.

Furthermore, we have noted that intersubjectivity is a process of unconscious communication, receptivity, and meaning making within each member of the dyad to bring idiosyncratic signification to the shared emotional field that interacts with an analogous function in the partner. The point here is that the shared emotional field is jointly constructed from the idiosyncratic characteristics of the patient and analyst and, once co-created, is experienced in accord with each member's unique mind. For example, in Chapter 1, Sam and I were immersed in shared affective territory defined by parental loss, yet each of us assigned a different meaning to that ambient mood (Sam, paternal absence; I, maternal loss). Our interaction progressed by virtue of the unconscious meaning-making function in each of us communicating with its "partner" in the other, thereby incrementally weaving together our "story" about the *mummy* from its skeins of personal meaning in each of us. Freud's comments about the transmitting and receptive aspects of the unconscious, Fliess's description of the "psychic working metabolism" of the analyst, and Reik's "reciprocal illumination" all capture the patient's side, but they do not deal with the analyst's experiences as a factor. Isakower comes much closer by alluding, in his concept of the analyzing instrument, to visual images that appear in the analyst's mind that are products of the joint unconscious encounter of two psyches. Arlow's (1969b) account of what he terms "unconscious daydreaming" by which we "dream along with our patients" most approximates the narrative-generating give-and-take between patient and analyst characterized by pre-conscious interactions in which each participant stimulates the other "to respond with a picture of his own" (p. 49). In addition, Ellman's notion of how the analyst and analysand must interpenetrate each other's psychological world in order to build analytic trust is another useful concept; however, he does not address implications of this model for joint meaning making nor the method by which the two selves achieve this interpenetration. Similarly, Renik's descriptions of a co-created narrative do not mention how this is accomplished.

I also said in the previous chapter that unconscious communication travels along many pathways including linguistic, pictographic, "extraneous" experiences (random thoughts, unbidden tunes), bodily sensations, and other yet-to-be-understood channels that, from a mystical point of view, may be called telepathic. Freud (1912) portrayed unconscious communication with the metaphor of the telephone, an analogy that emphasized the verbal/auditory channels. In other writings, he (Freud, 1905b, 1942) borrowed the word "empathy" [*Einfühlung*] from general psychology in order to explain how jokes or good actors surreptitiously convey strong emotions, thus opening up another conduit for unconscious transmissions. Ferenczi, Fliess, and Sandler asserted that the countertransference may be intentionally, though unconsciously, induced in the analyst and that projective, externalizing processes are the means by which this is accomplished. Isakower and Arlow underscored the importance of visual images as yet another channel by which one unconscious registers with another while in a mutual regressed ego state, and Jacobs (1991) acknowledges the importance of tactile, sensory, and bodily carriers of unconscious communication between the two subjectivities in analysis. Finally, states of mind that approximate dreaming seem to enable a capacity for two minds to engage in spontaneous and unconscious intersubjective work. Though Freud (1922) was skeptical, at best, about the existence of telepathy, he opined, if it did occur, "that sleep creates favorable conditions for telepathy" (p. 220). This speculation dovetails with Fliess's and Arlow's observation that the shared dream-like state of the two-person analyzing instrument enables the emergence of visual (preconscious) images in each partner. We will be returning to the role of dreaming as an aspect of intersubjectivity, but let us keep in mind Arlow's (1969a) statement that "we dream along with our patients" (p. 49) as we move forward.

The co-created narrative, ideally weighted more heavily in the direction of the patient's difficulties, owes its lineage not only to the psychic issues of each partner activated at the moment, but also contains, in part, a highly distilled historical record of each individual's family history. One factor that unifies the analysts covered in this chapter is their orientation toward helping the patient change through an uncovering of repressed "material" via the recollection of past trauma[10] and/or the externalization of internal object relations into the here-and-now of the analytic hour. Within this view, there is a hidden "truth" that is to be uncovered, interpreted, and worked though. Another perspective, advocated by Renik, is that there is no extant truth to be unearthed; rather, analyst and analysand are at work, on all levels of consciousness, to co-create an approximation of a "truth" about the patient's life in the form of a narrative that is not "cleansed" of tinctures of the analyst's personality but has been constructed with due consideration paid to the likelihood that his voice echoes in that narrative. Each analyst and patient comes to the analysis with his or her own cast of internal characters that meet and greet, marry and divorce, battle and make amends with their counterparts in the other member of the analytic duo. Jacobs (1983) has written most cogently about this phenomenon and notes

> the capacity of the patient's representations of his objects to stimulate in the analyst the reemergence of affectively charged self- and object representations which become linked with his representations of the patient's objects.

> (p. 627)

In this fashion, the histories of both the analyst and the analysand, memorialized in their respective *representational worlds* (Sandler & Rosenblatt, 1962), are unconsciously introduced to each other, not

44

unlike the experience of a newly married couple who, over time, get to know their partner's extended family.

Finally, we may view the intersubjective encounter as entailing growth in both partners of the analytic dyad by virtue of the influence they have upon each other, an influence that is achieved through the reorganization of aspects of their respective psyches that necessarily occurs as unconscious work constantly re-narrates the story of the analytic hour. Blum (1980), Reik (1948), and Jacobs (1991) all speak to ways in which the analyst and analysand experience emotional growth during the course of an analysis through reconstruction of the analyst's childhood (Blum), stimulation of conflicts in the analyst that allows for the investigation of his or her psyche "to profounder depths" (Reik), or identification with objects in the patient's inner world that triggers self-analytic work in the analyst (Jacobs). Growth in the analyst, according to these authors, occurs as a useful side effect of an analysis aimed at making the unconscious conscious. While this kind of mutual development surely unfolds over the life of an analytic journey, I would say that such overarching change is built from micro–moment-to-moment interchanges in each individual hour that accumulate over the course of treatment. It is from these small fragments of unconscious work, like Sam's invention of the *mummy* that instantaneously condensed the shared emotional field into a multifaceted complex character, that a jointly assembled narrative is slowly constructed. In addition to the mutual growth in patient and analyst flowing from unconscious aspects of themselves coming to light, the process of building a narrative that is neither the analyst's nor the patient's, but their conjoint handiwork, also brings about a maturation that is not unlike parenthood.

Notes

1   Writing a year before Fliess, Matte Blanco (1941) also enlarged upon Abraham's idea of psychic metabolism, saying that "the human mind is in a perpetual state of exchange with its environment, just as the human body is in a perpetual state of metabolism, taking from the outside, digesting, expelling what is not necessary and integrating the products of digestion into its own tissues" (p. 26) and later that "the mind is in a perpetual state of ever absorbing symbols . . . the *mental process of absorbing these symbols has, it seems to me, been completely neglected*" (p. 30, italics added). We can see that Fliess had much to say about the analyst's inner

process of metabolism, but Matte Blanco introduces the topic of how the transient introjection of the analysand's transference may be more than transient – that is, digested and thereby changing the analyst.

2 In Chapter 4, I present analytic work with an adolescent whose capacity to meaningfully associate was stimulated by my sharing a visual image that spontaneously arose while listening to her speak.

3 Lothane (2006), an expositor of Isakower's work, calls this process *reciprocal free association*.

4 A separate, but related, issue was the rejection of nonmedical analysts from the New York Psychoanalytic Institute (as a member of the American Psychoanalytic Association). Reik experienced a hurtful rejection by the Institute when he arrived in New York, which relegated him to teaching courses on applied analysis and prohibited him from clinical work (Reed & Levine, 2004). Thus, he was rebuffed on account of his professional identity as well as his theoretical outlook. Reik went on to found the NPAP at the urging of his nonmedical colleagues.

5 The contributions of this group of ego psychologists is considered in greater depth in Chapter 4.

6 Arnold Modell (1984) is generally credited with coining the "one-" and "two-person" distinction in the classical analytic literature.

7 Interestingly, Rickman's pioneering work at the Northfield War Hospital during World War II earned a visit from Karl Menninger in 1945 and a subsequent invitation from Robert Knight to move to the Menninger Clinic in Topeka, Kansas. Rickman was in the process of arranging the move when it was scuttled because his interests raised a "concern regarding your espousal [of] Kleinian ideas in training which may not assimilate well here" (cable from Robert Knight, 4 March 1945, cited in King, 2003, p. 51). Thus, like Horney and Reik before him, his "espousal" of ideas that did not "assimilate well" resulted in his exclusion and a rejection of "espousal" of ideas at variance with the predominant American psychoanalytic establishment. We will revisit Rickman's notions of the "field" in Chapter 3.

8 Actually, "re-introduced" would be more accurate, since Ferenczi had, in a letter to Freud (see above), mentioned his view of transference as aiming to induce a reaction in the analyst. Fliess also addressed this aspect of the transference.

9 Of course, Freud's (1914) paper, "Remembering, Repeating and Working-Through," forms the bedrock of analytic thinking about action and repetition as a form of remembering; however, my focus here is on the ways in which the patient and analyst draw each other into a shared pattern of action.

10 That is, actual events that have occurred or "screen memories" of experiences from the past that are fantasy elaboration of real occurrences.

3

Klein, Bion, and intersubjectivity: becoming, transforming, and dreaming

> In the end, it is impossible not to become what others believe you are.
> (From Naphtali Lewis, *Ides of March*, copyright 1983 by Edgar Kent. Reprinted by permission of Dundurn Press Limited. Quoted in Gabriel Garcia Marquez, *Memories of My Melancholy Whores*, 2005, p. 96)

The *guinea pig* is a common pet and also is a metaphorical subject of an experiment who is a research model for diseases in humans. Native to the Andes mountains, the guinea pig, or *cuy* in Spanish, serves as an important diagnostic tool to the folk doctors who tend to the indigenous people:

> Before diagnosing a patient's illness, the folk doctor often chews coca leaves . . . or alcohol to prevent diagnostic mistakes. The folk doctor rubs the patient's body from head to toe with a live *cuy*. . . . Then he slits the animal's abdomen, examines the rodent's organs and either diagnoses the illness or pronounces the patient's cure.
> (Morales, 1995, p. 75)

The "theory" underlying this diagnostic examination is that whatever ails the patient will be absorbed by the *cuy* and then reflected in the contents of the animal's internal organs. Thus, the native healer who finds a deformity in the guinea pig's spleen will confidently infer that his patient's malady similarly arises from some disturbance in *his*

47

spleen. These healers do not ask "tell me where it hurts," but instead rely upon a procedure that first requires the doctor to put himself in a receptive, but alert state of mind by chewing coca leaves and then "scanning" the patient's body with the *cuy*, which magically takes on the illness. It would be interesting to question such a practitioner and ask about his theory regarding how the patient's illness becomes the guinea pig's: Does the *cuy* "detect" the disease through the scanning? Does the patient's body actively convey in some manner its illness to the *cuy*? How important is the doctor's state of mind, modified by chewing coca leaves, to the diagnostic examination?

When Robert Fliess (1942) proposed that the analyst engage in trial identifications with the analysand, he was in essence suggesting that we become a guinea pig (as in an experiment) by introjecting the patient's "transference striving." And just as the *cuy* becomes the patient's illness, so the analyst "becomes this subject himself" (p. 215) and "tastes" the patient's suffering. He and Ferenczi believed that the patient induced countertransference feelings, but Fliess did not discuss the analysand's motives for doing this nor the psychological process by which this is accomplished. Likewise, Theodore Reik (1937) spoke of "an unconscious sharing of emotion" (p. 198), but we are left wondering how this occurs. And when a patient attempts to impose on the analyst a mode of interaction that is an externalization of an internal object relationship as Sandler (1976) has described, what does the patient do to actualize his or her inner world in the clinical encounter? Melanie Klein's introduction of projective identification in 1946 has provided an essential conceptual tool to explain how one mind evokes, induces, and recruits another mind to become a partner in an unconscious shared experience.

Becoming: the London Kleinian

Before reviewing Klein's ideas about projective identification, it seems relevant to consider the influence of her relationships, both analytic and collegial, with Ferenczi and Abraham on the development of her theories. In 1914, after her family had moved to Budapest, she read Freud's (1901) paper on dreams, was profoundly affected by the ideas, and sought out Ferenczi as her analyst (Grosskurth, 1986). We have already seen in the previous chapter how Klein gave Ferenczi's concept of *introjection* a central place in her thinking. Additionally, Ferenczi was impressed with her gift for understanding small children and encouraged her to pursue child analysis, just as Abraham, her second analyst, did. Grosskurth reports that Klein felt Ferenczi did not pay sufficient attention to the negative transference and overemphasized the healing power of a positive transference. Though Klein felt this was a shortcoming, her experience in analysis may have taught her the importance of dealing with the hostile transference, which she explored in her later analytic work. Furthermore, Ferenczi (1919) had been developing what he called an *active technique* that was employed with resistant patients in which the analyst actively intervenes to either prohibit or encourage certain behaviors in order to stir up affects too vigorously defended against. This technique was later the focus of much criticism, as Ferenczi in his later years (after analyzing Klein) pushed the limits of acceptable technique with *mutual analysis*, by which the patient and analyst literally took turns analyzing each other. Nevertheless, Klein's technique may have reflected Ferenczi's tendency toward activity in her practice of active interpretation, though well within established analytic traditions and respect for boundaries. Furthermore, Grosskurth notes that Ferenczi's (1913) well-known paper, "Stages in the Development of the Sense of Reality," had a significant impact on her and, in my view, especially with regard to her appreciation for concrete thinking. In this connection, Klein's references to Ferenczi are mainly to his work on symbol formation and the superego, and she rarely cited Ferenczi in her writings,[1] a fact that has been interpreted by some as a sign she secretly disagreed with his views; however, it also seems likely that "she may have absorbed much from his theory that was not explicitly formulated" by her (Likierman, 1993, p. 242). I believe another factor may have been Ferenczi's (1931) praise of Anna Freud's work with children over that of Klein's, a stance that may have been adopted in order to repair his frayed relationship with Freud (Berman, 2004). This must have been difficult for Klein, given Ferenczi's encouragement of her pursuing child analysis and their long friendship and analytic bond.

Klein moved to Berlin in 1921 following a reign of anti-Semitic terror in Hungary and began analysis with Abraham in 1924 after several years of his tutelage and encouragement of her to pursue child analysis. Sadly, their analytic work ended a year later upon his untimely death. As Aguayo (1997) points out, she began to shift away from some of Ferenczi's ideas to those promulgated by Abraham, such as their varying perspectives regarding children's sexual theories. Abraham also was an early pioneer in the analytic treatment of manic-depressive and schizophrenic patients (see Chapter 2), and, as a result of these researches, he promoted the notion that the most disturbed patients were those fixated at the earliest levels of development. He was the first analyst to describe the rapid oscillation between introjection and projection in the most troubled patients, an observation that Klein, in her early work, applied to her understanding of very ill children and that she later came to view as a normal characteristic (paranoid-schizoid) of early infancy. Klein took from Abraham (1916) his interest in the mother/infant dyad, expressed in his formulations about the early oral stages, and ran with it, offering detailed descriptions (some would say highly imaginative speculations) of the primal mother/child relationship that prefigured future analytic investigation as well as laid the groundwork for an intersubjective perspective.

In formulating the concept of projective identification, Klein (1946) was addressing the fate of that which is projected *into* the mother's body and how the experience of the mother is altered in the infant's phantasy. The preposition *into* is central to projective identification and reflects Klein's (1926, 1928, 1932) belief that the *epistemophilic instinct*[2] – that is, the drive to know – is first manifest as the infant's phantasies about the contents of its mother's body. When the baby's hatred begins to threaten its very existence, that hatred is projected *into* the mother, in which case

> the mother comes to contain the bad parts of the self, she is not felt to be a separate individual but is felt to be *the* bad self.
>
> (1946, p. 8, italics in original)

In this connection, the mother (in phantasy) becomes a persecutory object. Similarly,

> It is, however, not only the bad parts of the self which are expelled and projected, but also the good parts of the self.
>
> (p. 8)

The projected good (loving) parts of the self also transform the infant's experience of the mother, who in phantasy has become the idealized embodiment of all that is loving, protective, and nurturing.

Of course, an infant cannot place its hatred or love *into* an object; love and hate are not palpable entities with weight and mass to be transferred over a physical distance. In effect, Klein was suggesting a process not unlike the Andean folk doctors whose guinea-pig diagnostic technique assumed a transfer of the patient's illness *into* the animal. From her extensive analytic experience with very young children, Klein (1930, 1932) understood the *concreteness* of their thinking – that is, objects (inner and outer) are felt to be *perceptual/sensory*, rather than *conceptual*, in nature. This distinction has sometimes been difficult for analysts of other schools to grasp; thus, the first paper of the Controversial Discussions in London during World War II, by Susan Isaacs, "The Nature and Function of Phantasy" (1948), addressed this misconception. Isaacs observes:

> phantasies are, in their simple beginnings, *implicit meaning*, meaning latent in impulse, affect and sensation. They are the content of the archaic mental processes . . .
>
> (1948/1991, p. 213, italics in original)

Isaacs implies a development from the perceptual/sensory mode to a verbal, conceptual mode as the ego gains in strength. Yet we may also observe a reversal of this process, for example, in the formation of dreams when daytime experiences recorded verbally are re-encoded perceptually as dream images. Freud (1900) referred to this as *topographical regression*,[3] a term that I (Brown, 1985) used to describe one kind of concrete thinking in which "movement backward [away from conceptual mode] to an action, sensory or perception mode is toward concreteness" (p. 381). Although Storch (1924) had earlier described the concrete nature of the schizophrenic's internal world, Klein (1930) was the first to demonstrate the role of the analyst's interpretations, based upon an appreciation of concrete modes of cognition, in fostering the child's movement from imprisonment in a concrete universe to being able to engage in symbolic play. Thus, the notion that something is projected *into* an object rests upon an understanding of the concrete nature of unconscious phantasy. Moreover, Klein tied the maturation of abstract thinking to patterns of object relations, thereby setting the stage for Bion's (1958, 1962a, 1962b, 1965) theories of containment, reverie, and transformation that outlined an intersubjective model for the development of thought.

Klein's use of *into* with projective identification gave us a fresh way

51

of thinking about countertransference as having an emotional effect upon the analyst. Permit me a moment of concreteness: if something is projected *onto* the analyst, then one may wipe it off one's sleeve, as one would with lint. The lint may cause an emotional reaction, such as annoyance or embarrassment, but it hasn't found its way in through our pores. On the other hand, if an emotional state is projected *into* the analyst, then it has come to reside within him or her and cannot be swept away but must be dealt with by the analyst. The projection, as one of my supervisees once remarked, "is free to mix and mingle with people in my inner world, to meet my parents, attack my brother, or even marry my father." Projective identification, therefore, provides us with the means to comprehend how the analysand induces (Ferenczi) countertransference and how the analyst *becomes* (Fliess, Jacobs) an aspect of the patient.

Though Klein did acknowledge that it was sometimes difficult for the analyst to be the recipient of such projective identifications (Spillius, 2007) because of his or her associated inner objects stirred by the projection, like Freud she stressed that the countertransference was to be dealt with by the analyst in his or her self-analysis. Despite the fact that many of her devotees regarded countertransference, induced by the patient's projective identification, as a useful tool of analytic work, she remained skeptical of its relevance as a guide to emotionally understanding the analysand. She held this position firmly to the end of her career: witness her comments to a group of young analysts in 1958:

> I have never found that the countertransference has helped me to understand my patient better. If I may put it like this, I have found that it helped me to understand myself better.
>
> (quoted in Spillius, 2007, p. 78)

In the same meeting, Klein also distinguished between countertransference and empathy by stating that analysis of one's countertransference was often necessary in order to sustain empathic contact with the analysand. She would reject her adherents' view that projective identification was the mechanism that accounted for both countertransference and empathy.

It was left to Paula Heimann, one of Klein's analysands and most devoted followers, to first write about the positive use of countertransference (Heimann, 1950); however, though clearly influenced by the new concept of projective identification, Heimann was also a student of her first analyst, Theodore Reik. Her understanding of countertransference, though usually credited as an extension of Klein's concept of projective identification, is also reflective of Reik's influence. As we learned in Chapter 2, Reik was a flamboyant presence in the Berlin institute and a champion of the analyst's spontaneity as well as of using one's intuition as an instrument of the analysis. Heimann began training analysis with him in Berlin in the late 1920s, and then he impulsively left in late 1932 to return to Vienna before emigrating to the Netherlands. Nevertheless, she remained very attached to him, as evidenced in a 1933 letter that was recently published (Rolnik, 2008). Emigrating to London in 1933, Heimann began analysis with Klein, a figure whose sober analytic demeanor was strikingly different from Reik's. Where Klein would separate countertransference from empathy, Reik would emphasize the analyst's receptivity to whatever crosses his or her mind as indicative of one's empathic stance. Rolnik (2008) states:

> It has been suggested that the paper on countertransference was written as a reaction to Heimann's dissatisfaction with her analysis with Klein (Grosskurth, 1986, p. 379). However, her novel ideas on the subject may also be seen as an attempt to bridge Reik's radical, if somewhat self-indulgent, theory of analytic listening, to which she was exposed in Berlin, and Klein's notorious evasion of the topic.
>
> (Rolnik, 2008, p. 422)

Early on in this brief paper, Heimann (1950) dismisses the (then) widely held belief that countertransference is a negative phenomenon comprised of the analyst's transference to the patient's transference:

> I am using the term "counter-transference" to cover all the feelings which the analyst experiences towards his patient . . . [and] my thesis is that the analyst's emotional response to his patient within the analytic situation *represents one of the most important tools for his work. The analyst's countertransference is an instrument of research into the patient's unconscious.*
>
> (p. 81, italics added)

She also states that analysts tend to ignore the fact that analysis is "a *relationship* between two persons" (p. 81). But perhaps her most radical statement was that while countertransference was a normal and predictable event in analysis, it was also "the patient's *creation*, it is part of the patient's personality" (p. 83, italics in original).

Heimann's paper is written without any analytic jargon and with no references to other authors; however, we can see, especially in the last comment, a clear reference to projective identification. Her assertion that countertransference is the "patient's creation" and also is a "part of the patient's personality" clearly indicates that an aspect of the analysand has been placed *into* the analyst, ostensibly through projective identification.

In describing countertransference as the "patient's creation," Heimann was essentially restating Ferenczi's earlier view that the patient *induces* such emotions in the analyst, although Ferenczi (as well as Fliess and Isakower) did not identify the mechanism by which this occurred. These early explorers of intersubjective processes attributed the analyst's *becoming* an aspect of the analysand to introjection of the patient – that is to say, through the analyst's activity. Heimann's contribution, on the other hand, emphasized the active role of the analysand in *creating* emotional experiences in the analyst, a point emphasized by Brenman Pick (1985):

> The child's or patient's projective identifications are actions in part intended to produce [emotional] reactions.
>
> (p. 157)

Heimann and Brenman Pick are thus widening our view of projective identification from Klein's use of the term to denote a phantasy of the patient to a concept that includes an actual effect upon the recipient that is related to the analysand's pathology.

Roger Money-Kyrle's (1956) paper, "Normal Counter-Transference and Some of Its Deviations," continued with Heimann's observations and elaborated them further. Money-Kyrle had a brief analysis with Freud in Vienna, a more extensive training analysis with Ernest Jones in London, and another period of analysis with Melanie Klein (Jaques, 1979).[4] Like others before him, Money-Kyrle expressed the view that the analyst's mental functioning is engaged in a rapid oscillation between introjection and projection of his patient's inner world that permits him or her to maintain an empathic stance. There are, however, inevitable periods when the analyst fails to understand his or her analysand that occur when an aspect of the patient disturbingly coincides with an unanalyzed portion of the analyst's psyche.[5] It is at such times that the analyst is confronted with a "triple task":

> ...first, the analyst's emotional disturbance, for he may have to deal with this silently in himself before he can disengage himself sufficiently to understand the other two; then the patient's part in bringing it about; and finally *its effect on him* [the patient].
>
> (p. 361, italics added)

In highlighting the effect of the analyst's emotional state upon the patient, Money-Kyrle is raising for the first time in the Kleinian literature the impact of the analyst's subjectivity on the patient and is introducing a truly intersubjective psychology.

Money-Kyrle's recommendations regarding how one should handle the effect of the analyst's subjectivity upon the analysand frame a controversy that is still with us to this day: Should the analyst disclose his or her countertransference reactions, however relevant they are to the patient's difficulties, and, if so, how should one go about such a disclosure? In Money-Kyrle's opinion, it is important for the analyst to deal with a patient's comments about his or her mood, whether accurately perceived or not, by interpreting it as psychic reality that has personal meaning to the analysand. This stance was in contrast to Margaret Little's (1951) tentatively offered suggestion to confirm the accuracy of the patient's perception and then to encourage him or her to associate to it. Money-Kyrle raises the concern that Little's approach may forestall deeper analytic understanding:

> If . . . the counter-transference is too positive the patient may respond to our increased emotional concern. . . . We do not contradict him as we may wish. But it may be appropriate to tell him that he believes we are attracted to him and has to deny it in order to avoid the responsibility for a seduction. . . . As a child he may have been unconsciously aware that his caresses embarrassed one of his parents. . . . If so, the interpretation of the repetition of this pattern in the transference may enable the patient to reassess, not only his analyst's, but his real parent's attitude to him.
>
> (Money-Kyrle, 1956, p. 363)

Money-Kyrle's "intersubjective" perspective thus squarely places the emphasis on the unconscious meanings both the analyst and the patient attribute to their interaction. While acknowledging that the analyst's conscious feelings toward the patient may "confirm" the accuracy of the patient's perceptions, it does little to address the unconscious meaning the patient is attaching to the perception (accurate or not) of the analyst.

One critique (Benjamin, 2007) of the Kleinian focus on not confirming the reality of the patient's perception is that it deprives the analysand of an *authentic* interpersonal experience with his or her analyst. This raises the question of what constitutes authentic contact, and part of the answer rests with whether we are considering authenticity from a conscious or an unconscious basis. There can be little doubt that the analyst's remarks confirming an accurate impression of his or her emotional state by the patient can feel consciously reassuring, but attention to the analysand's associations to such reassurances may reveal an unconscious experience at variance with conscious expressions. For example, Feldman (1993) discussed Klein's (1961) treatment of Richard, a very anxious boy whom she reassured in one session that she saved an envelope that he feared she might have burned. Richard smiled and complimented his analyst that she was "patriotic"[6] and then immediately spoke of a girl who looked like a monster. Klein noted that her offering reassurance (on a conscious) level was felt unconsciously by the boy as doubting her "honesty and sincerity." Feldman comments:

> . . . what the patient would actually have found reassuring would have been to encounter an analyst who was able to understand and bear the patient's *and her own anxiety and pain* without trying to give an apparent reassurance to her young patient *or to herself.*
>
> (1993, p. 279, italics added)

Perhaps for theoretical reasons, or just simply British reserve, the London Kleinians have spoken very little of their private thoughts about their patients, thereby (inadvertently, I believe) conveying the impression of only being interested in the analysand's psyche. However, a close reading of in-depth case discussions clearly demonstrates their attunement to the patient's attempts to affect the analyst, to draw him into a specific role, its effect upon the analyst's emotions, and an appreciation of how the analyst's induced state of mind is experienced by the patient. I see this as a kind of "back-door" intersubjectivity that remains implicit in numerous Kleinian publications. In quoting Feldman above, I italicized "and her own anxiety and pain" as well as "or to herself" to underscore the implicit assumption that the patient is unconsciously attuned to, and making meaning of, the analyst's mental states.

Indeed, this unconscious reading of the analyst's emotional state is intimately connected to projective identification because the patient does not simply project into the analyst's mind in general but, rather, into a specific site in the analyst, as though the projective identification is a "smart bomb" aimed at an affectively resonant location and guided by an empathetic "GPS" system (Brenman Pick, 1985).[7] In addition to locating a "suitable target for externalization" (Volkan, 1976), according to Caper (1996) the patient engages the analyst by projecting an aspect of his internal world into the analyst's mind to learn about the analyst's reaction to what he projects. In this way the patient learns something about himself and his analyst by the reaction he obtains in response to his projective probe. In this manner,

> we learn about the minds of our objects by projecting into them our inner states (to see how they react), and we learn about our own inner states by *using the minds of our objects as instruments for measuring them (by seeing how they reacted).*
>
> (Caper, 1996, p. 862, italics added)

Caper's observation obviously applies to the two minds – analyst and patient – engaged in analysis and describes the means by which an *authentic* encounter is created, a connection between the analytic dyad that Betty Joseph (1971, 1985, 1987) often refers to as *real contact*. In her paper, "The Patient Who Is Difficult to Reach" (Joseph, 1975), she distinguishes between "*the* [patient's] *experience of being understood, as opposed to 'getting' understanding*" (1975, p. 79, italics in original). "Getting" understanding refers to offering the patient an interpretation culled from the analysand's verbal "material," an approach that does not include attention to what Joseph calls the *total situation*, which is comprised of nonverbal elements, how the patient makes use of the analyst's remarks, and, most importantly, "how our patients act on us to feel things for many varied reasons" (1985/1989, p. 157). Joseph would not disclose what she is privately feeling, but she states that

It is important to show, primarily, the use the patient has made of what he believed to be going on in the analyst's mind.

(1975, p. 80)

Furthermore,

> Interpretations dealing only with the individual associations would touch only the more adult part of the personality, whereas the part that is really needing to be understood is communicated through the pressures brought to bear on the analyst.

(1985/1989, p. 159)

Real contact, therefore, is achieved in the moment-to-moment aliveness of an analytic engagement that implicitly acknowledges the analysand's perception, accurate or not, of what is occurring in the analyst's mind and addresses the unconscious meaning that perception holds for the patient. I suggest that self-disclosures by the analyst that confirm the patient's speculations about the analyst's state of mind offer the analysand the conscious experience of *getting understood* on an adult level, but they do not convey an experience of *being understood* on a plane of deep unconscious phantasy.

At the start of this chapter I quoted Gabriel Garcia Marquez: "In the end, it is impossible not to become what others believe you are," which seems to capture the Kleinian intersubjective position. The phrase "it is impossible not to become" expresses the inevitability of the analyst identifying with what is projected into him or her and the clinical necessity of becoming that projection. We have seen how Klein's original concept of projective identification as an intrapsychic phantasy has been developed to include the effect that projections have upon the receiver by virtue of the analyst becoming/identifying with that which is projected. On the level of unconscious phantasy, the analyst's identification with the projection ensures that the analysand experiences him or her as having "become what others [the patient] believe(s) you are." *It is this unconscious recognition on the patient's part that the analyst has become the projection and can tolerate[8] this experience that creates for the analysand a sense of being authentically understood.*

In summary, the notion that the analyst identifies with an aspect of the analysand is not an idea originally conceptualized by the Kleinians. For example, Fliess's (1942) concept of trial identification

58

speaks to this phenomenon, but his emphasis was on the analyst's identification with the analysand's instinctually based "transference striving." In contrast, the English Kleinians have addressed the ways in which the analyst *becomes* the (or an aspect of the) patient through the combination of the patient's activity of projective identification and the analyst's activity of introjecting what is projected. Bion's (1957, 1958, 1959) extension of projective identification as an unconscious means of affective communication gives a theoretical underpinning to Heimann's and Money-Kyrle's assertion that the countertransference represents a barometer by which to understand the analysand. The perspective of the therapeutic dyad engaged in an unconscious intersubjective exchange grows out of the Kleinian assumption that the analytic situation is crafted by the oscillations of introjective and projective identifications, although, as we have seen, the impact of the analyst's psychology is recognized (Joseph, Money-Kyrle) but rarely discussed, except for attention given to the patient's phantasies of what is in the analyst's mind. The London Kleinians pioneered the view of the unconscious as populated (Brown, 1996) by phantasies of internal objects and other chimeras, inhabitants of the representational world (Sandler & Rosenblatt, 1962) that are externalized by projective identification into the transference and countertransference:

> ... it seems necessary for the patient that the analyst should become involved in the living out of some aspects of phantasies that reflect his internal object relations.
>
> (Feldman, 1997, p. 228)

While I am certain that Feldman scrutinizes his subjective reactions to the patient, the absence of any mention of such introspection has added to the tendentious judgment of the London Kleinians as removed, uninvolved, and inauthentic (Benjamin, 2009).

Becoming: the River Plate Group Kleinians

The emigration of Klein's ideas from Europe in the early 1940s to the River Plate region[9] in South America landed on fertile ground out of which grew a decidedly intersubjective interpretation of Kleinian concepts (de León de Bernardi, 2000). Many of the most influential

Spanish–language analytic papers published in Argentina and Uruguay were never translated into English, and so their influence was restricted to Spanish-speaking analysts. For example, Madeleine and Willy Baranger's exceptional paper, "The Analytic Situation as a Dynamic Field" (1961–62; revised in 1969), was not translated until its recent 2008 appearance in the *International Journal of Psychoanalysis*. Thus, its impact on analytic thinking is profound in Latin American institutes and also among many Italian analysts (Bezoari & Ferro, 1992; Ferro, 1992, 1993, 2002, 2005) who are at ease with Spanish. However, before launching into a discussion of the Barangers' paper, it is essential that we get a sense of the analytic climate in Buenos Aires that nurtured the growth of a particular perspective on Kleinian theories.

The cultural ambience of the Argentine Psychoanalytic Association (APA), which was formed in 1942, was one that combined psychoanalysis with input from social psychology, including the study of group phenomena, philosophy, and literature, giving the institute a broad intellectual tradition from which to draw (de León de Bernardi, 2008). Although there was some interest in psychoanalytic ideas prior to the outbreak of World War II, it was not until the influx of European analysts in the late 1930s that analysis took hold and was organized. Etchegoyen (2005) credits Angel Garma, a co-founder of the APA along with Pichon-Rivière (see below), as well as its first president (Etchegoyen, 1993), as the primary figure in establishing psychoanalysis in Argentina. A native of the Basque region of Spain, Garma moved to Berlin to obtain analytic training and was analyzed by Theodore Reik, as was Paula Heimann.[10] Garma's interests lay in the study of dreams (1946[11]), and in 1955 he published a paper entitled "Vicissitudes of the Dream Screen and the Isakower Phenomenon." Like Isakower, throughout his career Garma displayed a deep curiosity about dream-like experience. He also probed the nature of psychosomatic illnesses (especially peptic ulcers) and their treatment by analysis.

Enrique Pichon-Rivière, whose parents emigrated to Argentina from Switzerland in 1910, was an omnipresent force in the new institute of which he was a founding member and whose scholarly influence was attained largely through his seminars. He was analyzed first by Angel Garma (thus "inheriting" the analytic DNA passed down from Abraham to Reik to Garma) and then later by Marie Langer. He published very little, and none of his works have been translated into

English. Pichon-Rivière introduced Klein's ideas to Argentina (Etchegoyen, 2005) by bringing some of her books to Buenos Aires. He was also greatly influenced by the work of Kurt Lewin's social psychology, was familiar with the writings of Harry Stack Sullivan, and brought Lewin's Gestalt ideas of the field together with Kleinian notions of primitive object relations. When the Barangers moved to Montevideo, Uruguay, to start an institute there, they maintained a close tie with Pichon-Rivière, who frequently traveled to Montevideo to teach. Pichon-Rivière proposed a *spiral process* to characterize analytic work, in which there is a constant "spiral dialectic between the 'here, now, with me' and the 'there and then'" (de León de Bernardi, 2008, p. 781). Regarding the intellectual atmosphere that he elicited in Uruguay, Willy Baranger commented

> Pichon-Riviere shared with us the aim (partly the myth?) of a freer, more creative psychoanalytic institution, more permeable to insanity, not as limited by conceptual orthodoxies and rivalries over petty achievements as the mainstream institutes.
>
> (de León de Bernardi's, 2008, p. 777, translation of
> W. Baranger, 1979, p. 17)

We can begin to grasp a sense of the analytic perspectives promulgated by Pichon-Rivière and Garma with their emphasis upon notions of the Gestalt field, the spiral-like connection between the past and present as well as between patient and analyst, dream-like thought, and unmentalized experience observed in psychosomatics.

Heinrich Racker investigated the connection between transference and countertransference with greater discipline and focus, essentially expanding Pichon-Rivière's concept of a *spiral* process. Racker, born in Poland in 1910 and emigrating to Vienna with his family at the beginning of World War I, earned a doctorate in Philosophy and began his analytic training in 1936 at the Vienna Institute. He was briefly analyzed by Jeanne Lampl-de Groot, one of the first generation of psychoanalysts who were interested in child analysis and the psychology of women from a classical analytic perspective. Both Racker and Lampl-de Groot fled Vienna in 1938 with the arrival of the Nazi *Anschluss*: she returned to her native Holland, and he emigrated to Buenos Aires, where he resumed his training with Marie Langer as his analyst.[12] Langer, also a Vienna-trained (and born) analyst, similarly escaped Austria for South America, but shortly before the *Anschluss*. Langer was deeply interested in politics, having been a member of the Communist Party in Austria, active in promoting women's rights, and was sensitized to the potential for authoritarian power in analytic training. She wrote about group psychoanalysis and how unconscious phantasies operate to create "myths that reflect a traumatic social and political situation that can also become a political weapon" (Langer, 1957). Langer's passion about groups and associated phantasies, coupled with Pichon-Rivière's strong influence on the APA based on social and Gestalt (field) psychology, surely influenced Racker's views that ultimately led to his ground-breaking contributions to the study of the links between transference and countertransference.

Racker, like Heimann,[13] believed that the capacity to identify with the patient is the "basis of comprehension" (Racker, 1957/1968, p. 134) of the analysand, but he elaborates the nature of these identifications in considerably greater detail. In this regard, Racker delineates *concordant* and *complementary identifications* that comprise important elements of the countertransference. Concordant identifications denote the analyst's introjection of an aspect of the patient's self, in which case the analyst unconsciously feels "this part of me is you" (pp. 134–135). In contrast, a complementary identification signals that the analyst has identified with an internal object of the patient. Racker, more stridently than Money-Kyrle and Joseph, asserts that the analysand is attuned to the countertransference and that the patient's awareness of the fantasied and real countertransference is a determinant of the transference. Thus,

> Analysis of the patient's fantasies about countertransference, which in the widest sense constitute the causes and consequences of the transferences, is an essential part of the analysis of the transferences.
>
> (p. 131)

As a consequence of the unconscious interpenetration of the inner object worlds of the patient and analyst, Racker (1957/1968) writes that a "psychological symbiosis" (p. 143) will often ensue. This is not necessarily an unwanted situation; however, in other circumstances an intersubjectively complicated picture may emerge, which he terms the *countertransference neurosis* (Racker, 1953). One of many possible manifestations occurs when the patient has become (projectively) identified with an internal object of the analyst and the analysis becomes, in the analyst's unconscious, something other than a thera-peutic undertaking. Noting that some internal objects serve superego functions, Racker refers to other occasions when, from a structural point of view, analyst and patient may come to unconsciously repre-sent for each other the id, ego, or superego. A countertransference neurosis may follow characterized by, for example, the analyst project-ing his id impulses into the patient that stirs him or her to adopt the position of a superego toward the analysand. Unconsciously, or consciously, sensing that he or she is regarded as embodying poorly controlled impulses by the analyst, the analysand may react in a variety of ways, including anger, acting out, feeling misunderstood, etc.

It is my impression that Racker and South American Kleinian analysts in general are more at ease than their British colleagues in taking into account the effect of the analyst's subjectivity upon the patient.[14] O'Shaughnessy (1999) offered an example of the kind of intersubjective entanglements, described by Racker, that may develop when the analytic dyad devolves into two disgruntled individuals "who confront one another as abnormal superego to abnormal superego" (p. 862). More than most other London Kleinians tend to reveal, O'Shaughnessy addressed how she "found myself getting very depressed" (p. 867) in response to a patient's stance of superiority and "pressurized to condemn him in a way that would draw me into his cruel terrain" (p. 867). Though she is unmistakably linking her experience of depression and provocation to deprecate her patient in response to his unforgiving hostile arrogance, it leaves the reader wondering about the patient's awareness of O'Shaughnessy's feelings and their impact upon him. It seems that Racker's (1957) advice that "Analysis of the patient's fantasies about countertransference . . . is an essential part of the analysis of the transferences" remains an implicit supposition but is not discussed directly by O'Shaughnessy. Sadly, however, Racker died at the age of 50, at the height of his creativity; truly a great loss for the entire psychoanalytic community.

Leon Grinberg was another leading figure in the APA. He was born in Buenos Aires to parents who had emigrated from Safed, Israel (then Palestine), home of the mystical Kabbalah. According to R. Oelsner (personal communication in 2008), "he inherited some of the wisdom of the wise old men in Safed that came to Palestine from Spain fleeing the Spanish Inquisition." He was analyzed by Arnaldo Rascowsky, originally a pediatrician who as an analyst wrote about the infantile psyche, and later, like Racker, by Marie Langer. Thus,

Grinberg, like the Barangers and Racker, was a member of the second generation of Argentine analysts whose thinking about the analytic encounter was influenced by Pichon-Rivière's thoughts about the spiral process of analysis by which the minds of analysand and analyst became interwoven, and he underwent personal analyses by analysts who studied the infantile mind as well as group perspectives on unconscious phantasy.

Grinberg (1962,[15] 1990) coined the term *projective counteridentification* to describe the impact of the analysand's projective identifications upon the analyst's subjectivity. As we have seen, it is essential that the analyst *become* through a temporary identification what the patient is projecting; however, there are certain situations when the analyst "ceases to be himself and turns unavoidably into what the patient unconsciously wants him to be" (1990, p. 84) – that is, the analyst concretely experiences himself actually to be the projection (as Gabriel Garcia Marquez noted at the start of this chapter). I believe this is what occurred in the Chapter 2 vignette of Johnny, who coerced me into becoming a killer of women, a role I struggled mightily against accepting. I had fallen out of the play mode, and my resistance to entering the play must have been rooted in an unconscious concreteness: that to *play a murderer of women was tantamount to being such a killer.* It took Johnny's gentle reminder, "Dr. Brown, we were only playing," to restore me to my senses.

Grinberg (1990) emphasizes that the analyst experiences a kind of passivity when under the sway of a projective counteridentification and that

> the analyst's reaction is largely *independent of his own conflicts and corresponds predominantly or exclusively with the intensity and quality of the analysand's projective identification.*
>
> (p. 88, italics in original)

He contrasts the concept of projective counteridentification with Racker's idea of the complementary countertransference. When the analyst is under the impact of a complementary countertransference, his identification with the projected internal object of the patient stirs a personal reaction, based upon his or her idiosyncratic conflicts, in the analyst. By contrast, with projective counteridentification

> the same patient, using his projective identification in a particularly

intense and specific way, could evoke the *same countertransferential response* (projective counteridentification) in different analysts.

(Grinberg, 1990, p. 90, italics in original)

While I agree with Grinberg's observation that the analyst may feel passively drawn into the projective counteridentification (as I did with Johnny's forceful pressure to be a murderer), I question whether, even in the face of the patient's violent projective identifications, the analyst's emotional reaction is truly "independent of his own conflicts." I am inclined to agree with Ogden's (1994a) view that even in cases of disturbance in the analyst brought on by personally troubling preoccupations, such as having a child in the hospital, what passes through the analyst's mind while with a particular patient still refers in some way to the analytic situation of the moment. Regardless of one's stance on this issue, Grinberg's formulation of projective counteridentification was hatched in a climate that increasingly came to consider the subjective experiences of both the analyst and analysand as an interlinked affective double helix. Grinberg advanced our understanding of intersubjective processes by exploring in great detail the nature of the analyst's internal relationship to what the patient has projected.

In summary, we can begin to appreciate the cultural and psychoanalytic milieu of the River Plate Group of which the Baranger's (1961–62) paper, "The Analytic Situation as a Dynamic Field," was a creative extension (de León de Bernardi, 2000, 2008).[16] Both Barangers emigrated from France to Argentina in 1946 after having earned doctoral degrees in their respective areas (Philosophy for Willy, Classics for Madeleine) and received their analytic training at the newly founded APA. Their publication was a sort of *selected fact* (Bion, 1962a), bringing together several parallel trajectories that had already been launched and unifying them into a common pathway from which a unique perspective on the analytic relationship appeared. The concept of a *dynamic field* owes much to their close collaboration with Pichon-Rivière and his ideas (from the work of Kurt Lewin) about Gestalt, social psychology, and group dynamics and Klein's understanding of unconscious phantasy (de León de Bernardi, 2008). Additionally, Langer, Puget, and Teper's (1974) thoughts about the operation of unconscious phantasies in groups and their commitment to socialism,[17] coupled with Bion's (1952, 1961) notions of a pervasive unconscious phantasy shared by the group, surely found their way into the Barangers' thinking. However, we should not under-estimate the extent to which their concept of the dynamic field was a watershed in recasting Kleinian theory as an intersubjective psychology.

The concept of the dynamic field

The Barangers' paper begins with a modest, though seismic, comment:

> . . . the analytic situation should be formulated not only as a situation of one person who is confronted by an indefinite and neutral personage . . . but as a situation between two persons . . . involved in a single dynamic process . . . [and] *neither member of the couple can be understood without the other.*
>
> (Baranger & Baranger, 1961–62, p. 796, italics added)

The patient and analyst, therefore, unconsciously create an emotional field together that the Barangers term a *bi-personal psychotherapeutic relationship*, which was replaced with *intersubjective field* in 1979 (W. Baranger, 1979; see also M. Baranger, 2005).[18] In this regard, the Barangers are conceptualizing the analytic field as a small group of two persons joined together "in unconscious phantasy that structures the bi-personal field of the analytic situation" (1961–62, p. 805). And just as Bion delineated the three "basic assumptions" that are common phantasies of a therapeutic group, so the Barangers postulate a shared unconscious phantasy that affectively colors an analytic session. In language that describes what we would today call "co-construction," they further state that

> The basic phantasy of the session is not the mere understanding of the patient's phantasy by the analyst, but something that is con-structed in a couple relationship.
>
> (p. 806)

The key word is that the shared unconscious phantasy is a *structure*, which denotes the formation of a psychic entity that is extant for a period of time, often for not much more than a session, and defines what the Barangers call the *point of urgency*. Though they do not credit

66

Klein directly, she first used this term in connection with the timing of an interpretation that ought to be given at the "point of urgency" (Klein, 1932), identified as the moment of maximal anxiety for the analysand. Thus, the Barangers are in essence re-defining Klein's technical suggestion in intersubjective terms: there is a shared experience in the analyst's and patient's minds that comprises the point of urgency, and this is where the analyst should intervene. In this connection, they are amplifying Racker's concept of concordant identification and Grinberg's conception of projective counteridentification; however, the Barangers take these ideas a step further by stating

> This structure [shared unconscious phantasy] cannot in any way be considered to be determined by the patient's (or the analyst's) instinctual impulses, although the impulses of both are involved in its structuring. . . . Neither can it be considered to be the sum of the two internal situations. *It is something created between the two, within the unit that they form in the moment of the session, something radically different from what each of them is separately.*
>
> (p. 806, italics added)

Here we see the Barangers formulating for the first time in the analytic literature the concept of co-construction of a third entity, the structure of a shared unconscious phantasy that emerges spontaneously in the intersubjective give-and-take of the analytic hour. This model also enlarges Pichon-Rivière's notion of the spiral process to include the interconnected coiling of the analyst's and patient's psyches as well as emphasizing the importance of the here-and-now "moment of the session." Furthermore, it seems to me that they are applying Klein's (1928, 1945) concept of the *creative couple* to the analytic dyad and underscoring the vital importance of the pair's fecundity and receptivity to mutual influence and anticipating what Bion (2005) later called the "something fascinating about the analytic intercourse; between the two of them, they do seem to give birth to an idea" (p. 22).

As we have seen, the Barangers' paper was only recently translated into English, in 2008; however, their concept of the shared unconscious phantasy representing a third "something created between the two" envisaged some contemporary ideas. Thomas Ogden's (1994a, 1994b) formulation of the *intersubjective analytic third*, published thirty-two years after the Spanish publication of the Barangers' "The Analytic Situation as a Dynamic Field," describes a similar perspective on the development of a third subjectivity created by the interpenetration of the psyches of analysand and analyst. This analytic third is an amalgam of both partners' unconsciouses, a relatively independent creation that has a life of its own: it is constantly being shaped, then reconfigured, by input from patient and analyst, and in turn it affects the pair. Consequently, each individual's experiences are simultaneously idiosyncratic as well as being products of the intersubjective analytic third. Even dreams – those most personal expressions of one's unique emotional "fingerprint" – are a construction of the analytic third:

> As an analyst and analysand generate a third subject, the analysand's experience of dreaming is no longer adequately described as being generated in a mental space that is exclusively that of the analysand . . . and might therefore be thought of as a dream of the analytic third.
>
> (Ogden, 1996, pp. 892–893)

Although Klein's (1946) formulation of projective identification and analytic conceptions of couples is implicit in Ogden's work, the Barangers leaned more on it from a theoretical point of view. In accounting for the development of the intersubjective analytic third, Ogden (1994a, 1994b) initially tended to be more heavily influenced by Winnicott's (1953) theory of transitional space and phenomena, and later developments of Ogden's theory (2004a, 2004b) were achieved by an integration of Bion's (1962a, 1992) thoughts about *reverie* and *dreaming* (see below). The Barangers (1961–62) ask rhetorically how the analytic couple differs from other couples of friendship or enmity and state that

> The criterion of the difference is . . . that it [the analytic dyad] is a couple in which all other imaginable couples are experienced while none of them is put into action [and that] the analytic gestalt by its nature needs to be invaded by all the other couple gestalts if it is to stay healthy.
>
> (1961–62, p. 807)

And, furthermore, that

the analytic couple depends on the process of projective identification and the unconscious phantasy of the bi-personal field is an interplay of projective and introjective identifications. . . . *The situation is managed in such a way as to avoid or limit the phenomenon of projective counteridentification.*

(p. 808, italics added)

Thus, the analyst must place him/herself in a receptive stance and remain open to be "invaded by all other couple gestalts," yet be cautious about being drawn into a projective counteridentification – that is, to lose perspective and believe he or she *is* actually the object the analysand experiences the analyst to be.

Ferro (2002, 2005) also speaks of the *couple's fertility*, which is an important component of the analytic field and is related to the question of analyzability: can this analyst/patient dyad engage in a mutual unconscious process that transforms unrepresented emotional experience? One offspring of the patient/analyst interaction is the appearance of visual images, and Ferro asserts that it is irrelevant whether the pictograms "belong" to one or the other of the pair because these are manifestations of the field. However, it is my impression that Ferro tends to place greater emphasis on the separate minds of the analyst and the patient working together more than do the Barangers and Ogden, who view the analytic pair as creating a third area of experience in which it is not that important to ask "Whose idea was it?" (Ogden, 2003a). Regardless of the import Ferro places on this question, he introduces the concept of *narratives*, and the associated appearance of *characters*, as barometers of the aliveness in the analytic field. This emphasis on the development of narratives as vehicles for transformation of the shared unconscious phantasy is a unique contribution of Italian analysts who work with the concept of the field (Ferro, 2009). Building on Bion's (1965) work on transformations, Ferro views the transformation of unsymbolized emotional experience (β elements) into symbolic thoughts (α elements) as a chief task of the analyst whose proper stance in analysis is one of *transformational receptiveness.* When the joint analytic work is proceeding well,

The relationship [between analyst and patient], or the field, is now understood . . . as the medium for operations of transformation, narratives and successive small insights.

(Ferro, 2002, p. 28)

For Ferro, the emergence of a new character, such as a father, mother, boss, etc., in the patient's communications indicates that the patient is transforming/representing some affective experience. From the classical analytic perspective, this may be viewed as a break in the associative flow[19] secondary to anxiety, but for Ferro such a shift, while possibly defensive, is also a signal to the analyst that something is percolating unconsciously in the field. The analyst must be open to the possibility that a new character represents the analysand's unconscious commentary on the analyst's technique, especially with regard to his receptiveness to the patient's projections. Ferro comments on

> the deep emotional level of the couple, on which the projective identifications are used to establish the emotional foundation which needs to be narrated through the characters and transformed by working through, and which must be shared by way of a story.
>
> (p. 25)

Thus far in our discussion of the Barangers' paper, we have focused on the shared unconscious phantasy of the couple in the analytic field and on Ogden's as well as Ferro's contributions to our understanding of the field's dynamics. While a conceptualization of the field heightens our appreciation of the impressive intersubjective connection between patient and analyst, the Barangers (Baranger & Baranger, 1961–62; Baranger, Baranger, & Mom, 1983) also detailed how what they term *bastions* and *bulwarks* generate difficulties in the field. Bastions are walled-off enclaves (O'Shaughnessy, 1992) that protect

> whatever the patient does not want to put at risk because the risk of losing it would throw the patient into a state of extreme helplessness, vulnerability and despair ... [and are] aimed at preservation from intrusion by the analyst and the analyst's interpretations into a private sector of the analysand's life.
>
> (Baranger & Baranger, 1961–62, pp. 814–815)

Depending upon the analyst's particular conflicts, the patient's bastion may find common cause with an allied area of emotional turmoil in the analyst, his *countertransference neurosis* (Racker, 1953), which together create a bulwark that the Barangers describe as "a purely repetitive granite-like block ... [to] completely paralyze the analytic process" (p. 817). Thus, the bulwark rests atop, and is an expression of, the shared unconscious phantasy of the analytic couple, which is a "stable structure" (p. 816) co-constructed from the interweaving of the transference/countertransference entanglement.

Ferro (2002, 2005) discusses the possibility that a bulwark may develop into an impasse if the analyst is unable to detect its presence, and he reminds us of the Barangers' (Baranger, Baranger, & Mom, 1983) advice that the analyst stand back and take a *second look* at both the patient's and the analyst's contributions to the impasse. Adding Bion's (1965) theory of transformations to the Barangers' ideas, Ferro sees the impasse as a collusion by the analytic couple to keep fears in each partner unmentalized – that is, as β elements. Analyst and analysand may unconsciously collaborate to tell each other comforting lies in order to remain shielded from painful emotional truths (Grotstein, 2004). In a related vein, Maldonado (1984), from Buenos Aires, observes that an impasse may also be characterized by "the absence or marked diminution of the type of representations which make up visual images" (p. 264), an observation that may be accounted for by the relative failure in the transformation of β to α elements. However, Ferro points to a potentially positive and adaptive aspect of an impasse in which the analytic couple may have time to prepare, consciously and unconsciously, for facing the source of the shared unconscious phantasy that has become hardened into an impasse. Cassorla (2005), a Brazilian analyst, also cites positive elements of the bastion as expressed in *pathological enactments* that are characterized by massive projective identifications of unrepresented β elements. In such cases, the impasse represents what he calls "elements in search of a thinker" (p. 708), which paraphrases Bion's (1962a, 2005) concept of "thoughts without a thinker." In this connection, the seemingly impenetrable and endlessly repeating enactment may also be a search, so to speak, by the analysand for an analyst who can transform what the patient is unable to represent. In summary, the intersubjectively created bulwark (and possible impasse) is unconsciously knitted by the "collaborating" psyches of analyst and patient, aimed at protecting each partner from frightening emotional truths by keeping such verities unmentalized, yet, paradoxically, also searching for another mind to think what is unthinkable.[20] This brings us to what Ogden (2001) calls the "frontier of dreaming" and to Bion's theory of dreaming.

Bion: trauma, transforming, and dreaming

Wilfred Bion was born in colonial India in 1897 and was sent to boarding school in England when he was 8 years old, never to return to the country of his birth (Bion, 1991a). He served as a young tank commander in World War I and encountered first hand the horrific cruelty of that conflagration, which, together with the trauma of being sent to boarding school, left indelible and haunting memories. He was analyzed briefly by John Rickman prior to World War II, at which point both Rickman and Bion joined the British army, became professional colleagues, and promulgated theories of group relations from their work with military officers. Kurt Lewin's (1935) writings about *field theory* formed a theoretical basis for the so-called "Northfield Experiments" (Harrison, 2000); indeed, Bion and Rickman (1943) published an early paper on intra-group tensions in which Lewin's influence was in clear evidence. Rickman, we may recall (Chapter 2), was analyzed by Freud, then by Ferenczi, and later by Klein in London and was the first analyst to suggest a "two-person psychology"; thus, the "intersubjectivity gene" was passed to him from Freud (unconscious communication), Ferenczi (the concepts of introjection and "mutual analysis"), and Klein (through her "inheritance" from Ferenczi and Abraham) as well as directly in Rickman's analysis from her discovery of projective identification. Additionally, Rickman (1945) showed an early interest in Lewin's *field theory* and gave a paper at the British Psychoanalytical Society in 1945 (Churcher, 2008) on this subject. For Bion, this "gene" was inherited from Rickman and Bion's own analysis with Klein, a "gene" that probably was also expressed by his immersion in group processes, which, as in many of the River Plate Group, promoted a tendency to see the analytic dyad as a small group.

It is my impression (Brown, 2006 – Chapter 7, this volume; see also Symington & Symington, 1996) that Bion's challenges of coming to emotional terms with these nearly unbearable experiences in his early years and in World War I[21] contributed significantly to his life work of addressing how one processes overwhelming feelings in order to learn from experience. This processing requires the existence within the individual of what Bion (1962a) terms *alpha function*, which "works on" concrete perceptual/sensory experiences to transform these into conceptual events.[22] *It is important to note that α function is the internalization of a complex intersubjective relationship between the mother and infant*

72

and not, as other authors[23] *have written, simply the internalization of a maternal function.* Put another way, it is the mother and infant thinking together as a couple that is installed in the psyche as α function. Like other writers, Bion underscored the importance of the analyst introjecting the patient's projection, but he added another dimension to this notion when he described a patient who "put bad feelings in me [in order to] leave them there long enough for them *to be modified* by their sojourn in my psyche" (1958/1967, p. 92, italics added). Bion did not, in this early paper, address the process in the analyst that causes what is projected into him "to be modified," but he turned his thinking to this question in subsequent contributions (1962a, 1962b, 1992) when he proposed the concepts of α function, reverie, and transformation (Bion, 1965) and in his elaboration of Freud's theory of dreaming.

Bion's theories of α function, reverie, container–contained, transformation, and dreaming are closely related concepts, all of which dovetail around how the mind *modifies* sensory-based (β-element) emotional experience and turns it into conceptual representations (α elements) in order for mature forms of thinking to develop that may be linked together in narratives suitable for conscious and unconscious communication. According to Grotstein (2009a),

> Even though Bion did not neatly distinguish between dreaming and alpha function . . . [he] tends to treat "dreaming" and "alpha-function" either as identical, overlapping, and/or as the latter's being a component of the former.
>
> (p. 734)

In either case, the patient projects something (an affect, internal object, etc.), called the *contained* (♂), into the analyst, the *container* (♀), who permits entry of the contained for a period of time, the *sojourn*, during which the analyst "modifies" the contained (♂) through his *reverie*, which is an aspect of α *function* that acts to *transform/dream* the contained (♂). According to Bion's view of *dreaming*, we are dreaming all the time, while we are awake and while we are asleep – that is, our minds are endlessly engaged in absorbing and metabolizing (to go back to Abraham's, 1924, original concept) unmentalized experience that arises from within ourselves, from others conveyed by projective identification, or from encounters with the ineffable and unknowable mythical substrate of human existence, Bion's "O" (1965, 1970; see also Grotstein, 2000, 2004, 2005, 2007, with which we must all suffer (Bion, 1965; Levine, 2011) and face.

From an intersubjective perspective, the analytic session is a place where the analyst and patient create together the shared "unconscious phantasy of the couple" (Baranger & Baranger, 1961–62) that is constructed from the intertwining of the patient's transference neurosis with the analyst's countertransference neurosis, thereby creating an *intersubjective field*. From a technical vantage point, the Barangers relied primarily on the importance of interpretation, preceded by taking a *second look* when necessary. However, today, following Bion's ideas about dreaming, transforming, and reverie, we widen our view of the intersubjective field to include the analyst's reveries (Bion, 1962a; Ogden, 1994b, 1997a, 1997b, 2004a, 2004b), so-called "wild thoughts" (Bion, 1997), dreams while awake and asleep (Brown, 2007 – see Chapter 9, this volume), enactments (Cassorla, 2005; Jacobs, 1991; Sandler, 1976), and other nonverbal aspects of the analyst's experience. The shared unconscious phantasy of the analytic couple is additionally the embodiment of a third area of experience, neither the analysand nor the analyst, but an "offspring" with its own vibrancy.[24] The analytic bounty of this fruitful collaboration is the appearance of Ogden's (1994a, 1994b) intersubjective analytic third, the arrival of Ferro's (2002, 2005) characters, and unconscious perceptions of the analyst as receptively open to authentically suffering with the analysand. In what follows, I present a segment from an analysis of a woman who suddenly announced she needed to sit up, and I discuss how this "decision" was unconsciously framed by two dreams, one a countertransference dream of mine and the other her dream, both of which captured an aspect of the shared unconscious phantasy that colored our "couplehood" of the moment.

Clinical vignette: dreaming the field

About three years into her analysis, Ms. C. abruptly said she needed to sit up because she could not tolerate the loneliness of lying on the couch. I was surprised by the apparent suddenness of this and wondered what might be occurring in the intersubjective field of which her "symptom" might be an expression. Her anxieties about weaning Molly, her 2-year-old daughter, and the associated feelings of loss in general had been center stage for some time. This was a difficult challenge for her and for Molly because of the profound pleasure it brought to both and also, I believe, because it signified a partial relinquishing of the special, safe sanctuary that they shared as well as the associated gratification of Ms. C.'s needs for maternal care. Two dreams, one my countertransference dream and the other Ms. C.'s, dreamed within a few nights of each other, seem to capture some sense of what was unconsciously defining the underlying shared phantasy of the field. My dream came first, and it was dreamed the night of our talking about her husband saying that she was never satisfied with anything he did. I dreamed that:

> I am in the apartment in which I grew up, in the living room and watching TV. I have a relaxed and unhurried feeling, although I am also aware that I have a patient to see at the end of the show. Suddenly I realize that it's one or two minutes past the appointment time and I rush to set up my office, which is the old bedroom that my brother, sister, and I shared when we were small. The place is a mess and I start to tidy it up. There was a brownish sofa with the pillows upended. At this point I realize the patient is Ms. C. and also that there is no waiting room; that she'd be standing outside the door ringing the bell. I have a sinking/guilty feeling that she will feel hurt/ rejected if I'm not on time and that she would leave.

My associations (that have to do with Ms. C.) were to pleasurable recollections of being a child, my family of origin temporarily reconstituted for some lovely dreamy moments, something very precious but now merely a memory. Then I thought of watching TV as a time when my mother would often make demands on me as a child, that she had just recently come home from the hospital, and I thought about my elderly father trying to meet her needs. I thought about how easily Ms. C. could feel hurt and how sensitive she is to feeling excluded from my life. There is also a story about me as a small child in which I demanded my grandmother feed me while I rang the doorbell, and it brings to mind Ms. C.'s anxiety about not meeting Molly's demands to be fed in the manner she desires. Thus, I speculate that I was dreaming about something that was in the analytic ambiance, but I had not quite consciously grasped it, and that it had to do with feelings around losing a precious childhood sense of togetherness [Ms. C. weaning Molly] as well as about unreasonable demands [her husband's complaint about her; Molly's refusal to wean; the recollection of my mother's demands; my insistence on being fed while ringing the doorbell].

In the intervening sessions between our two dreams, Ms. C. talked with considerable anxiety about her fear of hurting Molly by weaning her, of shutting her out, worrying that she was being cruel and depriving. Molly had begun to speak and cried for her breasts, and with great sadness Ms. C. said, "today is the first day in the two years she has been alive that she hasn't had my breast . . . I started to fill with milk today; I had to express it." Ms. C. joked that I had put her up to this, and then she talked about hearing about a lovely home for sale on my street [she and her husband had been looking for some time], but it was unavailable to her because of its proximity to me. She talked about the loss of moving from where she lived to my town, the milk she was not giving to Molly, the mild disappointment mixed with relief that her daughter was thriving in day care despite the weaning struggle, and also her doubts about whether she would want a second child. When I suggested she might like some nurturing from me, Ms. C. dismissed that as a crazy idea, the kind of nutty talk that her mother would say. She added that her transference to me was as a father and that we both knew how unavailable he was. I said that it is very sad to have a mother who makes no sense and no father to turn to in her place.

Ms. C. missed the session prior to the one in which she reported her dream because of an emergency dentist appointment. She was relieved to miss the analytic session and that she noticed herself detaching from me because she felt I did not care about her. She said it was hard to count on anyone, including me, and worried that with the expense of their new home she would not be able to afford to come to analysis. Ms. C. then said she had the following dream:

"You invited me to your house and you showed me around and we talked about decorating. You showed me this little room you built with a swimming pool, and I really liked it. I was talking to your daughter and we were getting along. She was nice.

She said it was a nice dream, but also sad because she realized she would never be invited into my home, nor would I see her new house. She wondered if my daughters lived at home [she heard that I have two girls]. I said "It's like the dream is saying 'Look how nice it could be, but it will never be' and that it leaves you with a futile feeling."

76

Her thoughts turned to her upcoming trip to Washington, DC, and to the sniper who was still at large who had killed many people. Also, her husband was feeling sick and that worries her because his father died at 47. Just before time was up, she recalled that there was a jacuzzi next to the swimming pool in my house and that it had a "cottagey retreat feeling." I said "a dream house," and she nodded.

Ms. C. started to sit up shortly after this sequence of several sessions that began with my countertransference dream. In retrospect, it seems that a wellspring of deeply felt feelings had been gradually building, perhaps triggered by the struggle to wean Molly. My dream and hers might be viewed as bookends between which lay volumes of powerful affects, and both of our dreams seem to have been created from a prevailing mood that was initially out of our collaborative awareness. I worried about possibly injuring her through exclusion in my dream, an anxiety that suffused Ms. C.'s struggles with weaning her daughter. In addition, the "dream house," into which my home was transformed by her dream, surely expressed her wish to be sheltered there as one of my daughters and, on a deeper level, must also be the "dream house" of early mother/infant intimacy from which both she (through her identification with Molly) and Molly were being evicted. Finally, lying on the couch in the context of these formidable affects was unbearably lonely and disconnected from a transferential father (and probably mother, too) who seemed unable to provide a warm home and a "cottagey retreat."

Ms. C. and I initially explored her lonely feelings and the fact that these were so unbearable to her. This led to a fruitful understanding of some of the roots of such emotions; however, the understanding only achieved a somewhat improved ability to tolerate the lonely feelings. While she was able to examine her loneliness in the sessions, the underlying longings have been much more assiduously defended against. Thus, Ms. C. could talk about her mother's "not getting it" and how her mother's empathy was always many degrees off, but my suggestions that she pined for something different from her mother (or me) tended to be brushed off. For example, during this time, she told me of the importance of her maternal grandmother, who lived with them when she was small, and that her grandmother made up for her mother's shortcomings. I said to Ms. C., after some months of sitting up, that we might want to reconsider her decision to sit up: that while it offered her a greater sense of connection to me, it also seemed to keep us from learning more about her loneliness and why these feelings are so unmanageable for her. She wondered if I would be able to help her deal with the loneliness and worried that I would be like her mother or father, who asserted that her feelings were "made up" and not genuine. She said that sitting up felt right for the time being because it allowed her to feel in better touch with me, something she needed. She also felt when I brought up the issue from time to time that I was telling her she "wasn't doing it right," a familiar and painful experience for her.

We can see in this vignette that there was a shared unconscious phantasy expressed in our dreams of being exiled from a longed-for preserve of precious childhood intimacy. Ms. C.'s guilt of weaning Molly painted the intersubjective analytic field, but she was unable to experience her desire to be nurtured and needed me to dream – that is, to represent – that longing for her, in a narrative form for us to explore together. My dream, therefore, captured Ms. C.'s pining for a familial Shangri-la and signaled my having *become* that wished-for yearning when I pleasantly dreamed myself back in a warm memory from childhood. In other words, my dream unconsciously worked on the unexpressed passionate desire in the field by linking it with affect-ively resonant memories from my childhood – that is, by creating a narrative that enabled me to begin to formulate some notion of the shared unconscious phantasy.

But my dream had another side. After pleasantly being transported back to childhood, the situation becomes messy and I am alarmed about abandoning Ms. C. as well as possibly losing her. In the dream, I am thrust out of the carefree, playful world of boyhood and become filled with anxiety about being an irresponsible adult. I was not fully aware at the time of having become so completely Ms. C.'s guilty self, but this identification allowed me to "taste" her rueful feelings and know firsthand the degree of her self-blame. Thus, my countertrans-ference dream, prior to her dream and leaving the couch, indicated that I was in the midst of narrating the shared unconscious phantasy of the field, although I was unaware of the extent to which the dream was a transformation of powerful conjoint affects that she and I were dreaming together.[25]

Bion (1965, 1970) has described two ways of how the analyst may understand the patient. He calls one the "K" link, where K is short-hand for *knowledge about* the analysand gleaned from listening to his or her associations and speculating about meanings. The other way of knowing a patient is the "O" link, which refers to *becoming or being at one-ment* (Bion, 1970) with the emerging unknown emotional truth of the session. It is only once the analyst has become this evolving O that he or she can offer an "interpretation [that is] an actual event in an evolution of O that is common to analyst and analysand" (p. 27). This seems to be Bion's equivalent to the Barangers' concept of the shared unconscious phantasy, though he stresses the necessity of becoming the unfolding emotional truth (Grotstein, 1981, 2004), O, while they primarily emphasize interpretation.

It was not until Ms. C. decided to sit up that the affective truth[26] of the shared unconscious phantasy began to dawn on me. Though we had each been dreaming and transforming by our own narratives the mutual O of our interaction, it remained unclear what exactly to make of these experiences. However, when Ms. C. said she needed to sit up because of her unbearable loneliness on the couch, the dreams depicting our respective perceptions of the shared unconscious phantasy of the intersubjective field suddenly, and retrospectively, acquired meaning that had been evolving through the unconscious work each of us had undertaken. To paraphrase Ogden's (2004b) idea of the analysand dreaming himself "into existence," Ms. C. and I had been engaged in dreaming ourselves into existence as a *dreaming couple* (Grotstein, 2000; see also Chapter 7), busily at work unconsciously to transform the intersubjective O of the shared unconscious phantasy into a co-created narrative of a moment in our history together.

We will now proceed in the next chapter to a more detailed discussion of Bion's theories as they apply to a deeper understanding of intersubjective phenomena.

Notes

1   Klein never referred to Ferenczi's later papers and mentioned him less frequently over time – only twice after 1933.
2   Freud (1918) first mentioned the epistemophilic instinct in the "Wolf Man" case.
3   Not to be confused with his *topographic model* that proposed the systems of conscious, preconscious, and unconscious.
4   Ernest Jones, though not a "Kleinian," was very favorably impressed by her work and invited Klein to move to London in the mid-1920s, whereupon she analyzed his wife and two children (Grosskurth, 1986). He was her leading advocate at that time; thus, one must assume that his praise of her work was surely conveyed to Money-Kyrle, either

consciously or not, and was a factor in his joining the Kleinian contingent in the British Psychoanalytical Society.

5 A viewpoint already promoted by Freud's (1910a) statement that "no psycho-analyst goes further than his own complexes and internal resistances permit" (p. 145).

6 The analysis occurred during World War II, when it was "patriotic" to conserve paper.

7 Krohn (1974) spoke of the uncanny ability of many borderline patients to detect the vulnerabilities in order to disturb their analysts, a capacity he refers to as "borderline empathy."

8 Carpy (1989) also underscores the technical importance of *tolerating* "the patient's projections in their full force, and yet be able to avoid acting them out in a gross way" (p. 289) as having a therapeutic benefit in itself.

9 The River Plate forms the boundary between northern Argentina and Uruguay.

10 It seems that there is something about the analytic lineage from Abraham to Reik and then to Heimann and Garma that appears to "prime" its descendants with a propensity for attention to dream thoughts, preverbal experience, and their manifestations in the interlinked transference and countertransference.

11 Published in English.

12 Racker appears to have had a brief stint of analysis with Angel Garma but for unknown reasons moved on to Langer. R. Oelsner (personal communication in 2008) speculates that it may have been a fee-related issue, because Racker was quite poor when he came to Buenos Aires, and Langer, given her Marxist proclivities, may have been more flexible with regard to finances.

13 Racker's paper, "A Contribution to the Problem of Counter-Transference," was first given in Spanish in 1948, though not published in English until 1953. Coincidentally, Heimann first delivered her paper, "On Counter-Transference," in 1949, and it was published in 1950.

14 It is difficult to assess the reason for these differences, especially when we consider the close connection between the London and River Plate Kleinians. A contingent of Argentine analysts attended the 1949 IPA Congress in Zurich and had a rewarding meeting with Melanie Klein. This initial contact was expanded during the 1950s and 1960s with frequent visits from important figures in the Kleinian world, including Hannah Segal, Bion, Meltzer, Rosenfeld, Betty Joseph, and others. In addition, many analysts from Buenos Aires sought out supervision and analysis in London (Etchegoyen, 2005).

15 This is the English version of a paper originally published in Spanish in 1956.

16 However, according to de León de Bernardi (2008): "Ego psychology was less accepted in the Rio de la Plata ... [because of] the fact that it was not considered radical enough in its interpretation of the unconscious, the supposition that the concept of adaptation could lead to social conformity and, last but not least, because of lack of knowledge" (p. 234).

17 From its inception, many members of the APA have had a strong affiliation with socialist/communist politics and movements that were represented by the *Platforma* group that was a segment of the institute's membership. However, in the 1970s during the difficult Peronist years when leftist organizations were frequently persecuted, the *Platforma* group seceded from the APA. This secession had its theoretical parallel in which Kleinian thought was identified with the established power hierarchy because of its predominance and the supposed minimization of social influences. As a counterpoint, Jacques Lacan's ideas were viewed as revolutionary (Etchegoyen, 2005).

18 The Barangers also state that "The analytic couple is a trio, one of whose members is physically absent and experientially present" (Baranger & Baranger, 1961–62, p. 798) to refer to the analyst's necessary split between his experiencing and observing selves. Interestingly, the concept of the "analytic couple as a trio" has been given scant attention in our literature, and this aspect of the Barangers' view of the dynamic field is never referenced by other authors. However, some recent papers that address the triangular aspects of the Oedipal situation (Aron, 2006; Benjamin, 2004; Britton, 1989; Brown, 2002; Caper, 2000) deal with the observing component of the analyst's mind. The triadic features of an intersubjective approach are discussed in greater depth in Chapter 6.

19 See Chapter 4 for a more detailed discussion of the ego–psychological school and its comparison to Bion's theories of transformation.

20 American analysts (Ellman, Jacobs, etc.) tend to see enactments as a form of resistance against the emergence of repressed unconscious material in which either or both the analyst and the patient participate. However, these analysts (Baranger, Ferro, Ogden) see a jointly constructed *bastion* as established by the analytic pair to avoid painful truths, as a failure to transform the shared unconscious phantasy, and as an expression of thoughts looking for a thinker, all of which require a restitution of a capacity for unconscious waking thought (dreaming).

21 Nicolson's (2009) recent book, *The Great Silence 1918–1920: Living in the Shadow of the Great War*, graphically describes the tragic fates of numerous surviving English soldiers who had been so severely maimed and mutilated that they were obliged to wear masks when out in public. These Phantom-of-the-Opera outcasts could not be ignored, yet a "great silence" blanketed full recognition of their sacrifices. Surely, these

haunted and disfigured living ghosts who walked London's streets must have also jarred Bion's own traumatic memories.

22 I discuss α function as one of the functions of the ego in Chapter 4.

23 For example, Kohutian writers describe *transmuting internalizations,* in which certain maternal functions of self-regulation are internalized.

24 In classical analysis it was said that a woman's wish to have the analyst's baby indicated her having reached a level of psychosexual maturity. Taken from another vertex (Bion, 1970; Ferro, 2002, 2005, 2009), could we say that such a wish reflects a patient's perception that the *analytic partnership was in the here-and-now* a fertile dyad that had already produced a "child?"

25 It also became evident at a later point in Ms. C.'s analysis that her sitting up was linked with anxieties about being engulfed by her needs for me and her sense of a need for weaning from this feared loss of self, as well as a dread of that weaning. However, it took considerable analytic work – and time – for Ms. C. to be able to acknowledge her intense dependent needs.

26 This "affective truth" is judged to be "truthful" because in the moment: (1) it subjectively feels "right" to the analyst; (2) it brings a sense of integration or "selected fact" (Bion, 1962a) to disparate impressions that did not previously cohere; and (3) it moves the analyst's experience of the session from Ps→D – that is, from unintegration to integration. The last two points are discussed further in Chapter 5.

4

The ego psychology of Wilfred Bion: implications for an intersubjective view of psychic structure[1]

> And we have to judge how to tell the patient the truth about himself without frightening him.
>
> (Bion, 1994, p. 173)

> Thus, if a resistance is in operation, it indicates that the patient is experiencing his or her thoughts or feelings as a danger.
>
> (Busch, 1995, p. 40)

Freud's writings are frequently mentioned in Bion's work, yet, when they are referenced, these citations are invariably to Freud's texts up to 1920. This is curious, especially given Bion's much-deserved reputation for erudition, and one must assume that he was very familiar with the entirety of Freud's work. It is as though he lost interest in Freud after the introduction of the structural theory (Freud, 1923a). Bion, however, often spoke of the "ego," found the idea of a superego useful, and furthered our understanding of the relationship between these two entities by promoting the notion of an "ego-destructive superego" (Bion, 1959, 1962a). Nevertheless, Bion (1994) found the conception of the tripartite model of the mind as incomplete and overly simple, "a crude, but shrewd subdivision of the mind into various parts" (p. 286).

In my view, although Bion largely eschewed Freud's structural model, much of his major theoretical thinking may be considered as the development of his own view of an aspect of the ego, alpha (α) function, that is engaged in giving meaning to emotional experience. Bion produced a view of the functioning ego, without naming it as such, that dealt with many of the same theoretical and clinical matters that Freud and the ego-psychological[2] school addressed from their perspective (e.g., the two epigraphs above from Bion and Busch regarding "resistance"). My main point is that what I will be referring to as Bion's "ego psychology" leads to an appreciation of the inter-subjective nature of psychic life and also a different view of structure. Furthermore, with regard to the clinical encounter, I contend that the so-called classical/relational split, which has been promulgated by both sides of this supposed divide, is a false dichotomy and assert that a consideration of Bion's two-person "ego psychology" is a conceptual tool to bridge that split. Additionally, I offer the view that the traditional ego-psychological emphasis on the analyst working on the psychic "surface" should be broadened to include the mental functioning of the analyst. Finally, I conclude with a clinical example in which the analysis of an adolescent is discussed from the enlarged view of the ego that combines ego-psychological and Bionian viewpoints.

The "Bionian" view of the ego

Bion was profoundly influenced by Freud's (1911) seminal paper, "Formulations on the Two Principles of Mental Functioning." *Indeed, this paper is by far the most widely quoted work of Freud's in Bion's writings, and, in my view, it is probably not excessive to state that much of Bion's theoretical contribution may be seen as an elaboration of this paper.* Freud described in "Two Principles" how the *pleasure principle* had to be supplemented by the *reality principle* because the "psychical apparatus had to decide to form a conception of the real circumstances in the external world" (p. 219) in order for it to survive. The establishment of the reality principle was a "momentous step" (p. 219) that placed new demands on the psychic apparatus for adaptation.

Freud also delineated in "Two Principles" the important role of *action*, which, under the aegis of the pleasure principle, "served as a means of unburdening the mental apparatus of accretions of stimuli" (p. 221). However, with the appearance of the reality principle, action was now to be more directed toward a goal in order to accomplish an "alteration of reality" (p. 221). *Thinking* developed as a means of restraining motor action by allowing the mental apparatus "to tolerate an increased tension of stimulus while the process of discharge was postponed . . . [and was] an experimental kind of acting" (p. 221). Freud did not identify the force requiring that "the psychic apparatus had to decide to form" a relationship with reality that demanded these new maturations, but he does give us a hint in a long footnote. He said that the adaptive changes are necessary for survival and then dropped a bit of a teaser when he said that the supremacy of the pleasure principle is ended "when a child has achieved complete psychical detachment from its parents" (p. 220 fn). This statement suggests an intimate connection between what happens in a baby's object relations and the growth of ego functions.

The commensal relationship and the dyadic expansion of consciousness

The association between the infant's early relationships and the growth of the ego is a vast area that has been explored extensively, and its scope is too broad to be reviewed here. However, *Bion's unique contribution to this territory is how the infant, in collaboration with its mother, comes to know reality, gives emotional meaning to its experiences, and learns from those experiences.* Alpha function, according to Bion, is that aspect of the personality that is responsible for comprehending emotional reality and giving affective meaning to perceptions, that develops in a unique choreography with its counterpart in the mother. Alpha function "may be regarded as a structure" (1962a, p. 26) and deploys consciousness like a searchlight to "probe the environment" (Bion, 1963, p. 19) and ascribe affective meaning to the objects detected in that probe.

In my opinion, Bion, without saying so, is in essence offering α function as a supraordinate ego function that is responsible for ascribing emotional meaning to experience. Alpha function, therefore, is the mechanism underlying the reality principle and also makes thinking possible. As we discussed in Chapter 3, Bion (1962a) described two kinds of basic thoughts, the first of which are *beta* (β) *elements*, which are raw sense impressions and emotions that are "not so much memories as undigested facts" (1962a, p. 7). Beta elements are concrete things-in-themselves that are "thought" about in a muscular way (like Freud's description of the role of action in the primary process to "unburden the mental apparatus"), meaning that the mind expels them through projective identification, a mechanism that is akin to one that Freud (1915b) implied, but never described in detail, in his concept of the "purified pleasure ego" that evacuates unpleasure to the environment. The second kind of thought is necessary for the capacity for narrative and metaphor, with latent meaning that may be accessed by "reading between the lines" and depends upon the existence of α function. The constituents of this kind of thinking are *alpha* (α) *elements*, which are β elements that have been transformed (mentalized) by α function. Though Bion does not make the direct connection, it seems to me that β elements are equivalent to the "accretions of stimuli"[3] from which, Freud stated, the primitive psyche sought to unburden itself. It is important to emphasize here that both the primary process and the secondary process coined by Freud depend upon α function since both operations require the presence of a symbolic capacity.

Freud (1911) saw the emergence of the reality principle as something forced on the mental apparatus by the demands of reality, and Bion agreed with this as a partial explanation for the development of thinking. However, *Bion's great innovation was to accord the mother, and her α function, a central role in the evolution of the infant's capacity to think and, therefore, learn from experience.* How does this happen? In his 1958 paper, "On Arrogance," Bion reported the case of a patient who found Bion "stupid" because he could not understand that the patient's attacks were a form of communication. Then Bion realized that this patient needed to "put bad feelings in me and *leave them there long enough for them to be modified by their sojourn in my psyche*" (1958/1967, p. 92, italics added). This finding represented a significant extension of Klein's (1946) view of projective identification as primarily an evacuative phenomenon by emphasizing instead its role as a communication designed to elicit a response (from the object) that "modifies" the projected emotions. In addition, Bion's use of the word "sojourn" implies that what is projected into the analyst remains there for a limited period before returning to its source. Thus, the analyst's mind, and the mind of the transferential mother, is elevated to a position of heretofore unappreciated importance in the development of the capacity for thinking.

Bion is here describing a communicative interplay between the minds of the infant and its mother that transforms (Bion, 1965) unmanageable and concrete (β–element) experience by virtue of its "sojourn" in the mind of the mother. The receiving mother takes in the projection and subjects it to her *reverie*, which is defined as

> that state of mind which is open to the reception of any "objects" from the loved object and is therefore capable of reception of the infant's projective identifications whether they are felt by the infant to be good or bad. In short, reverie is a factor of the mother's alpha–function.
>
> (Bion, 1962a, p. 36)

Interestingly, he (Bion, 1962a) calls what is projected into the mother the "*contained*," denoted by the symbol ♂, while the receptive function of the mother is called the "*container*," which is represented by the symbol ♀. The container takes in the contained (β element), processes it through its reverie, which is a constituent of the mother's α function, and through that processing transforms the β element into an α element. Bion (1962a) views the mother and infant who interact in this manner as a "thinking couple," and the activity of this ♂ ♀ pair is introjected as the "apparatus for thinking" that is "part of the apparatus of alpha–function" (1962a, p. 91).

Bion considers this container/contained (♂♀) relationship as "*commensal*" (Bion, 1962a, p. 91) in nature, meaning that the infant and its mother are dependent on one another and also that both grow through the process by which meaning is made of experiences that previously were merely raw sensory and concrete (Brown, 1985) things–in–themselves. Thus, Bion's view of this inchoate thinking couple who are beginning to co-construct meaning is similar to what Tronick (2005, 2007; Tronick et al., 1998) observes in the interaction of the states of consciousness (SOC) of the infant and mother,

> in which the successful regulation of meaning leads to the emergence of a mutually induced dyadic state of meaning ... [by which] new meanings are created and these meanings are incorporated into the SOCs of both individuals. As a consequence, *the coherence and complexity of each individual's sense of the world increases,* a process I refer to as the dyadic expansion of consciousness model.
>
> (Tronick, 2005, p. 294, italics added)

Thoughts without a thinker, mutuality, and growth in the container/contained

Bion offers two models, one explicit and the other more implicit, for the development of the relationship between the container and the contained. The more explicit model that he emphasized in his earlier writings (Bion, 1958, 1962a) is an *alimentary* one: that the infant evacuates an internal emotional experience into the mother, who "digests" through her α function what has been projected and gives it back to the baby in a more palatable state after its sojourn in her, not unlike a mother bird premasticating food for her newly hatched offspring. In my view, this is not a commensal model that leads to an increase in "the coherence and complexity of each individual's sense of the world"; rather, it emphasizes what the mother does for the infant. In addition to this alimentary model, Bion (1962a, 1997, 2005) offers, largely in his later writings, a *sexual/pro- or co-creative* paradigm that is more implicit in his writings and is directly suggestive of an interaction between mother and baby, between container and contained, that results in the growth of both partners and the creation of new meaning. For example, in discussing the appearance of unbidden "wild thoughts," Bion (1997) argues that it is not important to be "aware of the genealogy of that particular thought" (p. 27), a statement that implies a lineage of the thought from the interaction between analyst and patient. More to the point, Bion (2005) in *The Tavistock Seminars* compares the germination of a child with the development of an idea in analysis:

> It certainly is a collaboration between the two, and there is something fascinating about the analytic intercourse; between the two of them, they do seem to give birth to an idea.
>
> (p. 22)

I have always found it puzzling that Bion chose the symbols of ♀ and ♂ to represent container and the contained since these are imbued with highly "saturated"[4] meanings of femininity and masculinity. I suggest that he employed ♀ and ♂ because he (consciously or unconsciously) intended for the reader to consider the procreative dimension of the container/contained relationship, the "something fascinating about the analytic intercourse" that creates new ideas and meaning. Thus, the new structure of the ego he is proposing – the apparatus for thinking (♀♂) – is modeled upon a pro-/co-creative "analytic intercourse"[5] that germinates, gestates, and gives birth to new ideas. Though he does not reference Melanie Klein's (1928, 1945) concepts of the "feeding" and "creative" internalized (Oedipal) couple (Brown, 2002), Bion's idea of the ♀♂ as the apparatus for thinking appears to be an elaboration of her description of the creative couple.

Mutuality, from the perspective of the creative mating of the minds in analysis, involves the interplay between the internalized creative couple (the ♀♂, or apparatus for thinking) in both the analysand and the analyst. This interplay, therefore,

> is also a meeting of a part of the patient's and analyst's mind that is both receptive to being influenced, affected and penetrated, yet, simultaneously, is not frightened of influencing, affecting and pene- trating the mind of the other . . . there is an internalization of a couple for whom mutual influence is felt to be an act of shared creativity.
>
> (Brown, 2004, p. 47)

This act of shared creativity involves the patient inseminating the analyst's mind with an unprocessed emotional experience that the analyst transforms into a thought through reverie. One way of regard- ing this process is to consider the exchange as a "thought looking for a thinker" (Bion, 1997), that the patient projects an unmentalized experience into the analyst with the expectation that the analyst will "think" (transform) the thought for the patient and then return this newly minted and transformed thought back through observations, interpretations, etc. The analyst's comments, now planted in the patient's mind, stimulate the growth of new associations of the analyst's ideas that subsequently evoke further elaborations in the analyst. Thus, analytic collaboration is also a cross-fertilization in which new meaning is mutually created by the interaction between the internalized container/contained (♀♂) of the analysand and the analyst.

Some clinical implications

Bion (1970) has called analysis a probe that expands the very area it is investigating, and Ferro (2005) contrasts this emphasis with the traditional analytic perspective on technique:

> Thus the analyst presents him- or herself as a person capable of listening, understanding, grasping and describing the emotions of the field and as a catalyst of further transformations – on the basis that there is not *an unconscious to be revealed*, but a capacity for thinking to be developed, and that the development of the capacity for thinking allows closer and closer contact with previously non-negotiable areas.
>
> (p. 102, italics in original)

While I agree with Ferro in principle, he does appear to draw too great a contrast between "an unconscious to be revealed" and the development "of a capacity for thinking" that permits "closer and closer contact with previously non-negotiable areas."[6] What are these "non-negotiable areas" if not unconscious contents of the patient's mind? I believe that Ferro (2002, 2005) is attempting to broaden our appreciation of the centrality of the analyst's mind (α function/rev-erie/♀♂/apparatus for thinking) working interactively with the patient's mind to give meaning to what has been "non-negotiable" or unconscious for the patient.[7] Ferro is stressing the mutuality of this undertaking as distinct from the classical analytic technique in which the analyst sifts through the analysand's associations to gather latent meaning from the patient's material and offers his view of how the patient's unconscious has been revealed.

It may be instructive at this point, to consider how, in the classical tradition, the analyst comes to know what is in the patient's unconscious. Freud (1923b) advised us to listen to the patient's associations, drew our attention to the importance of repetitive actions (Freud, 1914) and dreams (Freud, 1900), and underscored the vital role of analyzing resistance (Freud, 1926) as technical methods by which unconscious material may be detected. Freud (1912) also introduced what we might call today an intersubjective strategy when he stated that the analyst should use his unconscious as an instrument in the analysis, but he did not guide us as to how this is to be done (Brown, 2004, 2007 – Chapter 9, this volume). He did say that the *doctor's unconscious* is able, from the derivatives of the unconscious which are communicated to him, to reconstruct that [the patient's] unconscious, which has determined the patient's free associations.

(Freud, 1912, p. 116, italics added)

Interestingly, Freud here is underscoring the *unconscious work* that is done by the analyst when he says that "the doctor's unconscious" is responsible for "reconstructing" the unconscious of the patient from the analysand's free associations. Freud (1923b) later appeared to emphasize the *conscious work* the analyst does when he stated that

the patient's associations emerged like allusions ... [and that] it was only necessary for the physician ... to guess the material which was concealed from the patient himself and to be able to communicate it to him.

(p. 239)

In Chapter 2, we explored in detail how Isakower (1957, 1963) further developed Freud's notion of the analyst using his unconscious by adumbrating the idea that the patient's free associations and the analyst's free-floating attention were two sides of the "analyzing instrument" coin. He said that there was a "near identity" (Isakower, 1963, p. 207) between the ego states of the analysand and analyst while the analyzing instrument was in operation, a point that some of his followers have extended by describing the process of "mutual free association" (Lothane, 1994; Spencer, Balter & Lothane, 1992).

I suggest that what is inherent in Freud's concept of the analyst using his unconscious as an instrument of the analysis, in Isakower's notion of the analyzing instrument, and in Ferro's outlining "the development of the capacity for thinking" is the concept of an unconscious aspect of the ego capable of receiving unconscious (emotional) communication, processing that communication, giving meaning to it, and ultimately capable of communicating that meaning back to the sending unconscious. This is a mutual unconscious process that goes nearly unnoticed when good analytic work is "purring" along, and it constitutes an unconscious streaming that flows back and forth between the linked ego structures of α function in the analysand and the analyst. *By the time the analyst has become aware of an interpretation to give the patient, there has been much unconscious work that has already transpired.* This is the territory that has been so richly explored by Bion, who recommends that the analyst have "faith" (Bion, 1967) in his unconscious to eventually bring to him spontaneous and unbidden thoughts that offer a clue to the unconscious work occurring within him; thus, we should begin each session without memory and desire and give ourselves over to what Freud calls our "unconscious memory" (Freud, 1912, p. 112).

A clinical vignette: Sally and "Good Bye Lenin!"

Sally is an 18-year-old girl who has been in analysis for about one and a half years. Although exceptionally intelligent and without any noteworthy learning difficulties (as assessed in neuropsychological testing), she has significant problems in school because of intense anxiety she experiences with peers. At the beginning of analysis, she frequently adopted a haughty attitude toward the other adolescents and complained about their stupidity and general intellectual inferiority. However, our analytic work helped Sally understand the defensive underpinnings of this posture, and we were able to link this stance to a chronic sense of inadequacy she felt growing up with very high-achieving parents who were exceedingly sparse in any form of encouragement. She once remarked that "The closest I ever came to a compliment was the absence of criticism."

This work was initially promising and led to the realization that Sally felt she had nothing to say to the friends she was now beginning to make. There was an empty quality to her interactions with them: she generally tried to tack herself onto conversations, adding little of her own thoughts and avoiding any confrontation. She wanted to fit in and simultaneously remain anonymous. There was a paranoid quality to these interactions in that Sally typically felt under the watchful scrutiny of others, and this theme soon emerged in the transference. She often apologized to me for being a few minutes late or if she felt she was wriggling excessively in her chair or not having much to say. Although she appeared visibly uncomfortable, Sally would say she did not feel much of anything when I commented on her seeming to be anxious. Her Mona Lisa smile conveyed some vague sense of being discomfited, and, though she said she was quite at ease with me because I knew her, she was rather removed from her affects. We regularly spent long periods in silence during which she said she had no thoughts in her mind, yet she often complained of vague physical symptoms of muscle aches and difficulty sleeping. It was as though she were present through her emotional absence, an experience that engendered a "reverie deprivation" (Ogden, 2004b) in me characterized by an odd sense of enfolded inner silence and a lack of associations to anything she said.

At the outset of analysis, Sally lived in a world in which her relationships tended to be experienced in gradients of tolerable sensory encounters. Her mother told me that Sally was a thin-skinned infant and young child, easily overwhelmed by sensory stimuli and difficult to soothe. She only felt comfortable in loose-fitting, soft cotton clothing. She had few friends in childhood and always needed to be in control of activities during play dates. Sally was also exceptionally concerned with orderliness and appeared to erect a wall around herself, a barrier built from stony expressions of banal formalities and cemented by her prodigious intellect. Her mother contacted me when Sally was asked to leave her school for failing grades, and I was among several people that Sally "interviewed." The initial meeting was noteworthy for my sense of disconnection, though we managed to have some conversation about science fiction. Later, Sally said that she wanted to work with me because she found me "bright," though I was not clear whether that meant I was intelligent or whether perhaps it referred to some sensory experience of light.

We began meeting on a twice-weekly basis, although I had suggested we get together "as often as possible." Sally typically did not have much to say of emotional significance, and I frequently felt like I was speaking to someone who represented her, an acquaintance of hers perhaps, but someone who was remote from the actual Sally. I was reminded of some of Tustin's (1991) patients who were encased in "autistic shells," often highly intelligent individuals whose impressive IQs were used like moats around thick castle redoubts. However, one day she arrived in my office sobbing and hatefully criticizing herself for being stupid because she just got a flat tire on her new car, which was now parked outside my office. She was helpless, fearful, and terrified in a rampaging affective storm about what to do. I suggested we go to her car and see if there was some material in the manual that could help her out. I located a "roadside assistance" card and called for her, telling Sally that next time she would know what to do. She was still very distraught, though somewhat calmed, and I offered her an appointment for the next day, which she gladly accepted. At the next appointment I again suggested we meet the following day, and in this way we started meeting four times a week.

I am aware that I *was* Sally's "roadside assistance" in this interaction, yet she was barely able to recall the exchange when I brought this up in subsequent sessions. Any suggestion, however gingerly given, that she might be keeping herself from uncomfortable feelings about relying on me were met with a blank response, as though I were speaking a foreign language. And indeed, I was conveying my thoughts in an unfamiliar tongue since Sally was more preoccupied with sensory concerns such as her difficulty sleeping. She was genuinely confused whether she was sleeping or awake at night, reported being up for 48 hours and then sleeping for 30 hours, and also said she did not dream. I was reminded of Bion's (1962a) comments about those patients with disturbed α function "who cannot dream cannot go to sleep and cannot wake up" (p. 7). I had difficulty tolerating the emotional flatness of being with her, of not being able to get through, until I realized that she needed me to be like the loosely fitting cotton garments she preferred as a child: soft to the touch, close, but not form fitting.

Some months later, during the winter, Sally spent several sessions berating the glare of the sun that poured into her apartment so intensely she felt she would need to wear sunglasses indoors. She conveyed a sense of helplessness as though the sun pursued her from room to room, relentlessly bombarding her with its blaze that pierced through her window shades. I had difficulty grasping the meaning of this complaint, since the days had been very cold, until the word "azimuth" suddenly came to mind, a word that was foreign to me but strangely familiar. As I thought about it, I recalled the word from a college science class which denoted the arc that the sun cuts across the sky, a path that is low on the horizon in the winter. This permitted me to gain some contact with the emotional meaning that the sun's unceasing glare held for Sally, and I was able to speak with her about the sensory overload this caused that she could scarcely filter out. My interpretation eased her anxiety, and she began to talk about her mother who was "in my face and all over me." The meaning of her battle with the sun became more apparent, and I drew a connection with her experience of her mother invading her, but Sally could not comprehend what I was saying.[8] Needless to say, I felt encouraged on two accounts: first, that my capacity for reverie was coming alive, albeit with the lone word "azimuth" springing to mind; and, second, that Sally was able to make a link, however unconscious, between the persecutory sun and her experience of her mother. This was an important step away from a sensory world toward the object world.

A few comments on my technical approach seem warranted at this point. Some readers might correctly observe that Sally's "analysis" was not "classical" at this stage of treatment: I went to the car with her, called the roadside assistance, and "taught" her how to ask for help on her own. Unlike Ms. C. in the previous chapter, Sally's α function was seriously impaired; thus, she was ensnared in a sensory universe of concrete experience and lacked the capacity to see beyond the immediate moment. Ms. C. could work metaphorically and dream rich communicative dreams, but Sally was caught between sleep and wakefulness. In addition, the analyst's state of mind is quite different with these two kinds of patients.[9] When analyzing Ms. C., I was able to dream a vivid dream that re-enlivened dormant childhood memories, which signaled that my unconscious was alert to her unconscious communications. In sharp contrast, my capacity for reverie was severely constricted with Sally, and my α function could only eke out a paltry one-word reverie – azimuth. Therefore, from a technical perspective, I had to meet Sally in the world of action and sensation in which she lived.

One could say that treatment at this juncture was not "real analysis" because of the technical modifications I had to undertake; however, I would argue that work with patients like Sally is just as "real" but is of a different quality. I also believe that it would be inaccurate to state that this kind of work is "preliminary" to analysis; rather, *this is the analysis at this particular time*. The analyst has to learn to speak another language that is sensory in nature and to understand that the analysand does not comprehend his metaphors and interpretations. He must lend his α function for some indeterminate period until the patient develops/strengthens her own. Regarding the suitability of classical analysis with patients like Sally, Ferro (2009) says

This model is applicable when it is possible to work on the contents – whether repressed or split off – of the patient's mental life, but it is totally inappropriate where there is a need for upstream operations to overhaul, sometimes to a considerable extent, the patient's actual apparatus for thinking thoughts [α function].

(p. 18)

We will now turn to the slow emergence of an ability to think symbolically and interactively in Sally.

The sessions in subsequent months showed further gains, and Sally and I slowly evolving into a thinking couple with mutually enriching associations, though these periods of contact remained infrequent. One noteworthy hour began when Sally asked before sitting down if it was ok to put a little trash that she had in her hand into my waste-basket. I was surprised that she needed to ask since she had previously done so, and I said to her that of course it is ok. She sat down and took the last sip of the iced coffee she had brought with her, reached into her bag, searched around, and pulled out a fresh bottle of water. Look-ing embarrassed, she said "sorry," smiled awkwardly, and said "hi" to indicate she had settled in and the session could begin. I said she seemed particularly self-conscious today, a comment that felt off-target as I said it, but she said she was "fine." She stretched out one leg and then the other, something she generally did at the beginning of sessions, smiled again, and then lifted her hands as if to say, "so I don't know what to talk about." Sally said she just came from the derma-tologist, who had applied a peel to her face (for her acne), and she described the process when I asked about it. I said her face looked smooth, and I became aware of how "comfortable" she seemed with this topic about which many adolescents feel very embarrassed. She then put on her light jacket, smiled, and said "sorry." I said that talking about this seemed to make her self-conscious, that perhaps she had to apologize for her skin as though it was something that needed to be covered up. [I felt my comment was "correct," but obvious, yet it did not lead to any further thoughts by her.] Sally apologized again for something, and I said I often get the sense she felt under constant inspection, checking out whether people are checking her out, per-haps to criticize her. [I decided to make a general comment that was not "saturated" (Ferro, 2005) with transference references.] She said that she often felt inspected, not sure for what – not so much here with me, but with her friends and even with her parents.

[At this point I remembered a trip to Russia a few years ago in which I visited an outdoor museum in Moscow that was like a grave-yard for the discarded old statues of the former Soviet Union. The visual image was of overgrown grass, an untended place next to a new, well-maintained indoor museum. The words "Big Brother" came to mind, and I thought of saying something like "It feels like Big Brother is always watching you." However, it felt that comment would be hackneyed, like much of what I had been saying that felt "correct" but did not make real contact with her. I debated whether I should share my memory with her and decided to do that.] I said that as she was talking I remembered a trip to Russia I had taken and that I thought my remembering it at this moment must have something to do with what she was telling me [her feeling of being inspected by friends and parents]. I related the memory to her, and immediately there was a palpable sense of her relaxing, as though her mind and body had suddenly been loosened from some hold. Sally quickly said that my memory reminded her of a recent movie she had seen, *Good Bye Lenin*, about a woman who had been in a coma while East Germany transformed into a non-Communist state. [I had also just seen this movie.] She noted that because of a recent heart attack the woman could not tolerate the loss of her beloved Communist government, and so her family created a ruse to hide the shocking changes of a now-democratic, but more disorderly, society. I said that many people missed the strange kind of safety they felt during the Soviet era when they knew everything they were doing was inspected and watched. Sally said she had read about that, that it kept people in line and that some people could not handle the freedom of a democratic state. [I felt at this point that we were "clicking," that real contact had been made.] The session was nearing the end and I wondered whether her near-constant feeling of being inspected may be similar: that although she felt uncomfortable feeling inspected, there might also be, at the same time (Grotstein 2009b, 2009c), some measure of safety that being watched offered that was hard to give up. This comment interested her, and she said she would have to give it some thought.

Discussion

Despite Sally's overall significant ego strengths, her capacity to process unrefined emotional experience was severely limited. Consequently, she found it exceedingly difficult to understand the subtleties of interactions with peers and resorted to tagging along in a nearly invisible style as well as adopting a haughty attitude to keep this limitation hidden. Making emotional contact caused great distress: Sally easily felt overwhelmed, and her constant apologizing expressed her fear that this difficulty would be unmasked, thereby exposing her

to intense criticism. Her α function – that aspect of her ego functioning that was capable of receiving normal communicative projective
identifications of emotional input, processing these affects into
thoughts, and conveying these thoughts back to her peers – was quite
limited. Ferro (2002, 2005) states that when the patient's α function is
limited, the analyst must lend his to assist the patient in transforming
emotional stimuli (convert β to α elements). Thus, I am emphasizing a
technique that assumes the ego is something that is dyadically helped
into existence rather than presupposing it exists, is intact, and may be
actively followed as well as pointed out to the patient (Busch, 1999;
Gray, 1994). When the patient lacks substantial α function or if it is
disturbed in the analyst, then the analytic couple ceases to be a
creative pair engaged in the creation of meaning.

The difficulties that followed from Sally's disturbed α function led
to a situation in the transference where there was a significant restric-
tion in the capacity for our respective "states of consciousness" to
engage in a "dyadic expansion of consciousness" (Tronick, 2005;
Tronick et al., 1998). Put in the language of Ogden (1994a, 1994b,
1997a, 1997b, 2004b), there was little development of an intersubjective analytic third, and I experienced "reverie deprivation" in its
place. This deprivation was directly connected to my difficulty in
understanding that she and I, at certain times, were speaking different
languages: Sally, a sensory-oriented language, and I, a verbal one. In
this regard, I was guilty of the same "stupidity" of which Bion (1958)
was accused by his patient – not grasping that we were operating on
different communicative levels. However, when I was able to "tune
into" the sensory channel over which she was contacting me in the
story about the unrelenting winter sun, my α function picked up her
signals and converted these to one condensed word: "azimuth." This
product of my α function was simply a word, a dry and emotionally
distant scientific term at that, but it did signal a small shift in me that,
when shared with Sally, triggered a commensal and analogous change
in her. This exchange was surely a "dyadic expansion of consciousness" but was clearly not the rich associative dialogue that we
achieved in the session with my reverie about Russia.

I began that session with the assumption that Sally was capable of
interacting on a level of mutuality that was beyond her capacity. Thus,
when I said that she seemed particularly self-conscious, she was truthful in saying she was "fine" because she was not registering any
emotional distress, which is why I felt that my comment did not make

contact with her. She told me about the visit to the dermatologist, then put on her jacket, which I, again mistakenly, interpreted from the perspective of shame against which I thought she was defending. My interpretation presupposed that Sally possessed in that moment a proficient α function. It is more likely that I missed her communication that had more to do with a sensory experience of a doctor helping to soothe her irritated skin. She probably needed the loose-fitting, soft-cotton me rather than the interpretative me offering a transference comment too direct for her to manage. Thus, I instead proposed an "unsaturated," general observation about feeling inspected, which appeared to trigger the start of an unconscious process of thinking together that resulted in the feeling that we were "clicking."

As Sally continued to elaborate on feeling inspected, I had the reverie about the graveyard for the icons of the former Soviet Union. The words "Big Brother" came to mind for me, but it felt predictable to say that I was concerned about shutting off what appeared to be a rare moment of mutual engagement. I debated about sharing my reverie but decided to do so and put it in the context of my mind's reaction to what she was saying.[10] Telling her my reverie had the very positive effect of furthering our engagement as a thinking couple whose respective associations mutually enriched each other. In addition, this reverie-based response was an analyst-centered interpretation (Steiner, 1993) that helped to diminish her paranoid anxieties and lessen her sense of being watched by me. Sally quickly experienced a physical and psychological easing, immediately thought of the movie *Good Bye Lenin!*, and told me about the woman who had been in a coma who, now awake, could not bear too much reality. I thought this association was a commentary on her own often comatose state in which she was present through her absence and that it was saying to me that she was frightened of leaving the old emotionally blunted state too quickly. Staying with her elaboration of my reverie, but now informed by her unconscious about the nature of her fear, I added that some people missed the sense of security that the erstwhile Soviet empire afforded through watchfulness over its citizenry. We were now in a commensal frame of mind in which we were elaborating on each other's associations, a dyadic expansion of consciousness (Tronick, 2005; Tronick et al., 1998) that was creating meaning *in statu nascendi*.

Sally's association about the woman who was in a coma because she could not bear the reality of the political changes alerted me, in a stark manner, to the very real limitations she experienced in her ability to manage powerful affects. Put in the language of one branch of ego psychology (Busch, 1995, 1999; Gray, 1994; Paniagua, 1991), her defenses were fragile and required her analyst not to put undue strain on those defenses. These authors recommend staying on the "workable surface" (Paniagua, 1991) that Busch (1999) describes as

> that combination of the patient's thoughts, feelings, and actions, and the analyst's reaction to these, *that is usable by the patient's ego.*
> (p. 62, italics added)

While I agree with this perspective in general, it leaves out the ways in which the psyches of the analyst and patient interact in a collaborative way to generate meaning together *on an unconscious basis* – meaning that the analyst slowly becomes aware of that allows for him to make an intervention "that is usable by the patient's ego." By primarily paying attention to the conscious ego, the ego-psychological approach eschews discussion of the unconscious activity of the ego, except for its initiation of defenses in response to "signal anxiety" (Freud, 1926).[11] In this regard, Bion's "ego psychology," which addresses the unconscious ego activity of the linked (ego) α functions of the analysand and analyst, seems an important balance to the other point of view that largely emphasizes the conscious ego in staying with the "workable surface."

In the first session that dealt with her sense of being pursued by the sun, there was only surface, one of sensory overload, and no depth with, or from, which to work. I suggest that the appearance of a workable surface depends on the existence of an unconscious stream of communication between analyst and patient. Without such a connection, the two are not an analytic couple but, rather, are like a duo of meandering states of consciousness incapable of creating meaning together that would register on the surface as something to be worked with. Stated another way, *there can be no workable surface if there is not some commensurate unconscious work being done.* Something shifted, almost imperceptibly, when my α function picked up a signal from Sally and transformed it into the word "azimuth." Depth had suddenly emerged and, with it, a surface on which to work, like a lily pad apparently floating on the water, its roots to the floor of the pond unseen.

In the second session that addressed my Moscow reverie, by

contrast, there was greater emotional substance both on the workable surface as well as in the breadth of the unconscious interplay between Sally's and my α functions. There was definite movement from talk filled with seeming *non sequiturs* to a meaningful development of emotional exchange to which we both contributed consciously as well as unconsciously. It could be said from a traditional ego-psychological point of view that this change was effected by my shifting to deal with Sally in displacement, thereby allowing her to feel more at ease with collaborating with me. I do not disagree with this in principle; however, there is more to this picture than displacement. I had to override my feeling of impatience with Sally's tendency to speak about quotidian details and wait until either she or I were able to bring something of emotional significance from the depths to the workable surface. Talk about putting her trash in my wastebasket, acknowledging her iced coffee and commenting on replacing it with water, talking about stretching her legs out, etc., while possibly being displacements were, on another level, a kind of gathering together of day residues in order for them to be woven into a dream. Ogden (2007) has written about a certain kind of talk between patient and analyst that

> may at first seem "unanalytic" because the patient and analyst are talking about such things as books, poems, films, rules of grammar, etymology, the speed of light, the taste of chocolate and so on. Despite appearances, it has been my experience that such "unanalytic" talk often allows a patient and analyst who have been unable to dream together [i.e., their α functions not "clicking"] to begin to be able to do so.
>
> (p. 575)

It was from this "unanalytic" work that Sally and I were able to begin to dream together, a dreaming that promotes the enrichment of both conscious and unconscious life as well as the interchange between them.[12] From the perspective of the conscious ego in the session with Sally, my intervention about her covering herself up led to her apologizing, which registered consciously with me that I had put her on the defensive by making her feel inspected. I realized that I was assuming that she was operating on a less than symbolic level, and, thus, I shifted my focus to a general, "unsaturated" observation about her feeling under inspection by others. This statement stayed on the "workable surface" of what Sally's ego could tolerate and permitted her some increased flexibility to speak more openly about how she often felt inspected by others (perhaps also gratifying the wish to be watched over – see above). On the other hand, from the standpoint of the unconscious ego, there was significant "unconscious work" (Ogden, 2004b) occurring within the patient, within me, and between our communicating α functions that collaboratively generated a deeper understanding of the meaning of Sally's adherence to feeling inspected. My reverie about the outdoor museum in Moscow appeared "unbidden" (Bion, 1997) and was the product of my unconscious ego (α function) at work, elaborating pictorially the idea of being watched. On reflection, though I was not aware of it at the time, I think this particular memory also expressed unconsciously my wish for Sally to overthrow the symbols of oppression under whose watchful gaze she lived. Sharing this reverie immediately led to her relaxing, and her unconscious ego went to work to offer mine a response and a rebuttal. In effect, her association to the woman in a coma said "wait a minute, not so fast, I'm not sure I want to be iconoclastic because it frightens me." Her reply permitted me to become consciously aware of the nature of her anxiety, which I could then interpret to her in a manner that was now usable by her conscious ego. Thus, the unconscious work Sally and I were able to do together gave me sufficient conscious knowledge of her specific anxiety that enabled me to address her conscious ego.

What I am calling Bion's ego psychology allows for the coexistence of both an intrapsychic and an interpersonal point of view without having to opt for one approach over the other.[13] There is a tendency in the ego-psychological literature (as put forth by Busch, Gray, Paniagua, and others) to favor the intrapsychic over the interactional and an analogous bias in the American relational school that deemphasizes the role of the intrapsychic (Spillius, 2004). Pray (2002) identifies what he calls the "classical/relational split" and states that in the ego–psychological school, "the emphasis is on camouflaged, unconscious intrapsychic conflict, not on current interpersonal realities" (p. 252). Busch (1999) has praised the important ways in which the relational schools have raised our awareness of the actual interactions between the patient and analyst, but decries a leaning in this perspective "toward a treatment structure focused on the analysand's needing to grapple with the analyst's personality and associations"

(p. 95). I see this as a false distinction that denies the connection between the intrapsychic and the interpersonal.

Indeed, there has long been a parallel trend in other American analysts calling themselves "ego psychologists" (see Chapter 2), writing in the 1940s and 1950s, who would not advocate a "classical/relational split" and instead see the psyches of patient and analyst interacting together. These analysts (Fliess, 1942; Reik, 1948; Isakower, 1957, 1963, to name a few) extended Freud's concept of the analyzing instrument in important and creative ways; however, my impression is that their writings were often dismissed as throwbacks to Freud's topographic model, lagging developmentally (Gray, 1994) by not paying sufficient attention to structural issues and Freud's (1926) second theory of anxiety. In addition, their work was also criticized (Spencer, Balter, & Lothane, 1992) as excessively based in countertransference – a critique offered in 1963 (see Martin Stein's comment above, Chapter 2, p. 33, regarding Isakower's work) that still gains traction, as evidenced in Busch's (1999) comments about the American relational school.

Shill (2008), who has written about intersubjectivity from the perspective of traditional ego psychology, argues that "intersubjective or relational approaches are part of the psychology of the ego" (p. 4) – a point of view close to that offered here, though my emphasis is on the unconscious aspects of the ego (e.g., α function). Shill correctly notes that intersubjective and object relations-oriented analysts ignore the ego aspect of intersubjectivity, but he goes on to deny the existence of "a two person psychology outside the separate minds" (p. 15) of the patient and analyst. Furthermore, he claims that

> a "two person psychology" is an intrapsychic creation and is contained separately within the minds of each of the two people. Since intersubjectivity between people is contained separately, even if more or less simultaneously, in the minds of each, it is for that reason subjective. It is created by each mind from the experience of experiencing the other mind.
>
> (p. 15)

To state that intersubjectivity is an "intrapsychic creation" is to neglect the actual effects the unconscious experiences of the analysand and analyst upon each other. Of course, these effects are registered in each individual's psyche, but each unconscious ego, through the activity of its α function, is in constant communication with its companion in the other member of the analytic dyad. Shill's approach leaves no opportunity for the co-creation of a joint narrative constructed unconsciously that I see as the sine qua non of intersubjectivity and as an important role of the ego.

Chodorow (2004) has proposed another trend that falls under the umbrella of ego psychology which she terms *intersubjective ego psychology*. This movement combines aspects of traditional ego psychology with the contributions of Erikson and Loewald. Chodorow quotes a relevant passage from Loewald:

> The analyst in his interpretations reorganizes, reintegrates unconscious material for himself as well as for the patient, since he has to be attuned to the patient's unconscious, using, as we say, his own unconscious as a tool, in order to arrive at the organizing interpretation.
>
> (Loewald, 1960, p. 241)

These intersubjective ego psychologists have offered creative extensions of some traditional concepts. For example, Poland (1992), as though in counterpoint to the diligent attention paid by Gray, Busch, etc. to the psychic surface, argues that excessive focus on the psychic surface is itself a holdover from the topographic theory, which ignores the analytic space generated by the effect of the minds of analyst and analysand upon each other. Smith (1999) also argues against those analysts (e.g., Renik, 1995) who advocate a radical revision of some basic technical approaches, such as neutrality and abstinence, and encourages us to consider technique as "shaped to a large extent by the personal character of the analyst and by the practical exigencies of the analytic situation, including . . . the intersubjective field" (Smith, 1999, p. 467).

My purpose here is not to evaluate the traditional and "intersubjective" ego-psychological schools, but to compare them with what I call Bion's "ego psychology." The Kleinian perspective (Feldman, 1997; Money-Kyrle, 1956), in which Bion is rooted, by virtue of Klein's (1946) discovery of projective identification, has long considered how the patient's intrapsychic universe (Brown, 1996) is played out in the transference/countertransference dynamic and, in this regard, has considerable overlap with the intersubjective ego psychology that Chodorow (and others of this "school') adumbrates.

Bion's contributions, especially in *Learning from Experience* (1962a) and *Transformations* (1965), extend both the traditional and the inter-subjective ego psychologies by emphasizing not just the impact of the patient upon the analyst's mind, but how that impact upon the ana-lyst's mind is also a search for another mind to transform/dream what the patient cannot manage. It is a *procreative* endeavor that creates new meaning like a child born to two parents, an offspring that owes its lineage to both yet is simultaneously its own agency (Ogden's inter-subjective analytic third). Furthermore, what I miss from the "inter-subjective ego psychologists" is a discussion of the ego per se as a functioning structure, because they tend to focus on character rather than structure. Bion's "ego psychology," by contrast, minutely delineates the working of α function in the context of an intersubjec-tive matrix.

From a Bionian point of view, the analyst "rents himself out" (J. Grotstein, personal communication in 2004)[14] to the patient as a kind of processing agent to help the analysand manage emotional truth (Grotstein, 2004); however, "in practice it is much more difficult because one does not know whether the patient is strong enough to hear the truth" (Bion, 1994, p. 179). Where Bion's ego psychology differs from both the traditional and the intersubjective ego psych-ologies is in the emphasis it places on the analyst's role, through the unconscious operation of his α function with that of the analysand, to be a partner in pursuing emotional truth, which requires "a capacity to tolerate the stresses associated with the introjection of another person's projective identifications" (Bion, 1958/1967, p. 88). In this regard, the patient must always "grapple with the analyst's personality and associations," but the object is not to burden the analysand with the analyst's private reactions. The patient needs an analyst who can introject the analysand's projective identifications, tolerate the transference (Mitrani, 2001), and transform what has been projected (Bion, 1965), all of which is accomplished through the unconscious work of his reverie and α function independent of, and in conjunc-tion with, that of the analysand. Thus, the intrapsychic and the inter-personal are inextricably knitted together, which results in evolution and transformation in both partners: there is a constant elaboration of the analytic partnership, commensal growth in the container and con-tained, and a dyadic expansion of consciousness. Or, put another way, as Elvin Semrad[15] has stated, "every analysis is a reanalysis."

105

Conclusion

This chapter has explored how Bion's major theoretical writings may be seen as the development of his own view of a central aspect of the ego's functioning. Though he did not generally subscribe to the tripartite model of the mind, in my opinion Bion's elaboration of the ego's relationship to reality represented an expansion of ideas inchoate in the "Two Principles" paper from which Freud was later to craft the structural theory. In postulating α function, Bion introduced an intersubjective dimension to understanding how the ego makes meaning of emotional events, because α function represents the internalization of the infant/mother couple creating meaning together through a process best described by Tronick (2005; Tronick et al., 1998) as the "dyadic expansion of consciousness." This leads to a deeper understanding of the unconscious exchange between the analyst and the patient in what Freud (1912) described as the analyst using his unconscious as an instrument of the analysis. Thus, there is a constant unconscious interactional process between the linked α functions of the analysand and analyst by which meaning is constantly being created and expanded that, when treatment is going well, results in the mutual growth of the container/contained ($♀ ♂$). Bion's ego psychology has been compared to the various branches of ego psychology, and all perspectives are important in analytic work. The analyst's attention to what is on the "workable surface" of the clinical hour is greatly enhanced by his gaining access, through attention to his reveries, to the parallel undercurrent of "unconscious work" in which both partners in the analytic couple are simultaneously engaged. Thus, there is considerable clinical utility to expanding the notion of the "workable surface" to include the mental functioning of the analyst.

Notes

1   This is a slightly expanded version of an article published in 2009 in the *Psychoanalytic Quarterly*, 78: 27–55.
2   In this chapter, I will mainly deal with the work of those ego psychologists, especially Gray, Busch, and Paniagua, who have advocated therapeutic approaches that partly seek to diminish the import of the analyst's personality in the analytic relationship. However, these theorists have

also systematically explored the role of the ego as a psychic structure in analysis, which the "intersubjective ego psychologists" (Chodorow, 2004) do not address.

3 Perhaps another way of talking about "thing-presentations" (Freud, 1900)? The question of the relationship between thing-presentations and β elements is discussed in Chapter 5.

4 Bion used the term "saturated" to refer to psychoanalytic ideas that are imbued with such well-established meaning that the experiences to which these terms originally referred may be lost. Thus, he introduced symbols to denote some of his concepts in order to take a fresh look at phenomena unencumbered by a "penumbra of associations" (Bion, 1962a). The reader should take note that Ferro (2002, 2005) also uses "saturated" to refer to interpretations that convey the analyst's pronouncements of meaning, as contrasted with open-ended or "unsaturated" statements that await the discovery of meaning.

5 Since publishing this paper (in 2009) I have become aware of the contribution by Paulo Sandler (2000) in which he similarly delineated two models of thinking that he calls the "digestive" and the "reproductive" models.

6 More on this debate in Chapter 5.

7 The issue of discerning between "unrepresented" and "repressed" unconscious contents of the mind is discussed in greater detail in Chapter 5.

8 To have brought up the maternal transference at this moment would either have been meaningless to Sally or else would likely have been experienced as persecutory. However, it was some time later in the analysis, when Sally wanted to cut back to two sessions a week and her α function had developed further, that I was able to interpret the transference of experiencing me as some implacable and relentless figure from whom she could not escape, just as she had earlier felt about her mother.

9 See note 4 in Chapter 5 for further comment on these two types of patient.

10 This is a technique I frequently use with adolescents, in whom there is a fear of knowing about and expressing what is inside them. It is a kind of modeling aimed at increasing their receptivity to thoughts that are otherwise troubling. In addition, particularly with those whose α function is disturbed, sharing my reveries as contextualized in their communications offers an approach to thinking with which they may identify. After all, α function is the apparatus for thinking ($♀ ♂$) that is the introjection of the thinking couple.

11 Busch (2006b) has recently discussed what he terms "defense enactments" in which the analysand engenders a reaction in the analyst that is "an unconscious response to the patient's feeling of danger . . . [and is a]

role-responsiveness to the patient's defensive position" (p. 68) which leads the analyst to collude with the analysand's avoidance of painful affects. While this is a welcome expansion of Gray's rejection of the usefulness of countertransference (Phillips, 2006), I am addressing the uniquely collaborative way in which the unconscious of the analyst and patient create emotional meaning together that is different from the analyst unconsciously resonating with a role evoked by the patient in the service of the analysand's resistance.

12 Bion (1962a) believes that dreaming – that is, transformations of raw emotion by α function – performs an essential task in differentiating the conscious from the unconscious. A boundary is created between these two domains called the *contact barrier,* which is a permeable membrane that permits a constant dialogue between the *Cs.* and *Ucs.* This differs from Freud's emphasis on a strict separation of cs from uncs.

13 Grotstein (1997, 2000), writing from a Bionian perspective, raises the valuable concern that the increased emphasis on a two–person model may neglect the significance of a one–person point of view, partly because the former "model suggests that psychic reality owes its origin to actual events in the individual's life ... [that could] eclipse the concept of unconscious psychic determinism" (2000, p. 42).

14 Green (2000) takes a similar view in stating that "The essence of the situation at the heart of the analytic exchange is to *accomplish the return to oneself by means of a detour via the other*" (p. 13, italics in original).

15 Elvin Semrad was a well-known Boston analyst who published little but was known for his insightful aphorisms. This quote is part of the local Boston psychoanalytic lore.

5

Intersubjectivity and unconscious process: an integrated model

> It is a very remarkable thing that the *Ucs.* of one human being can react upon that of another, without passing through the *Cs*. This deserves closer investigation, especially with a view to finding our *whether preconscious activity can be excluded as playing a part in it*; but, descriptively speaking, the fact is incontestable.
>
> (Freud, 1915, p. 194, italics added)

We have defined intersubjectivity as largely an unconscious process of communication and meaning making between the two intrapsychic worlds of the patient and the analyst that results in changes between, and within, each member of the analytic pair. In this chapter, I wish to deconstruct this complex exchange into its constituent elements and explore how the two minds affect, probe, come to know each other, and, through that exchange, create new meaning and/or "uncover" previously constructed meanings that have been repressed. In our journey thus far, we have traced the development of certain ideas, evolved from the DNA of various analytic lineages, that in retrospect we may see as an important notion that went unnoticed at the time. For example, Otto Isakower's (Chapter 2) thinking about the two-person aspect of the *analyzing instrument*, which was analogous with Kurt Lewin's (1935) earlier formulations of *field* theory, largely lay fallow because political forces of the day marshaled against a full appreciation of Isakower's ideas, due to doubts regarding the creative use of countertransference (Lothane, 2006), thus effectively driving the notion of the two-person field into a theoretical purgatory in American psychoanalysis. However, as we have seen in Chapter 3, the climate in the River Plate region reactivated Lewin's theories of the *field* when Pichon-Rivière productively blended them with Kleinian views of unconscious phantasy. The concept of the analytic field was given further expression by the Barangers' notion of the *shared unconscious phantasy of the couple*, thereby mating Pichon-Rivière's thoughts with Bion's study of group dynamics. Unfortunately, since the Barangers' ideas remained in Spanish until 2008, they stayed foreign to English-speaking analysts until Italian colleagues (many of whom are at ease with Spanish), such as Ferro, brought them to our attention, but only after their "marriage" with Bion's (1965) theory of *transformations*.

Like a symphony in which a melody is introduced early in a work but then remains latent until it achieves prominence later, intersubjective themes have appeared and faded over time in psychoanalytic thinking; however, in recent years the interest in transference and countertransference has evolved into a sustained and widened consideration of the interacting subjectivities of patient and analyst. At the end of Chapter 2, I said (regarding classical analysis) "Like a cluttered garage with an entire toolchest of implements scattered haphazardly around waiting to be gathered together and organized, we have within the classical tradition most of the instruments necessary to fashion a comprehensive theory of intersubjectivity." In an analogous way, various analytic schools, often disconnected from one another, have formulated theories of intersubjectivity. In what follows, I propose a view of intersubjectivity that is largely based on an integration of ideas from the Kleinian, Bionian, and Freudian perspectives outlined in the previous chapters. I will deconstruct the elements that comprise intersubjective processes into simple questions in order to focus our thinking on the subtle complexities of two psyches engaged with each other.

How does one mind communicate with another?

Communications occur on conscious, preconscious, and unconscious levels, often simultaneously on all three planes between analyst and patient, and between these systems intrapsychically. However, it is communication that occurs unconsciously[1] that is the deep wellspring of intersubjectivity and creative co-construction within the analytic dyad. Even the most rational, discursive exchanges between analysand and analyst are accompanied by, and enlivened through, a synchronous unconscious "conversation" (Brown, 2009a – see Chapter 4, this volume) that operates as though it were like a "picture in a picture" on a psychic television – seemingly hidden, but infusing the larger view with emotional meaning. This "conversation" is initiated and sustained by what Ferro (2009) describes as an "ongoing activity of baseline projective identification" (p. 1).

In order to understand the role of projective identification in inter-subjective processes more fully, I find Grotstein's (2005) concept of *projective transidentification* an important contribution. He reminds us that Klein (1946) considered projective identification to be solely an intrapsychic phenomenon in which the patient (or infant) projected *into an internal image of the object,* and we saw in Chapter 3 that she was dismissive of the view that it could be employed as an "instrument of research into the patient's unconscious" (Heimann, 1950). Bion (1962a) introduced the notion of the communicative aspects of projective identification, which Grotstein (2005) expands on:

> The projecting subject *and* the object of projection constitute *two separate self-activating systems*, and the interpersonal process should consequently be renamed *"projective transidentification"* to designate its unique transpersonal mode so as to contrast it with the unconscious phantasy of intrapsychic projective identification proper.
>
> (p. 1059, italics in original)

Grotstein is thus emphasizing the bipersonal nature of this encounter, and he goes on to elucidate the manner in which projective transiden-tification is effected by two processes:

> (1) conscious and/or preconscious modes of sensorimotor induction and/or evocation or prompting techniques (mental, physical, verbal, posturing or priming, "nudging") on the part of the projecting subject, followed by (2) spontaneous empathic simu-lation in the receptive object of the subject's experience who is already inherently equipped (programmed) to empathize with it.
>
> (p. 1059)

The projection (what it is that is projected is discussed below) finds what I would call a group of "familiar strangers" awaiting it within

111

the psyche of the recipient, a fellowship that Grotstein states "always *potentially* corresponds to the analysand's projected emotions" (p. 1064, italics in original) and "Thus the source of the analyst's information [about the patient] is largely from within himself" (p. 1062). I do not think it is important how the analyst conceives those aspects of him/herself that resonate with projected aspects of the analysand: depending upon his or her theoretical bent (Brown, 1996), the projections may be considered as instinctual forces, internal objects of one variety or another, affects, selfobjects, id, ego, superego, etc. What does seem relevant is that an analogous element in the analyst's psychic world is "nudged" (Joseph, 1987) into emotional prominence and, together with what is projected, colors the intersubjective ambience. In this fashion, the analyst *becomes* (Bion, 1965; Fliess, 1942; Grotstein, 2000, 2004, 2005, 2007; see also Chapter 3, this volume) the patient's projection.

Finally, when projective transidentification is deployed, the projection, however it is conceptualized, is guided by a sort of GPS system (Chapter 3) that has a preconception (Bion, 1962a) of the targeted area that is its destination. Prior to the act of projection, an unconscious *scanning* (Fonagy, 2005; Sandler, 1976; Sandler & Sandler, 1992) has reconnoitered the potential "landing site" for as close as possible an "identity of perception" (Freud, 1900) between the preconception and aspects of the analyst's inner world. In these instances, an unconscious empathic connection is established of the kind Racker (1957) would term either a *complementary* or a *concordant identification*, or what in ego-psychological terms would be viewed as a patient/analyst match based on *character* similarities (Kantrowitz, 1993, 1995). On the other hand, when the projective process is of the evacuative sort, then any site will do; what is important is that the psyche rids itself of intolerable experience. In such cases, *projective counteridentifications* (Grinberg, 1962) are likely to prevail. As we discussed in Chapter 3, Grinberg believed that analogous aspects in the analyst's psyche to the projection are not stirred and that what is important is the experience of feeling passively and violently taken over by the projection.

What is projected and how is it encoded?

Depending upon the psychoanalytic school to which one belongs, there are a variety of sobriquets each orientation attaches to the unconscious contents of the mind (Brown, 1996) – for example, internal objects (Klein, 1945; Ogden, 1983), autistic objects (Ogden, 1989; Tustin, 1980), superego (Freud, 1923a), selfobjects (Kohut, 1971), just to name a few. Typically these inhabitants of the internal world are considered from a developmental point of view that, when external-ized (through projective transidentification) into the transference/countertransference matrix, color the experience of patient and ana-lyst with a particular emotional hue. However, these contents of the *representational world* (Sandler & Rosenblatt, 1962) may also be regarded from the perspective of how they are encoded or packaged by the psyche for their journey by projection to another mind. Depending upon the nature of encryption – or what we analysts call *representability* (Freud, 1900, 1917) – the receiving mind is challenged in various ways to transform the projection into an experience that may be thought about by him or her. We will now examine two models of representability – by Freud and by Bion – that account for the way in which contents of the mind are encoded for use in projective identification and projective transidentification.[2]

Freudian views on representability

In attempting to understand aphasia early on in his career, Freud (1891) distinguished between *thing-*[3] and *word-presentations*, which are two modes of representing an object. Thing-presentations are sensory in nature, while word-presentations tend to be comprised of *images* (visual and sound) that are linked symbolically to the thing-presentation. Later, in his paper "The Unconscious" (1915c), Freud addressed the transformation of thing- into word-presentations from the perspective of the topographic model (con-scious, preconscious, and unconscious), a process that is achieved by the journey from unconscious to preconscious and then to con-sciousness. Freud notes that the greatest difficulty in this transform-ation is due to

> the rigorous censorship [that] exercises its office at the point of transition from the *Ucs.* to the *Pcs.* (or *Cs.*).
>
> (p. 173)

Interestingly, Freud ponders the question of whether the transposition

113

of an idea from one level of consciousness to another involves a "second registration" (p. 174) of that idea – that is, another way of representing the same object. This may seem like an esoteric point, but it leads Freud to introduce the role of the analyst's interpretation in helping this transformation along. It is the analyst's communication that the analysand's conscious thoughts have unconscious meaning that creates the "second registration," which, at some later time, when affects are freed by the lifting of repression, achieves meaning:

> To have heard something and to have experienced something are in their psychological nature two quite different things, even though the content of both is the same.
>
> (p. 176)

Although Freud does not state it as such, he is implying that the transformation of an idea from one level of awareness to another depends, in the clinical situation, on input from the analyst's mind. Furthermore, there is also a change in *representability* ("second registration") that is an inherent aspect of this process. He reminds us that the instinctual contents of the unconscious themselves can never appear in consciousness, because the nature of instincts (which comprise the core of the system *Ucs.*) is that they are not represented; however, there are unconscious *derivatives* of instinctual forces:

> The nucleus of the *Ucs.* consists of instinctual representatives [derivatives] which seek to discharge their cathexis; that is to say, it consists of wishful impulses.
>
> (p. 186)

Unconscious derivatives seek expression in consciousness but are held back at two checkpoints: the *first censorship* at the frontier between the *Ucs.* and the *Pcs.*, and the *second censorship* at the boundary of the *Pcs.* and the *Cs.* Furthermore,

> The system *Ucs.* contains the thing-cathexes of the objects . . . the system *Pcs.* comes about by this thing-presentation being . . . linked with the word-presentations corresponding to it.
>
> (pp. 201–202)

And finally that

> what it is that repression denies to . . . the [thing-] presentation is translation into words . . . [and that] A presentation which is not put into words . . . remains thereafter in the *Ucs.* in a state of repression.
>
> (p. 202)

In summary, Freud (1915c) viewed the elemental contents of the unconscious as instinctual forces that are, by definition, a "borderland concept" between psyche and soma and therefore incapable of being directly known. However, instinctual *derivatives* in the form of wishful impulses are the emissaries of the instincts in the unconscious, stored and encoded as thing-presentations that, under the pressure of instinctual forces with which they are linked, press for conscious expression. These derivatives are kept as thing-presentations unless they are given entry (past the first censorship) into the preconscious, which is achieved through linkage with words and/or visual images, thereby creating word-presentations. The preconscious is a sort of "waiting room" for the word-presentations to be admitted into conscious awareness (through the second censorship), either through willfully directed attention or by the pressure of the underlying impulses. Thus, representability occurs along a continuum from the sensory (thing-presentation) to the linguistic/imagistic (word-presentation) that enables an idea to travel from the unconscious to consciousness. Additionally, this process can occur in reverse, as in the case of repression when preconscious contents are stripped of their word-presentation and then relegated to the unconscious. Moreover, though Freud tended to explain this process in economic terms (cathexes, etc.), he did hint at the role of the analyst's interpretation – and by implication his or her mental processes – in transforming the representability of contents of the psyche by offering a "second registration." Finally, for Freud, changes in representability were synonymous with shifts in the level of consciousness.

Before we move on to Bion's ideas, the domain of the preconscious deserves further attention, particularly when we consider Freud's question at the start of this chapter regarding how one unconscious may communicate with another and "whether preconscious activity can be excluded as playing a part in it." Freud does not discuss this query, but it seems to me that the answer might be, "it depends." If one unconscious (of the patient) "can react upon that of another," by

definition the recipient (the analyst) will remain unaware of the con-
veyance because it has affected the unconscious. The analyst may
experience some unnamed perturbation, which in Freud's terms
would be a thing-presentation. However, if the analyst is to grasp the
meaning of this disturbance, it must be linked in his or her own mind
with verbal/imagistic word-presentations, which involves overcoming the first censorship, thereby becoming a preconscious (usually
visual) experience to which he or she may attend on a conscious level.
Thus, following Freud's model, we may say that "the *Ucs.* of one
human being can react upon that of another," but that impact will
itself remain unconscious unless the receiving individual can connect
that experience with a word- (verbal/imagistic) presentation that is
then potentially accessible to consciousness by passing through the
second censorship. To say that what was originally unconscious must
be transformed into preconscious experience is to privilege the
importance of "preconscious mental processes" (Kris, 1950) that are
visual, dream-like (Arlow, 1969a), daydream-like (Busch, 2006a;
Kantrowitz, 2001) phenomena that hover in a "transitional space
between the unconscious and the conscious" (Green, 1974, p. 417).

Bionian views on representability

In many ways, Bion's view of how unconscious contents are represented is not all that different from Freud's; however, he expanded our
understanding of the process of representation to include an intersubjective dimension that was only hinted at in Freud. Just as Freud
described thing-presentations that were tied to word-presentations, so
Bion introduced the concepts of β and α elements and developed a
unique theory of how the former are transformed into the latter. Like
thing-presentations, β elements are sensory in nature and must be
represented by α elements that, like word-presentations, "comprise
visual images, auditory patterns, [and] olfactory patterns" (Bion,
1962a, p. 26) if they are to achieve a meaningful status. Unlike Freud,
whose model of thing-presentations becoming paired with
word-presentations was linked to the movement from unconscious to
preconscious and then to consciousness, Bion connected the
transformation from β to α to a psychic structure – α function –
that worked unconsciously but which Bion did not tie to Freud's
tripartite id–ego–superego system, which he (Bion) regarded as

116

overly simplistic. However, as I discussed in Chapter 4, α function ought to be considered an ego function whose task is to transform concrete and sensory experience into meaningful psychological events that may be joined together into dream narratives that convey symbolic meaning.

Though Freud and Bion both address the emergence of a more abstract form of representability from a concrete/sensory mode of representation, Freud accounts for this in economic terms: that there is an instinctual push toward consciousness that is blocked most stridently ("rigorous censorship") at the threshold of the preconscious. The thing-presentation must be linked up with a word-presentation as a sort of "ticket" to gain admission into the preconscious, as though the thing-presentation says to the censor, regarding the word-presentation, "I'm with him." For Bion, on the other hand, the β element is transformed into an α element, and the two are not joined. *The prime mover for Bion is not the instincts' push for conscious expression but the psyche's need for emotional truth that nourishes it* (Bion, 1970; Grotstein, 2004). Moreover, Bion is not concerned with the journey from unconsciousness to being conscious; rather, what is essential is that the psyche has at its disposal α elements that the mind can weave together into narratives. These narratives serve to make the truth more tolerable in order for psychic growth to proceed and also are the means of emotional communication with another person.

Where Freud and Bion differ significantly is on the nature of what is projected and how it is encoded. Implicit in Freud's notion of unconscious communication is the idea that disguised meaning is conveyed along some unnamed channel that then must be deciphered by the receiver. The analyst, reading between the lines, can draw out the unconscious meaning of the communication and offer an interpretation that is aimed at making the patient's unconscious conscious – that is, by applying standard classical psychoanalytic technique. However, Bion (1954, 1957) found in his early work with schizophrenic and borderline patients that treating such cases with classical technique did not address the real problem of *these* individuals. For example, in his (1958) paper, "On Arrogance", Bion was accused by the patient of being stupid, which, upon self-reflection, he realized was an accurate statement because he was approaching the patient as though the man was capable of communicating on a verbal symbolic level. Bion came to understand that the communication, though encoded in words, did not use words to impart meaning but, *rather, to*

117

have an emotional effect upon the analyst. As long as he attempted to apply a traditional analytic stance of making the unconscious conscious, Bion *was* stupid, but he "got it" when realizing that the problem was a lack, or destruction, of a symbolic capacity. Then the analyst's task shifts from one of deciphering hidden communications to dealing with a mind that lacks whatever it is that can transform concrete sensory experience into emotionally based narratives that carry metaphorical meaning.[4] His discovery of α function was the fruit of Bion's efforts to understand this clinical challenge.

What is α function?

In "On Arrogance", Bion commented about the purpose of his patient's projective identification to "put bad feelings in me and leave them there long enough for them to be modified by *their sojourn in my psyche*" (1958/1967, p. 92, italics added). However, he did not address how the feelings are "modified" while in his psyche or the agency responsible for this alteration, and much of his subsequent research focused on just this question. It was a few years later that Bion (1962a) identified *alpha* (α) *function* as that aspect of the psyche responsible for acting on sense impressions and emotions (β elements) to produce α elements that are "suited for storage and the requirements of dream thoughts" (p. 5), and soon thereafter (1965) he outlined in great detail the processes of *transformation* that are inherent in α function. Let us return to Freud's theory of thing- and word-presentations for a moment from the perspective of α function.

Freud approached the question of the relationship between thing- and word-presentations from the perspective of the fate of an unconscious derivative as it traversed the path from the unconscious to the preconscious and then to conscious awareness, but he did not identify how this transpires other than to allude to the push of the drives to achieve conscious expression. As mentioned above, he (Freud, 1915c) briefly discussed how the analyst's interpretation offered a "second registration" by suggesting to the analysand that his or her conscious utterances have an unconscious meaning, thereby alluding to, but not elaborating on, the analyst's thought processes. Bion's theory of α function expands on Freud's idea about the transposition of concrete/sensory experiences to abstract/imagistic representations in two ways: first, by studying the nature of the analyst's mental activity in this process; second, by introducing an intersubjective component to Freud's solely intrapsychic point of view. To the extent that the analyst offers an interpretation of what he or she deems to be the unconscious content hidden in the analysand's free associations, he or she is sharing, as we have seen in Chapter 4, a thought that is the end point of some process in the analyst that is rooted in his or her unconscious receptivity to the patient. Freud introduced us to this territory, and Bion's exploration of it led to his discovery of α function.

Bion's concept of α function brings an intersubjective dimension to the transformation of concrete/sensory-based mental content to those of an imagistic/verbally encoded nature. Briefly, Bion (1962a, 1992) views α function as comprised of several subsidiary components that are linked with the infant's early experiences with its mother. When a projection from the baby is *sojourning* in the mother's mind, that projection is considered *contained* (♂) by the mother's psyche, the *container* (♀), and Bion links these two together as the container/contained (♀♂), which is "part of the apparatus of alpha function" (1962a, p. 91) and also refers to the ♀♂ as the "apparatus for thinking" (1962a, p. 92). Furthermore, while in the maternal container (♀), the contained (♂) is subjected to her *reverie*, which "is a factor of the mother's alpha function" (1962a, p. 36). Reverie is the means by which the mother's mind transforms (Bion, 1965) β→α elements by a process that is akin to dreaming (see below). Later, Bion (1963) added another factor to α function: the *paranoid-schizoid to depressive position balance* (Ps↔D), which refers to the maternal capacity to tolerate the oscillation between states of relative disintegration (Ps) with experiences of integration (D), thereby reinterpreting, in nonpathological terms, Klein's original concepts of the depressive (1935) and the paranoid-schizoid (1946) positions. There are a number of terms that Bion uses interchangeably and this can be confusing, so I offer a diagram to depict this model of α function:

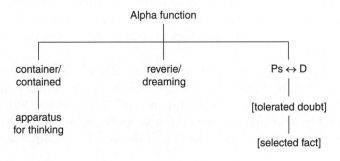

I have added two additional factors in brackets – *tolerated doubt* and the *selected fact* (Bion, 1962a) – that Bion himself did not include in his description of α function but which I see as integral aspects of the intersubjective implications of α function. These are placed under the Ps↔D balance because these factors are linked together: in order to withstand the oscillating pendulum of the Ps↔D situation, one must endure and *tolerate doubt* until a *selected fact* brings a sense of cohesion to what was experienced as disjointed. As we learned in Chapter 4, the *procreative* model of α function underscored the notion of two psyches mating and creating a third entity – a fresh idea produced by the analytic couple. The selected fact emerges, like a new and long-awaited child, born to a couple who may have spent long periods doubting their fertility (Ferro, 2002, 2005) but in the end their patience is rewarded. In addition, Bion (1962a) states that tolerated doubt is the medium in which there is mutual growth in the container and contained, or what Tronick (2005, 2007) calls the "dyadic expansion of consciousness." This mutual growth in both partners is furthered by their respective α functions working collaboratively to represent the shared emotional field, which inevitably involves recruitment of analogous areas of conflict that are reworked, re-imagined, and re-dreamed. We saw this process at work in the analyses of Sam in Chapter 1, Ms. C. in Chapter 3, and Sally in Chapter 4.

Before moving on to the connection between α function and dreaming, let us revisit the question of the role of the preconscious in intersubjectivity from the perspective of α function. Bion never used the term "preconscious" in any of his writings, but his theory of α function describes experiences that Freudian analysts would call preconscious – for example, Isakower's (1963) supervisee's visual image of the Mona Lisa. The difference seems to be that Bion did not address the *System Pcs.* (Freud, 1915c, 1923a) but instead explored *unconscious processes* without consideration of the distinction between the *Systems Ucs.* and *Pcs.* Instead, Bion was more interested in the development of thought, which occurs unconsciously through α function, more than its registration along the Freudian axis from unconscious to consciousness.

Several contemporary ego psychologists (Busch, 2006a; Kantrowitz, 2001) assert that intersubjective exchanges are "preconscious communication[s] between patient and analyst" (Kantrowitz, 2001, p. 25); however, I believe that the communication between one unconscious and another that includes the co-creation of a jointly assembled narrative remains an unconscious process for some time in analysis. *If we bring Bion's ideas about the transformation of β→α elements together with Freud's notions of the movement from thing- to word-presentations, we may conclude that an intact α function is necessary in order for concrete/sensory psychic experience to make the "jump" across the first threshold into preconscious-ness.* It is at this point that pictograms, characters (Ferro, 2002), α elements, and preconscious phenomena (Arlow, 1969a, 1969b; Busch, 2006a; Kantrowitz, 1999, 2001; Kris, 1950) emerge, and these are indicators that unconscious intersubjective work (Ogden, 2004b, 2005, 2007) *has already occurred.* For example, in the staccato give-and-take between Sam and me (Chapter 1), there was a dizzying proliferation of characters and phantasies that spilled into the play-room that from one (ego-psychological) vertex were preconscious phenomena, but from another (Bionian) perspective were the culmination of an unconscious simultaneous monitoring of our respective emotional states and the transformation of the shared emotional field, comprised of our individual unconscious subjectivities, into bearable images woven into a narrative.

What is the connection between α function and dreaming?

"Bion tends to treat 'dreaming' and 'alpha function' as being either identical, overlapping, and/or the latter being a component of the former" (Grotstein, 2009a, p. 734). The subject of dreaming in general, and Bion's ideas specifically, is a huge topic, and we will only consider its relevance to intersubjectivity. Thus, to state that the intersubjective connection between two minds is achieved through linked α functions is the same thing as saying that the analyst and patient dream a reciprocal dream together. We saw in Chapter 2 that many of the ego psychologists in the 1940s and 1950s, who were steeped in the psychology of dream-like ego states, explored the nature of these preconscious phenomena. Arlow (1969b) even spoke of how the analysand and analyst "dream together," although his emphasis was on the analytic dyad sharing an ego state and not on the mutual transformation of raw emotional experience into a jointly constructed narrative. A new theory of dreaming was needed that expanded Freud's (1900) notion that the function of dreams was to keep the dreamer asleep and also was a vehicle for expressing instinctually based wishes through the disguise of dream-work.

Freud's theory of dreaming was based on the *pleasure principle*, which guided the wish-fulfilling activity of dreams; while not appearing to reject this position, Bion (1992) did elaborate that

> The dream ... is in the domain of *the reality principle and the pleasure principle*, and represents an attempt to satisfy both.
>
> (p. 95, italics added)

Insofar as a dream is in the service of the *reality principle*, its origin is different from one forged by the precepts of the pleasure principle:

> Freud assumed that ... the latent content was the origin of the dream ... I say that the origin of the dream is an emotional experience ... and that this is worked on (rationalized?) to produce the dream.
>
> (Bion, 1992, p. 135)

In other words, frightening emotional truths are managed through the process of dreaming by their conversion from β→α elements that may then be given personal (and tolerable) meaning by linking the α elements into dream narratives. Put another way, when we dream we are providing a container (♀) for the unprocessed emotional truths (♂) that are subjected to our own capacity for reverie (α function). In this regard, we are telling ourselves bedtime stories,[5] an ability that depends upon the internalization of a *dreaming couple* (Grotstein, 2000).

   Thus, the capacity to dream meaningful dreams is actually a complex intersubjective event. The dreamer relates to the internal dreaming couple, a structural heir (Brown, 2008; see also Chapter 4, this volume) to the original dreaming couple – that is, the mother (and later father) and infant container/contained (♀ ♂) – that is introjected and becomes "part of the apparatus of alpha function" (Bion, 1962a, p. 91). I suggest that one implication of Bion's (1962a) use of the symbols for femininity (♀) and masculinity (♂) to represent the container and the contained, or the "apparatus for thinking" (or dreaming), is to underscore the intersubjective and procreative dimensions of thinking/dreaming:

> The use of the male and female symbols is deliberate but must not be taken to mean that other than sexual implications are excluded.
>
> (Bion, 1970, p. 106)

Dreaming has been linked with changes in representability, and, for Freud, the architect of this transposition was *dream-work*; however, we are left without an explanation of the psychic entity that constructs the dream. Following Bion's ideas, we can see that the "apparatus for thinking" ($\female\male$) – that is, for dreaming/transformation – is α function, which is the structural descendant of the infant and mother creating meaning together (Tronick, 2005).

Bion's theory of dreaming offers a clear model for understanding the transformation of β→α elements, but it leaves some gaps in explaining the formation of narratives. This raises the question of whether there are gradients of α function, an issue that has been addressed by some Italian analysts. Francesco Corrao (1992) proposes a "narrative–transformative–constructive model" that seems to describe a more advanced form of α function responsible for weaving α elements together into a narrative. Thus, α elements are like toys in a child's playroom that may be taken off the shelf and arranged in an infinite number of potential dream stories. In the clinical hour, the story is fashioned from the storehouse of various *narremes* (Ferro, 2005) – that is, α elements – that are suited to uniquely express the shared unconscious phantasy of the hour as it is registered respectively by the analyst and patient. Then, through processes of mutual projection and containment, the analytic dyad begin to weave a dream together[6] that becomes *their* dream; spun on a loom with threads that spool from the unconscious recesses of their respective psyches. This dream captures both the *growth and turbulence*[7] in the analysis and signals aliveness in that relationship, which is necessary for change:

> . . . if the person [or analytic couple] can dream, then he [they] can "digest facts" and so learn from experience.
>
> (Bion, 1992, p. 52)

And, also

> The analyst [or analytic couple] . . . must be able to dream the analysis as it is taking place.
>
> (p. 216)

This conjoint dream transforms the shared unconscious phantasy of the field (Baranger & Baranger, 1961–62) into an understanding in the analyst's mind of how he or she is processing the analysand's projections through his or her own metaphors, while simultaneously dreaming the patient into existence (Ogden, 2004b, 2007). However, this loom-work may become stalled when an unconscious collusion between patient and analyst leads to an "agreement" to "go on strike" because overlapping painful emotional truths in each are too difficult to confront. In this circumstance, "non-dreams-for-two" (Cassorla, 2009)[8] may emerge that is the product of the deadened emotionally interwoven situation, resulting in chronic enactments. When faced with such a benumbed process, the analyst must find within him/ herself the arrested α function and breathe new life into it in order to restart the "dreams for two." In what follows, I present a segment from the analysis of a young, self-destructive adolescent who was dedicated to not feeling; he initially needed me to dream/transform unrepresented experience for him, until we ultimately developed into an enlivened dreaming couple.

Jason's drawings: from affect evacuation to the co-construction of meaning

Jason was 13 years old when his parents contacted me because of his depression, self-injurious behavior, experimentation with marijuana, and extreme apathy about schoolwork. The middle of three boys, his two brothers had been diagnosed with bipolar disorder; while they often flipped into manic states, Jason tended to be depressed and listless. Most alarmingly, he engaged in self-cutting, and drinking whatever alcoholic beverages he could find until passing out, and he had recently attempted to set himself on fire. Understandably, his parents, both intelligent human-service providers, were deeply concerned; when I inquired as to what might be troubling Jason, they looked blankly at me. The notion that there could be meaning to any of their sons' emotional suffering seemed like a foreign idea, and they considered Jason as having a variation of his brothers' "biological illnesses." I had the impression that their pain at having three deeply troubled children was ameliorated by the belief that the boys had been stricken with illnesses akin to diabetes – that is, with no emotional or interpersonal meaning. Interestingly, when I later recommended analysis, they quickly agreed because one of their relatives had been significantly helped through analytic treatment.

Although all his teachers viewed him as highly intelligent, Jason simply showed no interest in his studies except for those assignments of interest to him. He demonstrated an impressive capacity for abstract thought (neuropsychological testing revealed no learning difficulties) and had a favorite male English teacher with whom he had wonderful conversations about poetry – in particular, the poems of T. S. Eliot. Jason felt especially drawn to Eliot's reflections on emptiness, which resonated with his own internal sense of impoverishment. However, despite his eloquent expounding on Eliot, he was completely unable to use language to capture his *own emotions* and, like his parents, grew dumfounded when asked to report his feelings. Jason also showed signs of being a talented artist, as evidenced in his constant doodling on a pad of paper during classroom lessons. These were very imaginative scribbles, usually scenes of drug paraphernalia and slogans from the marijuana culture, with which he entertained himself. "School," he told me, "is a mind-fuck, people trying to force an 'education' into you" and homework was the pinnacle of this disaster because "it's the teachers deciding that your after-school time belongs to them and they feel they have a right to tell you what to do with it."

Given Jason's extreme vulnerability to feeling impinged upon, I refrained from offering any "saturated" interpretations (Ferro, 2005) and instead adopted a "talking-as-dreaming" (Ogden, 2007) approach, as I did with Sally (Chapter 4). Initially we talked about Eliot's poems, particularly *The Waste Land* and *The Love Song of J. Alfred Prufrock*, and Jason immediately detected and discarded any of my efforts to gingerly offer comments about alienation and similar emotions. Sometime later, however, he allowed me to introduce an imaginary character, "Herr Professor Freud," with whom he was familiar, who speculated about the emotional meaning of whatever we were discussing. Jason would disagree with "Herr Professor" or not, and the character became my ventriloquist's dummy, speaking previously unacceptable ideas. Despite our beginning to talk about unbearable states of loneliness and *ennui*, Jason's self-destructive behavior continued unabated, and he was haunted by *nameless dread* (Bion, 1962a) – missiles of unrepresented β elements that bombarded his psyche from which he could only seek refuge by obliterating experience through drinking, cutting, and other maneuvers.

Jason asked to bring in the pets that he and his brothers shared, and I was "visited" by an array of rats, ball pythons, boa constrictors, and, on one occasion, an African millipede that I found particularly repulsive. These creatures seemed to convey something about Jason's

125

experience of himself that resonated with me as bizarre, un-human, frightening, and beyond words. They appeared to be what Ferro (2005, 2009) calls *balpha elements* – that is, mental contents that are slightly evolved versions of β but are not yet α, elements that are associated with a "shift [in] the balance from evacuation towards symbolization and thinkability" (2009, p. 86). Sensing that Jason was attempting to communicate something that lacked *psychic figurability* (Botella & Botella, 2005) and mindful of his artistic skills, I asked if he would care to draw during the sessions as a means of depicting what he was unable to comprehend in himself, and I said we could talk about the pictures if he liked. He readily agreed: I bought a sketchpad for him, and these drawings became a major part of the analysis. What follows is a recounting of how we used his drawings, and our interactions around them, as a means of giving meaning to the unknown specters that haunted him.

Jason began each session by starting to draw while talking about daily events, initially showing me the picture at the end of the hour. This evolved into my asking to see his creation in the middle of the session, our talking about it and offering our thoughts regarding possible meanings, then looking at it again at the end of the session and discussing how it had developed. In this way, the sketches came to reflect input from each of our minds and thus were an intersubjective creation. Figure 5.1 is an early drawing, not long after the pets were brought to my office, about which Jason had nothing to say. "I don't know what it is, it just came to me," he said, without any apparent emotion. In contrast to his apathetic demeanor, I felt invaded by an ill-defined nauseous feeling – just raw emotion experienced as a physical sensation. After regaining emotional equilibrium, my α function went to work to transform my initial somaticized response into an emotionally meaningful one. I noticed that the creature had no particular gender (though the eyes appeared feminine); it was both animal and bird-like, but with pathetically frail wings that rendered it incapable of flight. It had no mouth and looked as though it was captured or tied up, incapable of movement. I said that the picture suggested to me a sorry feeling of being neither bird nor mammal and that it seemed trapped or frozen. Jason was interested in my reactions and said, "Yeah, I see what you mean."

I believe that my first reaction of nausea, coupled with the unworldly animals Jason brought to the session, signaled his capacity to project into me some experiences that for him existed only as

Figure 5.1

repellant sensory events, as β or "balpha" elements, that required my α functioning to transform into a thought about which we could then converse. This process began with my transiently *becoming* (Bion, 1970; Fliess, 1942), or "working as a double" (Botella & Botella, 2005), that which was experienced by Jason as so repulsive that it had to be erased through extraordinary measures (drinking into a stupor, self-immolation, etc.). Thus, for some moments, both Jason and I occupied a psychic realm dominated by unbearable sensations that pushed for immediate evacuation: I did not want contact with the ill-defined monsters of his inner life, but knew I had to be touched by them. The words of Sartre's (1964) *Nausea* seemed suddenly appropriate:

> Objects should not touch because they are not alive. . . . But they touch me, it is unbearable. I am afraid of being in contact with them as though they were living beasts.
>
> (p. 19)

My thought about Sartre seemed to tap me on the shoulder and say, "nausea can have meaning, it can be transformed," and it indicated that my α function was beginning to bounce back from the initial impact of Jason's projections.[9]

About a year later, Jason said that what is so terribly awful about him is sexual in nature, but that he was not yet prepared to tell me the secrets in any detail. By this time, he had been speaking more freely to me, and his drawings in the sessions were similarly communicative, richly expressing his affects as well as capturing the emotional field of the analytic hours. These pictures, and our interactions around them, were indicators of the growth of Jason's α function and of the emergence of our connection as a fertile couple whose collaborating α functions created meaning out of what had previously been without form and emotional substance. Figure 5.2 is from a session during a

Figure 5.2

time that Jason was feeling defeated: he had achieved some notoriety for his painting but resented the drawing exercises his teacher required and was thinking about quitting. Similarly, he questioned whether the analysis (the "drawing exercises") was helpful because he could not bring himself to talk about his deepest, most disturbing thoughts.

Jason started the session as usual by drawing in the sketchpad and spoke of his mentor telling him to spend more time on drawing rather than painting, but that he prefers to paint. I said that his drawings in the hours have been uninspired lately, and he replied, "maybe I'm wasting your time and mine here because I can't talk about the sexual issues that I need to talk about; you expect me to talk about this stuff and I'm not cooperating." I said that there must be something that feels very dangerous about bringing these sexual feelings into the room, and he shrugged his shoulders. It was about midway into the hour, and I asked to see his drawing (Figure 5.2); at this stage, the background figure with the prominent eye had not yet been drawn. I asked Jason his thoughts about the picture, and he said there is a candlestick in the middle that reminds him of a still-life drawing he had originally refused to draw and had then destroyed. Then

ANALYST. I think this drawing tells us something about how difficult it is for you to talk about your sexual thoughts and feelings and why you feel our work here is a waste of time.

JASON. [*Immediately*] I'm not so sure about that creature [*in the foreground*], like it's me in some way. The object just below it reminds me of a mushroom cloud, as if the creature were taking it in, taking in a very powerful and potentially destructive force. That's all I have to say [*and he resumes drawing*].

ANALYST. I think the drawing expresses your fear that taking in the scary sexual parts of you, and our taking them in together to think about, might destroy you or you and I working together.

JASON. That might be so [*he appears to be giving serious thought to my interpretation while continuing the drawing quietly*].

ANALYST. It's nearly time to stop – what's happening with the drawing?

JASON. [*He has now added the background figure*] The "eye" in the drawing is a symbol of "I," you know, "me," as we have talked about before. That's my only thought.

129

ANALYST. I think it's the frightening sexual creature side of you that lurks in the background of your mind and in the background of our sessions, beginning to take some form for us to talk about, but perhaps felt to be too destructive to be brought more sharply into our focus.

JASON. You sound optimistic – at least one of us is.

Jason and I have clearly traveled a long distance from the exchange around the freakish image in Figure 5.1 that was largely encoded in sensory "language" that I had to decipher. For Jason, that picture carried no meaning he could explain in words; instead, it was solely a vehicle for the evacuation of an insufferable β^{10} experience, "thoughts" that required a thinker. In contrast, the images in Figure 5.2 were also disturbingly surreal, but they were expressive of meaning that we were able to jointly elaborate. There was a "creepiness" conveyed by the drawing that felt more communicative, rather than invasive, to me. This was a complex dialogue occurring on many different levels simultaneously: the transference implications of Jason's complaints about his teacher asking for more drawings, his feelings about the analysis (and his art tutoring) being a "waste of time," the destructive attack on his still-life drawing connected with fear of devastating the analysis, and, finally, the shadowy emergence of the ill-formed background apparition, drawn toward the end of the session, that hinted at what was to come. One could spend considerable time analyzing each of these important points, but what I want to emphasize is the growth in the complexity of our interaction and how our thoughts ping-pong or *squiggle* (Winnicott, 1965) with each other to create a narrative where previously none had existed.

Jason's comment at the end of the session that there was optimism, though it seemed to reside in me, appeared to kindle his own hopefulness, and the sessions became much livelier. Figure 5.3, drawn several weeks later, captures his renewed commitment to the analysis as well as being a product of a shared phantasy of the field (Baranger & Baranger, 1961–62). Jason picked up the sketchpad and began the hour by saying he had registered for a human-figure drawing class [I immediately felt heartened by his reinvestment in drawing/analysis] and that he had done most of a drawing assignment for his tutor. In fact, he had spent 5½ hours on it last night but had stopped short of finishing his homework because he got frustrated. When I asked about the task, Jason said it was a self-portrait and that it made him feel very uncomfortable because it was "narcissistic." He had recently completed a painting that was an homage to his grandparents and to his mother, but to draw himself was very difficult, though he was not sure why. He wondered if it had more to do with not wanting to do what his tutor asked, and, reflectively, he observed that "we've talked about how hard it is to do an assignment for someone else, except for my English teacher, and that's been the major problem in school."

It was now past the middle of the hour, and I asked to see what Jason had drawn, which was Figure 5.3 without the sweeping "tail of the lower fish" [my words to describe the portion of the sketch], and he said

JASON.   I have a lot of thoughts about this one. The figure in the center has a lower part that is a mermaid, which means that the bottom portion is only partly developed whereas the top part is more highly developed. Also, the sprout coming out of the head implies growth and hopefulness. So, what do you think of it?

ANALYST. I see what you mean, and that makes sense and I had some other reactions. That figure also looks like bait on a hook, and the lower part looks like a fish head about to bite. The round circle on top of the drawing makes me think of something on the surface of the water, as though we're submerged looking up at this entire scene.

JASON.   [*Immediately*] It could be like a fishing boat and the ripples of the water around it. So, I see what you mean. *I actually had a fleeting thought of what you just said when I handed you the picture to look at, but it never really reached my full awareness* [*italics added*]. Come to think of it, the bait could be like a sacrifice, like some pain to be endured, but for the greater good of getting something better [*he takes back the drawing and, in a subdued voice, says*] . . . like the pain I need to endure in order to deal with my sexuality.

ANALYST. Very scary to contemplate. [*I begin to think of how this phantasy of bait might be getting played out between us in the moment. Perhaps he's baiting me with his sexual phantasies to see if I'll bite and be the one who is allegedly forcing the issue on him? However, it's nearing the end of the hour, and this is not the best time to bring it up.*]

JASON.   I'm done [*and hands me the picture. He has added the*

131

"sweeping tail."] That round part [*at the end of the "tail"*] might be a pill, which stands for drugs, and I've decided to avoid the low road – that's behind me.

ANALYST.   The low road?

JASON.   That would be to destroy everything: quit painting, drop out of school and therapy too. Painting and therapy are related – they deal with expressing yourself.

This sequence of sessions, spanning more than a year in Jason's analysis, demonstrates the growth in his capacity to represent what had previously lacked figurability. This development occurred as a kind of Möbius strip: improvement in his capacity for representation

Figure 5.3

(from β→α) resulted from successful growth in the container/contained (♀♂), which, when internalized, enabled Jason's nascent facility to partner with me to produce jointly constructed symbols and, ultimately, a shared narrative that itself promoted further evolution in our dreaming together. Thus, *just as Freud and Bion link*[11] *changes in representation with the process of dreaming, so the capacity for symbol and narrative formation depends upon intrapsychic activity that derives from actual intersubjective exchanges that are internalized.* Our first "shared" dream was really a nightmare that occurred when my reaction of nausea to Figure 5.1 paralleled his feeling of self-repulsiveness. The shared "dream" was encoded exclusively as a sensory event[12] that initially was too powerful for me to "think" about in other than a concrete manner. My association to the line from Sartre indicated that I had intuited the depth of Jason's grisly sense of himself that at first fueled my "resistance" to transiently identify (Fliess, 1942) with him. In this regard, we were sharing an unconscious phantasy that there was something so revolting and awful about him that we dared not countenance it. This dyadic phantasy constituted a non-dream for two that, if left unanalyzed, could have initiated an ossifying analytic process of chronic enactments (Cassorla, 2005, 2009). Instead, I was able to tolerate Jason's projective identification although unable to transform it into an α element or, from another perspective, into a preconscious visual experience.

Prior to drawing Figure 5.2, Jason stated that his problems were largely sexual in nature and that he was unable to divulge these "secrets," an assertion I initially interpreted as the emergence of "repressed" material that he was consciously suppressing in the session. I felt annoyed that he was withholding, but I was unaware of Jason's unconscious seductive use of his "sexual" secrets to distract us from anxieties that I believe we collectively shared about his destructiveness. This catastrophic anxiety (Bion, 1970; Brown, 2008) was clearly evident in the session in his wish to quit working with his teacher and to stop analysis, but my mindset was geared toward thinking he was shamefully harboring sexual worries. However, Figure 5.2 refocused our attention to a more primal terror, an image of a nuclear-like apocalypse that was being represented, *in statu nascendi*, in that very moment by the drawing. The picture led me to shift my interpretive focus to Jason's anxiety of the disastrous effects to the analytic container, though I continued to think that this dread was ultimately about sexual concerns and not about destructiveness itself.

After my fixing our attention onto anxieties about damaging the analysis, Jason elaborated this theme further by drawing the vague background figure of the "eye" that seemed to say "there's more here than meets the eye and it's starting to come into view." My interpretation implicitly conveyed that I thought we could manage whatever (I was still thinking "sexual") felt so dangerously powerful, a comment that he found optimistic and comforting.

The discussion of whether Jason's severe anxiety resulted from the emergence out of repression of some organized sexual problem or from some unrepresented "nameless dread" (Bion, 1962a) frames a contemporary debate.[13] I think this controversy too easily polarizes (Renik, 2004) a very complex situation that may be viewed from multiple vertices (Ferro, 2005) that, upon closer inspection, demonstrates that repressed and unrepresented aspects may coexist within one expression. For example, it is quite possible that Jason was terrified of sexual phantasies that had surfaced from repression, stirring profound self-loathing and a fear that I would regard him with disgust if these were not withheld. It also may have been equally true that these formerly repressed phantasies are linked with powerful raw affective components that have yet to be transformed. In this regard, Figure 5.2 is especially instructive, in that it could be seen as containing the following facets: (1) Jason's conscious fear that his (previously repressed) sexual phantasies are dangerous; (2) an initial depiction (balpha element?) of his catastrophic fear of the destructiveness that until then had been unrepresented; and (3) a glimpse of a shadowy background figure, about which he had little to say, hinting at something about himself (an "eye"/I) that was largely unrepresented.[14] We can also see how positive growth in our ability to engage each other and co-construct a narrative through our dreaming together resulted in a nascent ability to represent experience that had formerly lacked figurability.

My optimism that the analytic container could manage his destructiveness infused Jason with hope and strengthened his α function, thereby enabling the productive "loom-work" in Figure 5.3. Although he said the humanoid figure suggested growth and hopefulness because of "the sprout coming out of the head," the fact that the skull was cracked open suggested something far more ominous to me. My attention was drawn to the fish circling below, and I was filled with a strong sense of foreboding, as though he were a worm on a hook, as bait. It seemed that once again Jason was recruiting me to be

134

the thinker for his frightening thoughts, and I was quite surprised, when telling him what I thought, that he quickly replied, "I actually had a fleeting thought of what you just said when I handed you the picture to look at, but it never reached my full awareness." It was rather stunning that Jason and I shared in this somewhat idiosyncratic take (being underwater, looking up at the figure used as bait) on the drawing. This was a true intersubjective moment,[15] resulting from the unconscious work each of us were doing on both intra- and inter-psychic levels in order to arrive at this shared thought, which was conscious for me and preconscious for Jason. Then he added his association of bait being "like a sacrifice, like some pain to be endured . . . in order to deal with my sexuality." This statement seemed to indicate his feeling of growing hopefulness that his inner container and α function had developed sufficient strength to be capable of handling "some pain to be endured."

While Jason and I shared the same visual perspective on the draw-ing, our associations went in different directions: his to the idea of sacrifice and suffering pain; mine to wondering whether his reference to sexuality was a kind of bait (what psychoanalyst worth his salt isn't interested in sex?) to lure me into an enactment in which I was seen as the one pushing the "dirty" thoughts on him. As I was considering whether he was baiting me, Jason's thoughts turned to his decision to leave the "low road" behind. There seemed to be a shared unconscious phantasy permeating the room about "dirty thoughts" and "low roads" that each of us was processing in our own way: I was concerned about being seduced into being a pusher of lascivious thoughts, and Jason struggled to eschew the "low road." By this point in Jason's analysis, we had evolved into a "dreaming couple" that had been successfully internalized by him into his α function, and in some respects the sexual themes in our communications were partly an expression that "implies a mental mating, or primal scene, resulting in the birth of new thoughts" (Ferro, 2002, p. 98).

I have underscored Bion's view that α function, and the associated capacity for "life-promoting" dreams, depends not only upon the internalization of the mother's α function but *also upon an internaliza-tion of the process of mother and infant making meaning together*. In the latter case, a triangular situation is established in the psyche that is comprised of the individual's self relating to the "dreaming couple" (Grotstein, 2000); thus, one's deployment of α function always implies a three-way interchange. We will now turn in Chapter 6 to a consideration of the triadic aspects of intersubjectivity, the relevance of the Oedipal situation, α function, and the role of the internalized Oedipal couple.

Notes

1   For the moment I will leave the distinction between *Ucs.* and *Pcs.* vague and discuss this below.
2   I do not mean to imply that authors from other schools (Kohutian, Freudian, etc.) subscribe to the notion that projective identification/ transidentification is the vehicle for intersubjective relationships.
3   In *On Aphasia* (1891) Freud uses the term *object-presentation* in place of *thing-presentation*, but in later writings refers only to thing-presentation. Thus, to diminish potential for confusion, I am using only *thing-presentation* here.
4   This issue of two kinds of mind – one capable of metaphorical thinking and suited for classical analytic technique, the other with a limited or absent capacity for symbol formation – has been the subject of numerous papers and books in recent years (e.g., among many others, Botella & Botella, 2005; Brown, 2005, 2006 (Chapter 6, this volume), 2007 (Chapter 9, this volume); Ferro, 2002, 2005; Fonagy & Target, 2007; Grotstein, 2007, 2009b, 2009c; Levine, 2008). The thrust of these studies, while often taking different theoretical perspectives, is that the analyst must use his own experiences as the means to "catch" a concretized communication that then must be "transformed," (Ferro, Grotstein, Brown), "mentalized" (Fonagy), or given "figurability" (Botella & Botella) through processes in the analyst. (See also p. 71 above regarding technical implications of this issue.)
5   In a recent paper, Parisi and Ruberti (2009), two Italian analysts, quoted Corrao (1987): "One could say that every phase in a child's development is marked by the child's fundamental request of the adult to *tell a story*" (p. 182, italics in original, translation from the Italian by Parisi & Ruberti).
6   This shared dream is what classical analysts refer to as a transference neurosis.
7   The conference title of the Bion in Boston 2009 conference was "Growth and Turbulence in the Container/Contained."
8   From the paper, "Reflections on Non-Dreams-For-Two, Enactment and the Analyst's Implicit Alpha Function," which received the Parthenope Bion Talamo prize for best paper at the Bion in Boston 2009 conference.
9   See Chapter 6 for a further discussion of disturbances in the analyst's α function.

10 Perhaps a *balpha* element (Ferro, 2009), since the drawing itself suggests a nascent transformational capacity?

11 Bion's (1977b) notion of "the developmental status" of a thought and Freud's (1900, 1915c) ideas about the movement from thing- to word-presentations.

12 A "topographical regression" (Brown, 1985; Freud, 1900), "transformation in hallucinosis" (Bion, 1965), or, in the Botellas' (2005) framework, "formal regression."

13 This was the subject at the Bion in Boston 2009 conference of a panel, "Dreaming into Being: Transformation and Representation in Non-Neurotic Structures," chaired by Howard Levine, with panelists Jaime Lutenberg, Renato Trachtenberg, and Rudi Vermote.

14 Perhaps a representation of his *ego-destructive superego* (Bion, 1962a) as well?

15 Are there any moments that are *not* intersubjective? One could argue that the moment two persons engage each other, all inter- and intra-personal moments are "intersubjective" phenomena of the field. However, something is lost if we ignore the "one-person" dimension; rather, these are two vertices from which to consider the analytic dyad (Grotstein, 1997).

6

Intersubjectivity and the internalized Oedipal couple[1]

In the evolution of our understanding of the analytic interaction from a one-person to a two-person psychology and from there to an inter-subjective perspective, some concepts that have been foundational to psychoanalysis have been left by the wayside. I have been attempting to demonstrate that many of the basic precepts of intersubjectivity have been nascent in our field from Freud's early contributions onward and that these ideas have not suddenly sprung into existence, like Athena from Zeus' head. However, perhaps because each gener-ation of analysts needs to establish its independence from its parents, those previous viewpoints are seen as outmoded (Kancyper, 2005). The Oedipal situation, once considered by Freud (1910a) to be the "nuclear complex" of development, has waned (Loewald, 1980) in the importance once accorded to it, even among classically oriented analysts. However, in recent years the relevance of "the third" (Aron, 1995, 2006; Benjamin, 2004; Britton, 1989, 1998, 2004; Brown, 2002, 2004; Ogden, 1994a, 1997a, 2005) to intersubjective phenomena has been explored, thus *reawakening interest in the triangular aspects of Oedipal dynamics.*[2] We will now briefly review Freud's and Klein's ideas on this subject in order to understand more fully the contemporary applications of "thirdness" to intersubjectivity.

Triangularity and the Oedipal situation

As a psychoanalyst trained in the American tradition, I was taught that the Oedipal phase began roughly in the fourth year of life and continued as the central focus of psychic development until its resolution ushered in the latency period. There was an implicit assumption about the Oedipal phase that was rarely questioned: that triangular relationships between the child and its parents achieve significance with the appearance of phallic-Oedipal strivings. Within this framework, triangularity and "Oedipal-ness" were inseparable qualities of the same phenomenon, and each was the sine qua non of the other. The developmental unfolding of the phallic-Oedipal stage was preceded by the pre-Oedipal period marked by, among other aspects, dyadic object relations. Indeed, just as the Oedipal phase was characterized by triangularity, so the pre-Oedipal period was the province of dyadic relationships. This perspective has remained one of the tenets of American psychoanalysis and, in a way, is somewhat unanalytic because the sudden appearance of triangular relatedness seems to have little or no preceding history: it was as though triangular relationships appeared on the scene suddenly and without apparent preparation.

This view of development – that there exists a sharp demarcation between the dyadic and triangular relational worlds – also had a significant impact upon our theories of psychopathology. The "neuroses" were generally considered to be responses to Oedipal triangular conflicts: patients at this higher level of pathology (Kernberg, 1967) either retain their triadic level of object relations or else are driven back by regression from Oedipal anxieties to pre-Oedipal dyadic conflicts. Borderline, narcissistic, and other "primitive" pathologies were seen as difficulties having to do with conflicts and/or defects of a pre-Oedipal – that is, dyadic – nature. Regardless of one's orientation in American psychoanalysis, whether orthodox, classical, ego-psychological, self-psychological, or contemporary Freudian, the view toward the more severe pathologies was that they were pre-Oedipal, hence dyadic, in nature and origin. Even today, one still hears in case conferences regarding sicker patients that such individuals "are not there yet" if the question is raised about possible triangular/Oedipal aspects of the treatment. It has been my feeling (Brown, 2002) that the "are not there yet" response to the question of triangular relationships in more disturbed patients may actually lead to clinical situations in which material important to the patient's life in general, and in the transference in particular, is left unexamined.

Although most psychoanalytic schools proudly trace their origins to the work of Freud, the Kleinians view their theoretical and clinical developments, however disparate from Freud, as a direct continuation of his work. In reading the classical and contemporary Kleinians, one is immediately impressed with the solid grounding in Freud. Indeed, during the Controversial Discussions (King & Steiner, 1991), when Melanie Klein and her adherents were challenged as to whether their contributions were "Freudian," Susan Isaacs (1948) took great care in the preparation of her paper, "The Nature and Function of Phantasy," to illustrate the continuity between Klein's views of unconscious phantasy and those of Freud (Grosskurth, 1986).[3] One of the most controversial of the discussions at the British Society centered on Klein's (1928) opinion that the Oedipal situation actually began in the first year of life, thereby obliterating the established notion that significant three-way interactions did not occur before the phallic period and throwing into question Freud's (1923a) view of the "pre-Oedipal" period that

> At a very early age the little boy develops an object-cathexis for his mother . . . on the anaclitic model; the boy deals with his father by identifying with him. *For a time these two relationships proceed side by side,* until the boy's sexual wishes become more intense . . . from this the Oedipus complex originates.
>
> (pp. 31–32, italics added)

Intersubjectivity and the primal scene

A central feature of the Kleinian approach to the early Oedipal situation is the importance of the primal scene. Freud (1918), of course, introduced this as the primary unconscious pathogenic factor in the case of the Wolf Man, who had repressed primal-scene material he had witnessed at age 18 months. Implicit in the description of the Wolf Man's primal-scene phantasy is an idea that Freud did not choose to further develop: that at 18 months a child has the capacity to form a representation, which emerged from repression later in the analysis, of his *parents engaged as a couple.* This was a perception of parental intercourse as a violent act, which became linked with other sadistic trends in the Wolf Man's life. Following this case report, Freud appeared to shelve the concept of the primal scene and "never incorporated the primal scene and its associated phantasies as a principal component of the Oedipus complex" (Britton, 1992, p. 36). Thus, though Freud did

not expand on the relevance of the primal scene, the concept introduced the importance of phantasies about the triad of mother, father,
and child together.

Klein (1932) was also impressed with the relevance of primal-scene
material in her analysis of a very disturbed 6-year-old girl, Erna,
whom she analyzed in the early 1920s. As Freud had observed in his
analysis of the Wolf Man, so Klein also discussed the hatred stirred in
Erna's viewing of her parents' sexual encounters. However, Klein
found that Erna's hatred was motivated by a profound "oral envy of
the genital and oral gratifications which she supposed her parents to
be enjoying during intercourse" (1932, p. 46). Thus, Klein here is
emphasizing that Erna's hatred is an envious response to feeling
excluded from a primal-scene phantasy of endless intercourse, which
depicted her parents as engaged in an inexhaustible exchange of a
"special food, which was eaten by the father and mother alone"
(p. 40). In Freud's view, the Wolf Man saw the sexual act itself as
inherently sadistic, while, from Klein's standpoint, Erna's hatred
stemmed essentially from *a situation of deprivation and loss*: that she was
left out of something incredibly special going on between her mother
and father. Klein returns to the issue of loss again at the end of the
paper and states that "the process of weaning . . . sets the Oedipus
conflict in motion" (p. 55), and she talks about the child's fantasy that
its mother has incorporated the father.

Klein's view of the Oedipal conflict being triggered by conflicts
around loss was not yet formulated when she presented the case of
Erna at the First German Conference on Psychoanalysis in 1924.
Frank and Weiss (1996) compared the unpublished manuscript Klein
delivered to the conference with the report of Erna's analysis published eight years later in *The Psychoanalysis of Children* (1932). It is
interesting to note that in the initial presentation Klein (1924/1925)
explained Erna's complicated phantasied relationships with her parents as a "regression from the genital stage that has already been
partially attained to the anal and oral-cannibalistic stages" (p. 13,
quoted by Frank & Weiss). This perspective was consistent with the
prevailing view of the time in which the appearance of more primitive material was seen as a regression from phallic-Oedipal conflicts.
Thus, Klein's ideas about the existence of an early Oedipal conflict
must have matured shortly after her first discussion in 1924 of Erna's
treatment, since she published in 1928 her initial paper devoted to the
Oedipal situation in which the role of loss in the weaning process was

emphasized. Frank and Weiss note that the analysis of Erna was nearly simultaneous with Klein's analysis with Karl Abraham, who died in 1925. One could speculate about the possible role that Abraham's loss, coupled with earlier significant losses in her life (Grosskurth, 1986), played in Klein's shift in being able to appreciate the connections between the inception of the Oedipal conflict and difficulties with early object loss.

Klein advanced her understanding of the emergence of early Oedipal anxieties with the introduction of the depressive position (Klein, 1935), thus expanding her having previously linked the appearance of Oedipal conflicts with the loss associated with weaning. In "The Oedipus Complex in the Light of Early Anxieties" (Klein, 1945), she stated that the inception of the Oedipus complex and the depressive position are coincident. One aspect of the depressive position, owing to the lessening of reality-distorting projective mechanisms, is the increased capacity for knowing reality. In terms of the baby's object relations, the most important reality is the acceptance of the mother having a separate existence from the child. In addition, the awareness also grows that the mother has a relationship with the father, from which the child is excluded. This experience of the parental relationship becomes internalized into what Klein called the "combined parental figure," who may be felt as a cooperative and creative couple or, paradoxically, as a dangerous pair bent on tormenting the child. Thus, Klein asserted that beginning in the second half of the first year of life the infant moves into a triadic world and that these experiences of triangularity are internalized. The important defining features of these internalizations are the knowledge that parents have a relationship independent of their connection to the child, the small child's fantasies of what the parents are doing together, and the potentially painful emotions of envy and feeling excluded.

Contemporary Kleinian perspectives build upon Klein's linking the depressive position with the emergence of the early Oedipal situation. Britton (1992) states that the resolution of the Oedipus complex is achieved by working through the depressive position, and vice versa. In the greater capacity for gaining knowledge that accompanies the maturation of the depressive position lies the danger of discovery that one is left outside the mother and her involvement with the father, a knowledge that may imply unbearable grief and resentment. This realization, according to Britton, presents a fearful question: "Will our love survive knowledge, particularly our growing awareness of the separateness of our love objects and their relationships with others which exclude us?" (p. 45). O'Shaughnessy (1988), speaking of an "invisible Oedipus," asserts that the analyst should always be on the lookout for Oedipal material, regardless of the diagnosis of the patient. She would assert that issues of loss are inevitably interwoven with fantasies of exclusion from a parental couple, trends that are evident in the patient's relationships with others and also become manifest in the transference.

Britton (1989) writes that the internalization of a parental couple experienced as loving and creative generates an inner comfort with being a part of a relationship that is observed by a third individual and also permits the person to accept being the observer of a relationship between two others. However, catastrophic consequences may result when the internal combined parental couple is experienced as hostile and exclusionary, and this may be felt in the transference as an intolerance of the analyst communing even with himself. Caper (1997) has written cogently about this phenomenon and describes how the analyst having a "mind of one's own" is perceived by some patients as an unendurable agony. Here, Caper is stressing the patient's experience of the analyst doing his job as an analyst – that is, his connection with psychoanalysis as an internal object, and how this may be felt as the analyst forming a couple with himself that forbids the patient. Caper states:

> . . . emergence into the depressive position must involve acknowledgement of the object's sovereign object relationships. And if awareness of these relationships places the patient in a triangular situation in the transference, then emergence into the depressive position is the same as accepting one's position in the oedipal situation.
>
> (p. 277)

Furthermore, there are often triangular and early Oedipal components of certain clinical situations that are traditionally seen as exclusively dyadic in nature. I (Brown, 2002) wrote about my analytic work with a very troubled and narcissistically vulnerable woman, Ms. D.,[4] whose terror of being abandoned by me was interpreted from the vertex of the early mother/child matrix. Although this approach was helpful to her, she still remained very depressed until I realized that *what I had been interpreting as fear of loss of a dyadic connection by*

143

abandonment was additionally a fear of loss by exclusion from an archaically organized Oedipal couple. This was an extremely important distinction that allowed me to hear the material in a different way and to understand the transference/countertransference manifestations in a new light. Thus, her experience that I had failed her empathically was linked to a phantasy that my capacity for attunement had been directed to someone else, thereby leaving her painfully excluded from a couple thought to be in perfect emotional synchrony. Britton (1998), further developing Rosenfeld's (1987) ideas about "thin-skinned" narcissistic patients, describes the sense of "malignant misunderstanding" that patients like Ms. D. may experience: the introduction of a third person

> creates in phantasy the third object as the source of malignant misunderstanding forever threatening the mutual, empathic understanding between the self and the primary object.
>
> (Britton, 1998, p. 56)

Intersubjectivity and thirdness: American relational perspectives

Aron (1995) accurately notes that

> Relatively little use has been made of Klein's concept of the combined parent figure especially outside the circle of Kleinian analysts, even though the combined parent figure is particularly an important contribution.
>
> (p. 213)

Writing from the perspective of gender issues, he sees in Klein's concept two central roots of intersubjectivity. First, Klein's notion of the combined parent figure is an internalization of the primal scene in which the viewer identifies with both the male and the female participants, which Aron sees as an early step towards the ability to place oneself in another's shoes – a necessary precondition for intersubjective experience. This internalized primal scene is "a valuable and organizing structure" (p. 197) that "regulates self and object relations between our phantasies of masculine and feminine selves" (p. 213). Regarding the analytic situation, Aron adds a gender-related

144

perspective to the Kleinian point of view about the primal scene (Britton, 1989, 1998; Caper, 1997; O'Shaughnessy, 1988) by asserting that these masculine and feminine identifications need to be integrated with relative comfort, which enables the analyst to flexibly shift from empathic and receptive (feminine) modes to more firm and penetrating (masculine) interactions. These are two components, expressed through the metaphor of gender, that comprise part of one's analytic function. Aron notes that for some patients contact with the analyst's internalized primal-scene couple stirs an envious need to divide these two aspects, which is equivalent to "enacting attacks on the primal scene in which the two sides of the analyst have come to represent the two parents" (Aron, 1995, p. 222). (We shall see later in this chapter how this dynamic got played out in my treatment of an adult woman in analysis.)

A second connection of the primal scene to intersubjectivity is the development of a sense of "triangular space [that] is the basis of the integration of self as both subject and object and . . . [is central to] the development of intersubjectivity" (Aron, 1995, p. 217). Here Aron is expanding on the contributions of Britton (1989) by underscoring the importance of being able to hold seemingly disparate identifications (masculine/feminine; self/object) in mind in order for the analyst, for example, to step into the patient's experience without losing sight of his or her own point of view.[5] In later contributions, Aron and Benjamin (1999) and Aron (2006) expand on the Kleinian tendency to view the primal scene mainly in terms of emotions around loss associated with feeling excluded from the parental couple's intimacy and consider instead that

It may turn out that primary triangular processes exist from very early on in life and that what is most characteristic of the oedipal stage is not triangularity per se, but rather symbolic thought, narrative structure, and reflective self-awareness.

(Aron, 2006, p. 353)

However, Aron seems to be overlooking the main thrust of Klein's reinterpretation of the Oedipal situation: that it, including triangular relationships, begins in the first year of life with the infant's initial glimpses that mother is separate and has a relationship with father from which the baby is excluded. Thus triangularity is extant from the dawn of relational life and does not grow out of dyadic

145

interactions but, instead, has its own trajectory that runs parallel to dyadic relating. (More about this in the following section of this chapter.)

Triangularity, for Benjamin (2002, 2004), grows out of dyadic experience and does not have a developmental line of its own. She delineates two patterns of triadic interaction that are facets of inter-subjectivity, the first of which is termed the *one-in-the-third*. In this mode, the "third" refers to a co-created "rhythm" of two people being together that is forged by mutual accommodation to each other's individuality, and it is through this accommodation that a joint way of being, a kind of couple-hood, spontaneously evolves. Benjamin asserts that the one-in-the-third emerges in the space between the two – that is, from the pre-Oedipal mother/infant pair. The couple surrenders to the third, so that each is directly influenced by the established third, and Aron (2006) notes that

> this form of thirdness may well be pre-oedipal [and] . . . does not require an oedipal father to sever the child's connection to mother.
> (p. 353)

The second form of thirdness conceptualized by Benjamin is called the *third-in-the-one*, which she also refers to as the *symbolic* or the *moral third*, and it arises in the space between the two individuals when they are no longer in a state of oneness. This differentiation between them is prompted by the inevitability of the mother (or analyst) to fail in accurately mirroring an affective experience, thereby marking the separation between the two. In this case, the "third" is the recognition of a space between the two in which mentalization and affect regula-tion may be undertaken. An example of the third-in-the-one is the analyst's self-disclosure, which in effect introduces a third element – his or her formerly private thought – to the dialogue.

In summary, it seems to me that the primary difference between these two points of view, the Kleinian and the Relational, centers on the question of whether thirdness emerges out of a dyadic matrix (the Relational perspective)[6] or whether triangularity is an inherent fea-ture of relationships that is independent of, though connected to, dyadic interactions. Aron's (1995) earlier thinking that considered the internalization of the primal scene as an important structure, which would highlight issues of exclusion and loss as well as the mother–father–baby triad, seems to have evolved toward a view that regards thirdness as an epiphenomenon to dyadic relating. However, on a clinical level, there is overlap between the positions taken by Britton and Caper and those by Aron and Benjamin in terms of the effect upon the patient of becoming aware of the analyst's personal musings. Both schools see this as an indicator to the analysand that the analyst is separate: for Benjamin and Aron, it is a sign that the third-in-the-one is marking the differentiation; for Britton and Caper, it demonstrates to the patient that the analyst is communing with him/herself, thereby excluding the analysand from an unconsciously experienced (by the patient) Oedipal situation. We will shortly explore Bion's contributions to this discussion, but first a brief detour to some developmental studies that may shed further light on the question of early triangular relationships.

Early triangular relationships – the developmental perspective

Kleinian theories of an early Oedipal situation are often considered to be overly inferential, imputing relatively sophisticated states of mind to the infant that are beyond its cognitive capacities. A major argument raised in the traditional analytic literature against the notion of early triangular relationships is that the relative absence of symbolic thought and the infant's limited ability to form three-way relationships preclude the internalization of the parents as a couple until around age 18 months (Sharpless, 1990). I would argue that the appearance of classical Oedipal triangular relationships is the final outcome of many prior epigenetic steps beginning early in infancy and that this perspective is increasingly supported by contemporary studies of early development. Even within more recent studies, there is scant attention paid to the very young child's relating to both parents simultaneously. Several of these reports will now be reviewed.

This apparent reluctance to consider the centrality of early triangular relationships because they are not represented on a mature symbolic level continues to perpetuate the notion of the "triadic" classical Oedipal phase and the "dyadic" pre-Oedipal period and essentially denies that there is a continuum of triadic experiences from early life onward (Brickman, 1993). However, Herzog (2001) believes that the very young child is constantly monitoring the relationship between the parents. He commented in an earlier paper

147

that the relationship between mother and father is recorded, represented, resonated with and continuously monitored, and that it
serves as an antecedent for the development of classical, e.g.
Oedipal object relations.

(Herzog, 1991, p. 3)

Herzog underscores the young child's need, beginning in the first
year of life, for two different kinds of interaction: a pattern of
homeostatic attunement and one of *disruptive attunement*. Homeostatic
attunement, which generally is the maternal style, involves empathic
interactions of "being with" the child affectively. On the other hand,
disruptive attunement, typically a paternal style, involves interactions
with the child that "stir things up" by introducing stimulating new
elements to where the child is at the moment. Both interactive patterns are necessary for healthy development and have important
implications for the child's capacity to regulate its emotions, to play,
and to endure trauma. Herzog's findings show the necessity for
healthy development, beginning in the first year, of an internalized
parental couple interacting collaboratively (one homeostatically
attuned and the other disruptively attuned) with the child.[7]

In a fascinating study of triadic play between parents and their
infants, Von Klitzing, Simoni, and Burgin (1999) also highlight an
inborn need for three-way relationships with the actual mother and
father from the outset of life. Most significant for this discussion is
Von Klitzing et al.'s observation that

the infant, as early as four months, is not only responsive to the
parental interactional offerings but also *actively contributes* to the
triadic family interactions.

(p. 82, italics added)

The authors describe a very rich interaction in which a 4-month-old
actually worked to draw the other parent into an ongoing dyad in
order to form a triadic interaction, and they conclude that this is an
inborn need of all infants. Speaking intersubjectively, they emphasize
that the interaction of the infant's inborn need for triangular relationships with the parents' representational worlds fosters the behavioral
appearance of triadic play. One implication of their findings is that
the later emergence of the classical Oedipus complex can be seen as
"a culminating stage in a continuum of triadic experience" (p. 86).

148

Fivaz-Depeursinge and Corboz-Warnery (1999) present the find-ings of an extensive study of the development of triangular relation-ships beginning in infancy in their book, *The Primary Triangle*. Acknowledging that psychoanalytic studies have tended to focus on the effects of exclusion from the parental couple, they set about tracing the growth of collaborative triads. They approach the subject from an intersubjective perspective and, leaning heavily on Dan Stern's (1985) work, they emphasize the unfolding of affect attune-ment within early triangular relationships. They noted instances in which 3-month-olds in an experimental play situation alternated their attention between the mother and the father in a manner that fostered three-way interactions. In addition, these infants also initiated emotional interchanges with their parents that created affectively attuned experiences. The authors note that these early exchanges between the infant and its parents anticipate later patterns of mother, father, and baby together at the intersubjective stage (Stern, 1985) at 9 months when complex interactions of mutual affect attunement and regulation are observed in triangular relationships. At this age,

> shared individual representations generate a collective triangular imaginary representation – that is, a subjective experience simultaneously shared by the three parties.
>
> (Fivaz-Depeursinge & Corboz-Warnery, 1999, p. 169)

In summary, from the perspective of developmental studies, there appear to be two lines of thought regarding the relevance of early triangular relationships. The first point of view is that early triadic relationships are observable, they grow out of dyadic interactions, and their connection to later Oedipal manifestations is questionable. The other point of view – of which Brickman, Herzog, Von Klitzing et al., and Fivaz-Depeursinge and Corboz-Warnery are adherents – holds that there is a direct epigenetic line from the earliest triangular rela-tionships that culminates in the classical Oedipal complex. These authors also assert that there is likely an inborn predisposition to triadic modes of relating that is apparent from the dawn of inter-actional life and connected to, but independent of, dyadic exchanges. These studies would seem to support Kleinian views that relating to the parental couple is a central feature of object relations that begins in early infancy and that these early patterns may prefigure later Oedipal manifestations. Furthermore, the infant's often active efforts to create triangular connections with its parents, beginning at 3 or 4 months, bolster a view of a "mentally" active baby already aware of its involvement with parents by the middle of the first year of life. With regard to the mental activity of the infant, it is of course impossible to ascertain the baby's phantasies about its parents; however, it seems not too far-fetched to assume that just as the small child's interactions in the "primary triangle" become increasingly complex, so too do its "ideas" about its parents' relationship become more sophisticated. At the earliest times, the infant's notions about the connection between mother and father would be organized at the level of concrete operations, with subsequent transformations as thinking matures and development proceeds (Brown, 1985, 1996).

Thus, these observations cast considerable doubt on the view that triadic interactions grow out of dyadic connections in a linear manner. It is probably more correct to say that dyadic and triadic relationships develop in tandem with significant transactions occurring between the two modes of relating (Herzog, 1991, 2001). So what are the implications for intersubjectivity in the analytic consulting room that we may draw from these studies? It seems to me that Aron and Benjamin, in adhering to a more classical view of the Oedipal situation maturing in the 3- to 5-year-old range, miss the dimension of intersubjectivity that devolves from the interaction between the internalized primal-scene couple in the analysand and the analyst (see the clinical vignette later in this chapter). Aron (1995) initially addressed this dynamic, but only from the perspective of an Oedipal couple in the classical phallic-Oedipal stage, thereby de-emphasizing the importance of affects around loss, exclusion, and envy that characterize the early Oedipal situation. This has unfortunately led to the tendency to see "pre-Oedipal" (before 3 to 5 years) relations as solely dyadic in nature and centered on issues of sameness/difference, attunement/empathic failure, and "either submission or resistance to the other's demand" (Benjamin, 2004, p. 10).

The primal scene, container/contained, and alpha function

In contrast to Freud, Bion saw the capacity for thinking as arising within the matrix of the mother/infant relationship (Brown, 2005, 2009a [Chapter 4, this volume]). The infant projects the contained

(♂) into the container/mother (♀) who subjects the ♂ to her reverie in order to transform it into a thought (α element) that is suitable for being woven into a narrative. We learned in Chapter 5 that Bion intentionally used the feminine (♀) and masculine (♂) symbols to connote a sexual interpretation to the act of thinking, likening the appearance of a new thought in the emotional field to an offspring of the analytic couple. Hence, the container/contained (♀ ♂), which is subsumed into α function, is created by the introjection of the trans-formational thinking capacity of the first couple – that is, the infant (♂) placing into the containing (♀) mother emotional experience too difficult for its weak ego to manage. Though Bion did not link the container/contained (♀ ♂) to the early Oedipal situation, I believe that, intentionally or not, he meant to promote a model for thinking that was linked to Klein's (1945) idea of the creative Oedipal couple. Thus, he was sketching a picture of the earliest interactions, depicting two individuals creating something new that did not previously exist. In this regard, this earliest couple (container/contained, or ♀ ♂) may become a template that prefigures the infant's later experience of the mother and the father as a couple in the early Oedipal situation, which, in turn, colors the emergence of the classical phallic-Oedipal complex.

I have been arguing that intersubjectivity depends upon the unconscious collaboration of the linked α functions of analysand and analyst, who together create a joint narrative that only slowly comes to their collective awareness. However, insofar as the analyst's think-ing – that is, "consultation" with his or her internalized thinking couple (♀ ♂) – is experienced as a threat, then the patient may strive to attack that analyst's capacity to think. We will recall that Bion (1962a) stated that the activity of the ♀ ♂ is introjected and becomes "part of the apparatus of alpha function" (p. 91). Thus, injury to either the ♀ ♂ or to α function inevitably hobbles the other. For the pur-poses of this discussion, I will also, following Grotstein (2000), refer to the ♀ ♂ as the "thinking couple." I add this emphasis to highlight the interpersonal activity that thinking represents. Much has been written about how severe trauma disrupts the connection to the internalized mother (Brown, 2006; Laub & Auerhahn, 1993), leaving the trauma patient unprotected and stranded internally as well as externally. In addition, I suggest that significant trauma also severs the tie between the patient and his or her internalized thinking couple (♀ ♂). Sensing the analyst's capacity to commune with him/herself, the patient may

151

strive to enviously destroy the link between the analyst and his or her internalized thinking couple *as well as seek to enviously attack the links that join the container and contained that comprise the internalized thinking couple of the analyst,* a point also made by Aron (1995).

Clinical vignette

Ms. B., a single woman in her twenties, developed a phantasy during analysis that I was under the sway of a callous analyst (I was not in analysis at this time) who instructed me to treat her cruelly; thus, this imagined analyst and I comprised a dangerous tormenting couple. This phantasy was intimately connected to the traumatic events in her life that had brought her to analysis and was directly linked to her inner experience of the parental couple. As this phantasy of a destructive couple came to dominate her experience of the analysis, she sought to dismantle the relationship with my imagined analyst. This stirred strong countertransference responses in me that made it extremely difficult to gain contact with my own internal supervisors (Casement, 1991), and therefore I was often unable to think. The work temporarily ran aground at the point of interaction (Brown, 2004) where I had become for the patient the embodiment of a malevolent thinking couple whose spiteful collaboration she sought to tear apart.

Ms. B. consulted me because she was unable to mourn the tragic loss of her brother, six years her senior. He was her admired protector and worked as a foreign correspondent who was often posted in very dangerous parts of the world, an occupation their parents considered risky. She once accompanied him on an assignment where he introduced her to some politically unsavory, though quite exciting, characters. Several years before contacting me, her brother was killed on assignment in what she regarded as a highly suspicious car crash. Ms. B. believed he had been murdered while investigating a story and wanted to pursue an inquiry into this matter. Her parents, understandably, were grief stricken and took the position that their son had lived a suicidal lifestyle; therefore, they wished no further inquest. Thus, for Ms. B., the factual reality of her brother's death was denied by her parents, and she alone was left to bear witness to what she believed to be the truth of his murder.

Socially isolated, Ms. B. desperately needed to talk to someone about her brother's tragic death, yet also thought no one would believe her. In the early sessions she told me about her frequent nightmares involving mutilations and gruesome deaths. She had tried in vain to contact her brother a few days before his alleged murder and was consumed by the thought that she might have been able to save his life. When I suggested that she appeared to feel guilty about his tragic death, Ms. B. became infuriated because I supposedly turned the reality of his murder into an intrapsychic fiction. I replied that if that were so, then I would be treating this horrible experience as did her parents. In response, Ms. B. grew more angry, claiming that I was now avoiding responsibility for my failure to understand her and was blaming it on her parents.

In the sessions, Ms. B. often railed against me, asserting that I was doing little to help with her distress. I assumed that her guilt over this loss was so powerful that it threatened to overwhelm her; thus, I said we needed to take our time and recognize that her difficulty in speaking must be a way to feel safe from unbearable emotions. Ms. B. angrily rebuffed this stance as evidence that I did not want to understand her; however, my gentle interpretations aimed at conveying my understanding of her terror-filled experiences were met with the accusation that "you sound like a fucking syrupy school marm!" If I sought to engage her with noninterpretative comments aimed merely at describing how she felt unsafe and not protected by me, then Ms. B. would angrily denigrate this stance by saying that my words were the equivalent of attempting to offer a picture of food to someone starving to death.

Ms. B. filled me with the sense that I could do nothing right and that I was the source of her excruciating distress. I thought she was projecting into me her intolerable experience of tormenting guilt, and I commented that I was now in a position with her that required me to carry terrible feelings of failing her when she needed my help the most. She shouted at me not to blame my emotional struggles on her and to take them up instead with my own analyst. Ms. B. then had a series of automobile accidents that frightened her terribly, and she blamed these on me, asserting that I was killing her. It now became clear to me that the traumatic loss of her brother was being enacted in the transference/countertransference matrix: I was identified with her guilty self whose alleged lack of protectiveness was now dangerously leading to her death (through identification with her brother) by automobile accident. All my attempts to describe this situation to

153

her fell to naught and seemed only to raise her ire further. Her constant criticisms were difficult to endure, partly because her incessant projective identification of guilt joined forces with unforgiving aspects of my superego, and also had the effect of creating a divide within me: that the interpretive aspect of my analytic self was transformed into a brutally hurtful visage and that the holding/containing aspect of my analytic self was completely ineffectual. This made it very difficult for me to think, since Ms. B. actively drove a wedge between these two components of my analytic function – that is, my internalized thinking couple – and also devalued each of these capacities.

At this point in the treatment I had the following dream:

> I was with female colleague, A.R., who was accompanying me because I was working for the press on an assignment somewhere in the Middle East. We went into a coffee shop that was filled with intimidating Mideastern soldiers and I said "We'd like to see Saddam Hussein." They asked why, and I said we were reporters. After an uncomfortable silence, one of them said "He's not available at the moment." Then they separated A.R. and me, at which point I started to feel frightened. I began to feel a loss of safety because A.R. and I were not together and started to worry that some awful harm could come to both of us, which also made me feel guilty that I had imperiled A.R.

My associations to this dream that were relevant to Ms. B.'s treatment were on several levels. The feeling of guilt for A.R.'s endangerment was prominent and seemed parallel with Ms. B.'s constant refrain that I was responsible for her suffering and, in this regard, represented an identification with her guilty self. On another level, I was also identified with her brother, casting myself as a reporter, and was recklessly exposing my companion – the patient as A.R. – to danger just as Ms. B.'s brother left her unprotected by his death. Finally, *I believe this dream also captured the experience of my analytic function or internalized thinking couple* ($♀ ♂$) being attacked by Ms. B. In fact, A.R. is a close colleague of mine, and she and I have worked collaboratively to help many child patients. We are a couple in the beginning of the dream but then are separated and ganged up on, so that we are both in great danger when apart. I often felt that Ms. B. was ganging up on my efforts to be a thoughtful analyst, and the dream appears to express that feeling: Ms. B. as the threatening soldiers that divide A.R. and me

154

(my internalized thinking couple), rendering us helpless and ineffectual.

About one month after my dream, she developed the phantasy that I was in analysis with someone who encouraged me to treat her badly, a phantasy she could not explore. However, we were able to begin to make some inroads into this impasse in a Monday session that began with her saying she had been up a good part of the night thinking about why I treated her so poorly. Her cell phone then went off in the session and she took the call, which turned out to be an annoying work colleague. This woman tried over the weekend to "crash" Ms. B.'s plan to go to see the movie *Panic Room* with another friend. She told the woman from work she could not join them, but worried that she was now being punished for excluding her. I said she has been feeling panic in the room here with me in the sense that my supposed analyst has crashed our being together by instructing me to be mean to her. I added that it was curious she left her cell phone on during the session, which seemed to invite someone to intrude on us and exclude me, perhaps to let me know something of what she feels. Ms. B. said, "I still think you're getting analyzed and that's where you come from on Tuesday mornings. I think that's who tells you not to say anything to me anymore." She then reported a dream:

> I'm with my brother, but he's in danger. I'm happy to be with him again, then this man and woman appear, saying they could be of some assistance. Although they act friendly, there's something untrustworthy about them. They want him to admit to "reckless endangerment," and he says he has to do it. He says they are stronger than he is and that he can't protect me anymore. The man of the couple is useless and tries to say something, but just sputters. Then I hear some news about a man who died in a car crash. I wake up really scared.

Ms. B. said caustically that she was sorry she told me this dream and expected that I would now have a "field day" with it and try to force some hurtful psychoanalytic interpretation on her. I said I actually did have a lot of thoughts because it was a powerful dream that conveyed something of why she is so frightened. She told me to shut up, that she was not interested in my stupid theories that make her feel worse by blaming her and not appreciating the reality of how hurtful I am. I replied that she feared I would be like the man and woman in the dream who pretend to be helpful but who are really untrustworthy.[8]

155

She softened in response to my comment and sarcastically asked, "so what other brilliant insights do you have?" I said I thought she needed me to be alive for her in a protective way, like her brother in the beginning of the dream, but that when she thought about me and my supposed analyst, it felt like I became a useless sputtering man, someone who was dead to her, and that frightened her terribly. Ms. B. grew uncharacteristically pensive, remained quiet for a while, and then joked warmly: "Well, I guess if you never did talk to anyone else about me, it might make me feel like I wasn't very important." I chuckled a bit and said it was nearly impossible to believe that if I did discuss her, it would be a friendly effort to really understand her and not some wounding plot like her parents who force their version of reality on her. She listened quietly, and the session ended on an unusually positive note.

Much has been written about how the patient may attack the analyst's capacity for thinking. Bion (1959, 1962a, 1962b, 1992), of course, detailed how violent projective identifications and envious attacks seriously disrupt the analyst's α function. Britton (1989) and also Caper (1997) offer an additional Oedipal motive to understanding these assaults: that the analysand may experience the analyst consulting with himself in reflective thought as equivalent to forming a couple that excludes the patient. Therefore, the effort to break apart the analyst's thinking capacity is tantamount to separating him from his analytic partner – that is, his contemplative self. I suggest that one implication of Bion's (1962a) use of the symbols for femininity ($\female$) and masculinity ($\male$) to represent the container and the contained, or the "apparatus for thinking," is the idea that one's reflective self is actually the structural heir (Brown, 2009a) to what was originally the thinking couple ($\female \male$).[9] Thus to attack the analyst's thinking is also to attack the internalized thinking couple on whom he depends for his reflections.

Ms. B.'s unrelenting harangues that I was killing her were successful projective identifications that burdened me with her split-off guilty self. Like a boxer wilting from the incessant pounding of his adversary, I could not find a neutral corner to serve as an "island of contemplation" (Sterba, 1934) in which to think. Furthermore, and unbeknownst to me at first, her withering assaults on everything I did had the additional effect of tearing asunder the constituents of my internalized thinking couple on which one's apparatus for thinking depends. Although it was very difficult to think in Ms. B.'s presence,

I was able to muster enough α function at night to dream the internal catastrophe that I was experiencing, depicted in my counter-transference dream (Brown, 2007 – see Chapter 9, this volume; Heenen-Wolff, 2005) of helplessly looking on as A.R. and I were torn from each other. Analysis of the dream enabled me to understand and tolerate Ms. B.'s attacks, thereby permitting some forward movement in treatment.

Interestingly, Ms. B. reported her fantasy of my being under the control of a sadistic analyst as I regained my thinking capacities following analysis of my countertransference dream. The focus shifted from her attacks on my *internalized* thinking couple to feeling brutalized by me and my *externalized*, imagined analyst. Her enactment in the session of inviting an intrusion into our relationship by leaving her cell phone on gave me the opportunity to interpret the role she played in creating her panic of exclusion and torment. This intervention led to Ms. B.'s complex dream, one aspect of which highlighted the untrustworthy couple who disingenuously offered assistance. I believe this couple captured her experience with both the external and the internal parents, a couple who forcefully collaborated to use thinking to invade her mind with their version of reality and whose partnership she needed to destroy to preserve herself. This dynamic was played out clearly in the transference as she sought to dismantle my capacity for thought by obliterating the connection between my internalized thinking couple, represented by A.R. and me, in my dream.

Ms. B. was ill equipped to handle the trauma of losing her brother, because her internalized thinking couple (or $♀♂$), upon which one's α function depends, was felt to be a cruel pair out to poison her with intrusive false realities. We will now turn in Chapter 7 to examining in greater depth the destructive effects that trauma has upon one's capacity to think and dream, which leaves the traumatized patient in a cognitive wasteland of concrete experience from which he or she is unable to escape.

Notes

1   Parts of this chapter were previously published in my 2002 paper, "The Early Oedipal Situation: Developmental, Theoretical and Clinical Implications," *Psychoanalytic Quarterly*, 71: 273–300. In addition, some

portions of this chapter were presented in a paper, "Catastrophic Change and Trauma: Damage to the Internalized 'Thinking Couple'," given at the Rome Bion Conference in January 2008.

2   The Oedipus complex is a multifaceted phenomenon that includes notions of psychosexual development, primitive (oral) and penis envy, competitive and destructive phantasies directed at the breast and penis, etc. However, the primary focus of this chapter is on the triadic aspects of the Oedipal configuration and its implications for a theory of intersubjectivity.

3   There is a "classic" story, told by Grosskurth (1986), about an encounter between Melanie Klein and Anna Freud in which Klein was reported to have said, "I *am* a Freudian, just not an Anna Freudian."

4   The termination phase in Ms. D.'s analysis is also discussed in Chapter 9, which deals with countertransference dreams.

5   A challenge to the analyst that had earlier been considered by Fliess (1942) and Grinberg (1962).

6   And also the traditional Freudian point of view.

7   The importance of the imago of the father as a third object in early infancy has been discussed extensively by Lacan (1977). Michael Parsons (1999), a British "Independent," has also described the role of the internalized parental couple in the capacity for playfulness.

8   I also thought that the man and woman represented parents – both internal and external – who, she felt, forced their "reality" upon her; however, I did not comment on this thought because I knew it would disrupt the momentary contact between us.

9   I believe this also links with Freud's (1912) description of the communicating (Bion's ♂) and receptive (Bion's ♀) aspects of the dynamics of unconscious communication.

7

Julie's museum: the evolution of thinking, dreaming, and historicization in the treatment of traumatized patients[1]

> But what humans forget, cells remember. The body, that elephant . . .
>
> (Eugenides, 2002, p. 99)

Some 60 million years ago, an enormous meteor, too large to be incinerated as it penetrated through the multiple levels of the earth's protective atmosphere, crashed into the Yucatan peninsula and raised a cloud of thick dust that choked off much of our planet's life at the time. This destructive meteor, originating from an unknown place external to the earth, created a caesura (Bion, 1977a; Freud, 1926), a sudden break in the extant way of life, and required new adaptations in order for organisms to survive. The reign of the dinosaur kingdoms came to a rapid end – the demise of a powerful dynasty of leviathans relegated to the annals of natural history whose greatness paleontologists were later to discover and which provides an endless source of fascination and awe for many children. The latency-age child's fascination with the world of dinosaurs seems to resurrect the sense that there was an epoch in his own history when he was an invincible titan, an era that has been lost and that requires new adjustments. However, for some children, the demand to slowly let go of an omnipotent world and evolve into the practical realm of latency is experienced as a premature and devastating end to a way of being from which he may never recover. These children must often resort to

159

desperate maneuvers, such as brittle narcissistic structures, which restore a semblance of the lost omnipotence but also stifle evolution of the self.

Severe trauma similarly creates a sharp break in an individual's life that establishes a deeply felt sense of dislocation from a previous existence, as though life as it had been came to an abrupt halt. Early in my career, I treated a young man hospitalized for psychosis following traumatic experiences during the Vietnam War. This handsome and childlike veteran appeared physically unscarred by combat but nonetheless brutalized by the psychotic illness that rendered him unable to function. Although his speech was often incoherent, he frequently uttered in a very clear voice, "When I was a baby I knew everything there was to know, but now I don't know anything." It was not until many years later that I began to understand what this patient was trying to tell me: that the war trauma destroyed both his capacity to know and to think in the present and that he had a sense that there had been a time in his life, as an infant, when he was protected by a shield of omniscience. Indeed, his lucid statement, offered periodically in the midst of a garble of broken words and phrases, stood as a kind of testimony that there still existed within him some shred of a former ability to think clearly, even with a sense of irony. Paradoxically, his statement was also like a lifesaver to which he clung – one last desperate vestige of a bygone era of greatness that had been eradicated by the trauma of war. Finally, his fantasy of an all-knowing infancy seemed to be a frantic attempt to restore the self shattered by the horrific trauma of war.

In this chapter we will explore the effects of severe trauma upon the individual's capacity to think, imagine, dream, and evolve. I hypothesize that severe trauma has a splintering effect upon the personality, which then triggers attempts at restitution that struggle to piece together the shards of a blown-apart psyche to achieve some semblance of coherence. However, these restitutive efforts frequently lead to the formation of a brittle and rigidly constructed traumatic organization (Brown, 2005). This organization is characterized by concrete thinking (Bass, 2000; Brown, 1985) that dooms the patient to repetitive enactments and he is unable to learn from experience (Bion, 1962a). Additionally, the traumatic organization remains split off from a part of the psyche that is in touch with reality; thus, because it has no access to experiences in reality, the traumatic organization cannot evolve, thereby further entrapping the traumatized person. Put in the language of Wilfred Bion, severe trauma results in the reversal of α function, a regression from α to β elements, the cohesion of the disparate β elements into a rigid β screen, and an arrest in the normal balance of the PS$\leftrightarrow$D interchange. I also discuss the implications of this model for the psychoanalytic treatment of severely traumatized patients and present a detailed clinical case to illustrate these points.

This chapter applies many aspects of Bion's theories regarding psychotic functioning to an understanding of traumatic experience, which I (Brown, 2005), as well as some other authors (Gibb, 1998; Ingham, 1998), have previously done.[2] Bion's (1962a, 1962b) theory of thinking and its disorders were developed from his work with psychotic patients and he (Bion, 1957) differentiated between the psychotic and nonpsychotic parts of the personality. In my view, we may also distinguish between traumatic and nontraumatic segments of the personality, especially in those severely traumatized patients in whom a seemingly impermeable traumatic organization is dominant. It is particularly curious that Bion does not directly discuss trauma in any of his writings despite the fact, as we have seen in previous chapters, that he endured much trauma in his personal life. From this perspective, therefore, Bion's theories of thinking and its disturbance devolve from both his personal experiences with trauma as well as his work with the psychotic portion of the mind.

What is a psychological trauma? Just as the earth is surrounded by layers of atmosphere that dissolve or greatly reduce potentially harmful meteors, so the psyche, according to Freud (1920), is enveloped by a "protective shield" [*Reizschutz*] that is a barrier to excessive stimulation. And just as the earth may be struck by objects from outer space too large to be burned off in its atmosphere, so the ego may be traumatized by "any excitations from outside which are powerful enough to break through the protective shield" (Freud, 1920, p. 29). Although Freud viewed the "protective shield" in exclusively neuro-physiological terms, current thinking is that this shield is also built upon internalized object relations. Khan (1963) underscored the importance of the mother as an auxiliary ego, and therefore a primary component of this shield, while Laub and his collaborators (Auerhahn & Laub, 1984; Laub & Auerhahn, 1993; Laub & Podell, 1995) have discussed how massive trauma destroys the link to the internal empathic mother. This protective shield has also been likened to a skin that enfolds the ego – an impact-absorbing rind that has the effect of a "second skin" (Anzieu, 1993; Bick, 1968, 1986) or what

Gerzi (2005) has termed a "narcissistic envelope." Thus, a contemporary view of the protective shield is that it is comprised of those internal objects that are involved in the regulation and management of powerful affective experiences that may be associated with neuro-physiological correlates (Schore, 2002).

The capacity for symbolic thought is one of the first casualties when major trauma strikes, a fact that led Ingham (1998) to observe that "Trauma and thought, trauma and knowledge are indivisible" (p. 99). My emphasis in the present chapter is that one of the central pillars of the protective shield is the capacity for thinking, dreaming, and imagining. Thinking, dreaming, and imagining, in turn, are dependent upon positive early experiences with the mother containing and transforming what the infant has projected, and it is this containing–transforming interaction that "becomes installed in the infant as part of the apparatus of alpha-function" (Bion, 1962a, p. 91).[3] Ingham (1998) states, using Bionian terms, that α function is broken down by trauma, giving rise to a psychic experience in which there is a preponderance of β elements. I have previously addressed the reversal of α function and emphasized the defensive and adaptive aspects of the regression from α to β elements:

> Emotions that are unbearable to experience in a meaningful way (alpha function) are coped with via a defensive concretization . . . that offers the embattled ego a kind of adaptive plea bargain: instead of having to manage unbearable alpha element experience, the ego can shift defensively into an active muscular mode (Bion, 1962a), attempting to expel concretely felt β elements through violent projective identification.
>
> (Brown, 2005, p. 404)

Furthermore, from the perspective of Anzieu (1993), the "psychic envelope" is the mental space in which imagination and dreams are generated, and damage to this envelope impairs the capacity for thinking, imagining, and dreaming. In the case of severe trauma, psychic experience may lose its three-dimensionality (Gibb, 1998) and the patient may feel caught in a "black hole" resulting from a deficiency in mentalizing (Gerzi, 2005). Gerzi asserts that

> where relations between the self and selfobject are optimal they become internalized and are manifested in the development of a

container, an internal structure (skin or envelope) able to contain all of the affective expressions of the self . . . while trauma is akin to a knife stab rupturing the skin. It is experienced as a rupture in the containing envelope.

(pp. 1036–1037)

While I agree with Gerzi that trauma may result in "a rupture of the containing envelope," he does not address the cognitive implications (Brown, 2005) of this tear, and this is precisely where Bion's ideas are helpful to elaborate a broader picture. The ripping of the psychic envelope, from a Bionian perspective, involves not only a disturbance of affect regulation as Gerzi suggests, but additionally leaves the psyche crushed by concrete, raw sensory experiences (β elements) from which the mind may only unburden itself by means of violent projective identification and acting out. Trauma, from this perspective, fragments the psyche as a consequence of its explosive effect upon its organization. Furthermore, because the traumatic event is too unbearable to think about by ordinary secondary-process means, the pieces of shattered experience are encoded concretely as β elements. This enables the psyche to have some sense of mastery over the trauma by being able to project the bits of experience and manipulate them through the musculature (Bion, 1962a) – that is, through force-ful projective identification. In addition, in an effort to recover from the destruction of the trauma, the disparate β elements, in which the traumatic experiences have been concretely encoded, are now patched together into a rigidly constructed β screen (traumatic organ-ization). This reestablishes a sense of coherence in the psyche that is really more of what might be called an "organized chaos" and comes at a very high cost; it is a narrative that holds the trauma victim's mind together to which he or she desperately clings as an "explanation" for his or her brittle state. The concrete nature of the traumatic organiza-tion ensnares the patient in repetitive enactments that aim at achiev-ing a feeling of mastery but leave the person caught fighting the tar baby of Disney's *Song of the South*: the more he struggles to free himself, the more deeply he becomes stuck. Finally, the crippling of α function and the associated concreteness of the β screen creates a segment of the patient's mind in which the capacity for play/imagin-ation (Auerhahn & Laub, 1984; Brown, 2005; Herzog, 2001) and dreaming are significantly curtailed or absent (Bion, 1962a, 1992).

In earlier chapters we have seen how Bion (1962a, 1965, 1992) viewed dreaming as a process by which α function transforms raw sensory and emotional data (β elements) into α elements that are capable of being joined together in an emotionally meaningful narrative. Dreaming, from this perspective, occurs while we are awake as well as asleep and is constantly processing emotional experience to enable psychic growth: "if the person can dream, then he can 'digest' facts and so learn from experience" (Bion, 1992, p. 52). The destruction of α function leading to the formation of a traumatic organization renders the patient unable to dream about the traumatic events in a manner that would permit him to mentally assimilate the trauma and therefore personally evolve. This personal growth is also tied to the ability of the psyche to endure moments of relative disintegration that lead to new integrations, what Bion (1965) refers to as the PS↔D balance (see Chapter 5, this volume). However, for the traumatized person, the "organized chaos" of the traumatic organization (β screen) rapidly descends into massive confusion that prompts the return of the old fragile order. New experiences are seen as carbon copies of the original trauma, and the hope of enrichment from a reality experienced as fresh and new is dashed. The trauma remains as an "undigested fact" (Bion, 1962a) and cannot be transformed into memory; instead, the traumatic experiences are registered as ego-alien and concretely encoded dissociated incidents. As a consequence, the traumatic experiences are never "historicized," meaning that they are not integrated into the patient's identity, and the traumatized person becomes a "subject without a history" (Baranger, Baranger, & Mom, 1988, p. 125). Thus, the process by which emotional growth occurs is arrested.

The analysis of severely traumatized patients is aimed at restoring the normal developmental process by which β elements are converted into α elements by α function, transforming previously "undigested facts" into memories, and, ultimately, helping patients integrate/historicize these memories into their ongoing sense of identity through "re-writing" their narrative. Some patients have been so damaged that their ability to think, imagine, and dream has been foreclosed, thereby interring them even more deeply in a "life within death" (Tarantelli, 2003). In such cases, the analyst is called upon to offer his α function to help the patient bear what is unbearable, to think what is unthinkable, and to transform the "undreamable experience" (Ogden, 2004b) into a symbolic and three-dimensional occurrence that is a true dream (Weiss, 2002). We turn now to discuss the psychoanalytic treatment of a woman profoundly traumatized during her childhood whose α function was crippled and who needed to "borrow" mine for some time in the analysis. This was very difficult and challenging work that demanded that I endure countertransference experiences of a concrete nature in order to transform these into psychological events that enabled her to slowly move out of an obdurate traumatic organization. My work with her additionally focused on the importance of my being a *witness* to her suffering that furthered her recovery.

Clinical illustration

I had been seeing Julie, a 48-year-old married woman with no children, for about fifteen years by the time of this period in her treatment, the last five or so in analysis. We began working together when she was an inpatient, admitted for severe, overwhelming panic attacks. As she slowly came to trust me, she began to reveal a "history" of horrible trauma from her childhood. "History" is in quotation marks because the "facts" of what occurred were reported as a swirling conglomeration of experiences that were difficult to decipher. She had many flashbacks of dissociated bits of "memory" that swept her up in reliving frightening, somatically encoded events. She also reported experiences that she felt when going to bed at night, not being able to discern (as was the case with Sally in Chapter 4) whether she was awake or asleep, whether these were dreams, "memories," or phantasies. In fact, she did not have any real dreams in the sense of symbolically meaningful narrative stories to which she or I could associate. She had fragments of "traumatic dreams," but even these remained in the confusing netherworld of uncertain reality.

Thus, her traumatic "history" was revealed to me. She "remembered" that her father began sexually abusing her when she was about 5 years old and reports that she was forced to have sexual intercourse and perform fellatio on him. These were terrifying memories that were recounted through flashbacks, fears of harm from me, etc. However, more troubling to her were memories of abuse from her grandfather, a respected public figure whom she revered and the only person in her family who felt interested in her as a person. On the traumatic side, she recalled (in an avalanche of flashbacks, etc.) his lovingly stroking her back at night and then moving his hands to her genital area. At first this touch felt pleasantly arousing, but then became too exciting, which frightened her. He slowly began to introduce penetrating her and ultimately to have sexual intercourse. In addition to the traumatic overstimulation and forceful penetrations, this behavior was also traumatic in that she felt powerfully betrayed by him and had also lost the protection of what had previously been her only loving relationship.

These abuses notwithstanding, Julie said that her mother's abuse was far more devastating than that of her father or grandfather. She felt that her mother had essentially attacked and destroyed everything that was vital to her sense of who she was. I said it was like a soul murder, and she agreed. She reported that her mother treated her as a trophy piece to be made over in whatever way her mother pleased and, in the process, to snuff out anything that was inherently Julie. She loved to dance as a child and seemed to show some talent; however, her mother tore her away from these lessons and made her take piano instead, forcing her to play for any visiting company. This pattern happened with other abilities, but the one that troubled her most deeply was the capacity to draw. When she was young, her mother bought her some colored drawing pencils, and Julie quickly took to this. She felt that drawing permitted a degree of self-expression that she had never previously experienced. One day her mother found her drawings, drawings that were mainly of penises. Outraged, her mother demanded to know what this was about, and she told mother that the drawings were about what her father and grandfather were doing to her. Her mother flew into a rage, threw all her drawing utensils away, and pushed her downstairs into the scary basement. She remembers being beaten – not just physically, but beaten down emotionally and spiritually.

In the many years leading up to analysis, these "memories" were worked on, words were put to them, and the powerfully disruptive affects associated with them were abreacted. My role in the transference shifted, often many times within the same session, from that of protector to possible abuser, to guardian of her sacred drawings, to someone who would snuff out the embers of a flickering self. A significant part of our early psychotherapy work focused on her wish to be known by me, to be understood in a way that felt true, yet that very contact simultaneously was seen as enormously dangerous. After many years, she began to have a more consolidated sense of herself, was better able to communicate verbally and less through enactments, had fewer and fewer flashbacks, and gradually began to express herself through some artwork. This artwork, which she often brought to sessions, consisted of geometric shapes that were each assigned a different color and represented people in her past.[4] Julie deployed these rather creatively to depict themes of penetration, conquest, and intrusion. This development felt significant to her as a brave step forward in expressing something genuine about herself and, additionally, was an opportunity to work on one aspect of the maternal transference – that is, overcoming her fear that I, like her historical mother, would seek to destroy such creations.

As Julie's formerly splintered personality became increasingly integrated, the more blatant post-traumatic stress disorder symptoms decreased markedly. However, it soon became clear that a murderous superego reigned tyrannically within this better organized psyche.[5] Every step forward for her seemed to trigger a sense of internal catastrophe. Although progress continued to be made, there was a sense of being up against deeper-seated resistances and transferences that appeared to be inimical to further progress. In addition, she reported that she remained unable to think, remember, and draw. Thus, I brought up the idea of analysis with her as a means of our being able to understand more fully the internal forces against which she battled. This was frightening to her at first, particularly the fear of giving herself over to me and my possible controlling influence. She also expressed, for the first time, some underlying feeling, for which she barely had words, that there was something very scary about the idea of "getting better." We discussed fees, the use of the couch, appointment times, etc. I left using the couch up to her, but she wanted to use it to try to access her "true" feelings better with less attention to my reactions.

We will now review a period of about eighteen months' analytic work in which there was considerable evolution in Julie's capacity to think, to dream, and ultimately to historicize her traumatic past. This was accomplished very slowly as traumatic material was relived in the moment-to-moment fluctuations of the transference and countertransference. Overall, my experience as her analyst evolved from one of helping her bear unbearable experiences to one of bearing witness to a traumatic past that had become part of her identity. She began a session early on in this segment of the analysis by stating, "I had this dream or something this morning; well, not really a dream because I don't know if I was awake. *My mother was walking toward me with this box and I was angry and upset that she took all my words away from me.* When I awoke, maybe I didn't wake up, I'm not sure, but later I was really angry that she had taken all my words away from me, any thoughts or feelings or ideas, that she had taken them and they were in the box."

She had no associations to this "dream" other than to say that it was exactly what her mother had done. My association was to the previous session in which she was angry with me because she felt I was not paying sufficient attention to what she was saying, and she had left me an angry telephone message that evening. I said that I thought her angry message was in response to feeling I was exactly like her mother in the dream, someone with whom she wished to share her feelings but who instead stole these from her. She went on to criticize me for not being more enthusiastic about her hard work in and out of analysis and how this flattened her.

This "dream," or, more properly, this experience that Julie had during the night when she was unsure whether she was awake, demonstrates a nascent capacity to give emotional meaning to what had occurred in the previous session. Paradoxically, this beginning ability to symbolize was employed to convey her experience of thoughts, feelings, and ideas as concrete things that can literally be stolen. For Julie, the "dream" was simply an exact replica of her mother's actual behavior. My interpretation that in the previous hour I was "exactly like her mother in the dream" not only made the obvious link to the dream but also emphasized her experience that I *was* her mother in the session. I had learned with Julie to stop making comments such as "it's as if I was your mother," because she inevitably rejected these words as a sleight of hand by which I supposedly avoided responsibility.[6] The two incidences – in the session with me and in the "dream" – had collapsed into one concrete experience, each equivalent to the other, and whether she was awake or asleep was of little consequence. Thus, there was no distinction between her inner phantasy life and reality, little appreciation that I was not her mother, and consequently a diminished ability to learn from her experiences in analysis.

Some months later, as Julie worked to break the attachment to her tormenting internal parents, she came to realize the powerful affects that cemented this connection. She described being caught between two unbearable choices: to either continue in the excruciating life of persecution and torture or to be confronted with insufferable emptiness. At one point, these emotions overwhelmed her so that she regressed to a state in which this conflict was experienced concretely as an actual urge to vomit. This struggle was depicted graphically in one session:

> I'm trying to get rid of my [internal] parents and I thought I won't be able to draw until I vomit up something. I woke up last night and I felt like I want to throw up all this garbage, but I can't get them out of my system. Then I had this vision of myself drawing: an easel came down with a canvas and another with a drawing pad and I could see myself drawing and I felt happy . . . A voice said 'you have to get them out of your system' and I said I already vacuumed them out. Then I actually had dry heaves and asked my husband to get me a wastebasket. I feel scared about what will I do without them.

As Julie was speaking I began to have the feeling of needing to sneeze, being close to sneezing, which then turned into a sense that I would burst out in tears. Her thoughts went to a powerful antibiotic she was taking and her worry that the strong medication would also destroy the necessary "good" bacteria. I said that when she vacuums out the bad parents who feel so real inside her, it's like she has also gotten rid of aspects of them that can help protect her; that she feels so bereft and intolerably empty that she needs to bring them back. She replied, "I was screaming at you the other day because you were going to leave me alone and I couldn't bear it; that's when I called you back because I wanted to die." I said that she wanted to scream the bad me out of her, but that only made her feel more empty, an emptiness so unbearable that dying was preferable. She began crying heavily and said despondently, "I will never have parents that live inside me."

This session conveys Julie's being in the painful throes of what feels to be an impossible dilemma: she is caught between the Scylla of persecution and the Charybdis of profound emptiness. She is able to tolerate a portion of this conflict that signals some forward movement, yet the affects overwhelm her and the conflict is represented concretely in her struggle to throw up. One difference from the earlier "dream" of her mother robbing her words is that I was deeply affected by her projected sadness, an emotion that I also experienced as overwhelming. However, it is important to note that I initially experienced Julie's unbearable sadness through a reversal in my α function when her pain was first registered concretely as my urge to sneeze and then cry. Julie then spoke about the good and bad bacteria, and, putting this association together with my urge to sneeze and cry, this allowed me to regain my capacity for reverie (α function) in order to interpret her anxiety about losing the "good" protective bacteria when the "bad" bacteria were expelled. This brought to mind her anger at me from a previous session, which she was now able to link to the theme of unbearable loss. Thus, Julie's resorting to a concrete mode of expressing her struggle through the vomiting symptom was transformed by my α function, and the session evolved to permit her to bring the affects of loss into the transference. In that transference, I became a complex figure of emotional depth about whom she felt much ambivalence that was a far cry from her former "dream" in which I was simply interchangeable with her mother.

Julie began to experiment with drawing, and while at some moments this felt restorative to something vital about her that she feared had been snuffed out, at other moments she felt the terror of being killed for this forbidden activity. I commented that her drawings on paper had originated in her mind and were also drawings that created scenes in my mind. At first she was very fearful that I would want to destroy this capacity, just as her mother had obliterated her drawings, but as this anxiety was addressed she grew more comfortable in drawing pictures in her own mind, knowing that they simultaneously registered in mine. Thus, I found that *she was engaging me not only to bear her intolerable affects but also to bear witness to* a final transformation of her traumatic experiences into symbolic pictograms (α elements) that were on display in both of our minds. I saw this as a signal that she was *historicizing* her traumatic past, and we came to call this Julie's museum.

Julie began a session by saying she had been phantasying a museum that was a maze of narrow hallways with drawings of hers on display for visitors, drawings of her life that were meant to evoke intense emotions. One was a "canvas with a knife sticking out with frozen tears stuck to it . . . [while another was] a painting of my head and all the skin was pulled back to the hairline and you could see my brain with penises sticking into my brain and also a picture of my mother naked on all fours, screaming something into my brain." She continued to take me on this tour and elaborated the various rooms and pictures for over a week. Julie said that these imaginative drawings, though upsetting to conceive, also felt strangely calming to produce. I found this deeply moving and was reminded of my visit to Yad Vashem, the Holocaust Museum in Jerusalem, and realized she was

170

now showing me her own apocalyptic history. As our "tour" continued over the week, Julie interspersed her descriptions of her displays with telling me about a book she was reading authored by a black woman who had researched her heritage of slavery in order to gain some perspective of its role in her life. It was clear that Julie was doing the same with her personal museum.

The following exchange demonstrates the process of historicization in the context of our touring Julie's museum:

ANALYST. So, I'm the first visitor to your museum?

JULIE. Yes, so what do you think of all this?

ANALYST. I think it's important for you to have me here in your personal house of horrors, for it to be in both of our minds.

JULIE. I think I want people to be scared and terrified; want them to be so terrified that they can't forget it, that it soaks into their skin like it did mine; partly so they'll understand me better, not just the words.

ANALYST. A picture is worth a thousand words.

JULIE. Right, and how do you live with that and function as a normal contributing human being when you have all of that inside of you? . . . My museum says you have to make a place for people to talk about it . . . a place where people can say this happened so it doesn't have to live in their muscles or brains – it has someplace else to go.

ANALYST. Into the minds of others to bear witness.

JULIE. Yes, to say this wasn't your fault, you don't have to hate yourself because it was inflicted on you, so you don't have to feel like a monster.

This session highlights several important changes in Julie's mental functioning in general and in the transference in particular. The tour through her museum evoked powerful emotions in me through her use of projective identification that now was not evacuative but communicative (Bion, 1959) instead. I did not feel invaded, as one would feel being the target of a projective counteridentification, but, rather, deeply affected. Each of us had our own associations to her museum: I was poignantly reminded of Yad Vashem, and she thought of the author who struggled with integrating slavery into her own history. The analytic exchange between us was three-dimensional, with our having individual associations that breathed life into Julie's museum, associations that built off each other and created a vibrant narrative that was a living testimony to what she had endured in her life. Finally, my bearing witness, where previously I had to solely bear intolerable emotion, had the effect of fostering Julie's historicizing the trauma so it no longer had to live in her "muscles or brains."

Discussion

When severe trauma strikes an individual, her entire sense of being can be shattered: that life as it had been known has been irretrievably changed. Thus, the trauma victim is left quite literally to pick up the pieces of a blown-apart self and to try to reassemble these shards into some semblance of a former self. One of the first casualties of that devastation is the capacity to think, and psychic experiences may be re-encoded concretely. In Bionian terms, this process is described as the undoing of α function in which α elements are reconfigured as β elements. This is an adaptive maneuver on the part of the ego that allows it to gain a sense of mastery by expelling through projective identification concrete bits of experience that are unable to be thought about through ordinary symbolic means. Furthermore, in order to restore organization to the splintered psyche, the disparate β elements are cobbled together into a coherent β screen that really is a brittle, chaotic traumatic organization, but one which nevertheless creates a unifying personal narrative. This is a self-enclosed system, split off from ordinary reality, that allows no new ideas in – therefore precluding dreaming or evolving – and is unable to learn from experience. The traumatic organization (β screen), constructed from a shaky agglomeration of β elements, has a life of its own perpetuated by repetitive enactments that serve to reinforce a traumatic view of the world; therefore, the trauma becomes timeless and cannot be historicized. Encounters with this β screen leave the analyst feeling helpless because no new ideas are permitted, and he may experience a constriction in the capacity for reverie/dreaming.

In working with traumatized patients in analysis, the analyst can be helped by understanding the properties of this traumatic organization. His provision of an auxiliary α function is essential in assisting the patient to transform β to α experience. In this regard, he is called upon to help the patient suffer insufferable affects so that through a process of identification the patient can take in the analyst's α function and gradually increase her own affect tolerance. In addition, the patient and analyst gradually evolving into a thinking couple – as Julie and I became when she thought of the author writing about slavery and I remembered going to Yad Vashem – is internalized as well to become part of the analysand's α function or "apparatus for thinking" (Bion, 1962a). My work with Julie demonstrates how the analyst must withstand being equated with the patient's traumatic objects through violent projective identification. Events are felt to be things in themselves and therefore carry no latent meaning. Over time, however, the patient's capacity to think more abstractly increases and is connected to successful experiences with the analyst as an effective container. For example, after considerable work in analysis, I was able to feel not only that I would burst into tears, but also that I could use this to formulate an interpretation that was useful to her. She and I both had associations to her phantasy of vomiting up her parents, and this permitted the start of exchanges between us that gave form to previously unrepresented traumatic experience. Finally, her construction of Julie's museum signaled the ability to think abstractly, to engage me in a mutually enriching process of unconscious communication that brought a three-dimensional perspective to her traumatic experiences. This important evolution allowed for the historicization of her traumatic past so that her horrendous prior experiences no longer had to live in her "muscles or brains." This final step was accomplished with the help of my bearing witness – that is, providing my mind as a place where the horrors of her past have been indelibly registered and having my mind survive.

Historicization has been described (Auerhahn & Laub, 1984; Baranger, Baranger, & Mom, 1988) as the process by which the traumatic event(s) is integrated into the person's sense of identity, a process that is intimately linked to the existence of an internal "empathic dyad" (Laub & Podell, 1995) between the patient and an inner mothering figure. We should add the notion of an internalized thinking (or dreaming) couple, a central component of α function, to the presence of an inner empathic maternal figure. This would create an additional perspective that views historicization as the end point of a continuum of activities subsumed by α function that foster evolving cognitive transformation. Bion's (1962a) writings describe its most essential form: that α function is that *aspect of the personality which transforms raw emotional (β element) experience* into α elements that are capable of being combined into dream narratives that have latent psychological meaning. This process could be observed in Julie's analysis when her urge to vomit was transformed by my α function into a sneeze, then into sadness. A second level of α function has to do with the *formation of a narrative*, which has been most pointedly addressed by Italian analysts (Corrao, 1987; Ferro, 1992, 2002, 2009), and extends the concept of α function to include how the α elements are joined together in a narrative − a narrative that is a jointly constructed production of which it is unimportant to ask, "What's true and whose idea was it?" (Ogden, 2003a). Julie's museum was a prime example of this facet of α function at work. Finally, we may think of a more evolved form of α function, *bearing witness*, which entails an affirmation of the reality of an independent personal narrative, separate from the personal narratives of others (Poland, 2000). Bearing witness, which is especially important in the treatment of trauma patients (Brown, 2005, 2009b), transforms a subjective sense of having been invaded by an alien trauma into a consensually validated experience of integration and coherent identity. My tour of Julie's museum, with her as the guide, bore witness to her newly conceived personal narrative of what had happened in her traumatic past. Although this narrative was intersubjectively constructed, it was now *her* story to share with me as an independent observer.

In conceptualizing the progression toward the historicization of a trauma, it may be helpful to consider the vertical axis of Bion's Grid, which "indicates [the] developmental status" (1977b, p. 3) of a thought.[4] The potential thought begins as a concrete sensory experience, a β element and must be transformed by maternal α function into an α element. When an experience is transformed into an α element, which is a pictogram, then it may be woven into a dream that is imbued with latent symbolic meaning. The capacity to dream furthers cognitive transformation by leading to the generation of new concepts since α elements, now free from their sensory antecedents, are available to join with other α elements to create new concepts. These newly formed concepts may then be wedded to other concepts that permit the continued evolution of higher order models and even more advanced deductive hypotheses. I believe that this is precisely what occurred in the analytic work with Julie. Initially, her traumatic experiences were registered as concrete β-element experiences (I was equivalent to her mother in the dream; her urge to vomit) that were transformed by my α function into α elements (my urge to sneeze–cry leading to her deep sadness over losing her internal parents).

Continued analytic work enabled her to integrate these newly born α elements into the individual (imagined) pictures that lined the walls of Julie's museum, which itself represented a supraordinate concept. This final transformation, for which my bearing witness served as midwife, signaled the historicizing of the trauma into an overarching conception of herself.

The capacity to engage in artistic expression has been an important factor in the recovery of some patients (see also Chapter 5) who are otherwise unable to represent or mentalize their traumatic experiences. I have emphasized that a hallmark of many severely traumatized patients is the reversal of α function, leaving them stranded in an unthinkable world of frighteningly real, overpowering experience. Laub and Podell (1995) comment that "Art has the ability to revive the enshrouded past of a trauma through a dialogue in the present" (p. 993). Julie's strong desire to recover a lost artistic ability, felt to have been crushed by her mother's destructive assaults, was associated by her with an inability "to think and remember." Thus, she expressed an intuitive understanding of the capacity of art to represent what cannot be initially symbolized due to a damaged α function that is incapable of transforming the raw sensory events of the trauma into a "memory" (Bion, 1962a). Following an internal calling, Julie engaged in attempts to represent what happened to her by creating collages of geometric shapes that stood for the abusive figures in her life. These creations were immensely fulfilling to Julie and allowed her a beginning sense of mastery over the trauma, partly because her traumatic past was now something she was learning to think about. Additionally, sharing these constructions with me fostered the working through in the transference of her terror that I would be the covetous and enviously ruinous mother – that is, an ego-destructive superego.

Laub and Podell underscore the importance of a "dialogue in the present" in which the analyst provides what Rose (1995, cited by Laub & Podell, 1995) calls a "witnessing presence," which for the art of traumatized individuals "confirms the reality of the traumatic event" (Laub & Podell, 1995, p. 993). It may seem paradoxical I am emphasizing Julie's artistic expressions since, apart from the collages she showed me during the psychotherapy, she produced little actual works of art while she was in analysis. However, regarding the "art of trauma," Laub and Podell write that

Its definition should be radically expanded to include the

"imaginative acts" that occur spontaneously within the process of survival itself. . . . They produce emotional responses parallel to those produced by conventional art forms, and . . . are themselves a form of art.

(p. 998)

Indeed, Julie's capacity for imagination was broadened significantly during the eighteen months described of her analysis. Initially, she was simply incapable of imagining the trauma that befell her; however, as the treatment progressed she slowly developed the capacity to represent, in an increasingly more complex manner, the traumatic experiences that had been stored ("The body, that elephant . . .") as "undigested facts" (Bion, 1962a). From this perspective, Julie's museum, though crafted in the atelier of her imagination, was a major work of art even though it existed solely as a private exhibition for my viewing. The creation of this museum, therefore, was like a patient being able to successfully turn a nightmare that interrupts sleep into a successful dream that permits the dreamer to remain asleep. This is reminiscent of those patients who see us because of nightmares and who "need the mind of another person . . . to help him dream the yet to be dreamt aspect of his nightmare" (Ogden, 2004b, p. 861).

Conclusion

Einstein's well-known saying that "Imagination is more important than knowledge" may be paraphrased as "Imagination is necessary for knowledge" in order to appreciate one aspect of the dilemma for severely traumatized patients. Caught in an endless cycle of evacuative dreams that lead to repetitive enactments, these individuals are unable to experience "true dreams" (Weiss, 2002) that could be "felt as life-promoting" (Bion, 1992, p. 67). Imagination and the capacity for play are foreclosed, and therefore new knowledge – the key to unlocking the traumatic organization – cannot be gained. In addition, the analyst's mental processes, at least early on in analysis, may also be pre-empted and limit his ability to help because he "must be able to dream the analysis as it is taking place" (Bion, 1992, p. 216). This puts considerable pressure on the analyst to access his imagination in order to bolster or, in some cases, completely provide the α function that has been hobbled in his patient. The analyst's imaginative capacity – that is, his containing and transforming reveries – serves as midwife to assist the birth in the patient of increasingly sophisticated ways of giving meaning to the traumatic episodes in her life. Spontaneous "imaginative acts" (Laub & Podell, 1995) in the patient, which are in essence artistic productions, are milestones that mark the forward movement. In successful treatments, the patient's capacity to represent the trauma evolves from the concrete to the progressively more abstract, culminating in the historicization of the previously unthinkable experiences.

Notes

1   This is somewhat expanded version of a paper originally published in 2006 in the *International Journal of Psychoanalysis*, 87: 1569–1586.

2   The relationship between trauma and psychosis is a fascinating topic but is beyond the scope of this chapter. The reader is referred to Laub (2006) for further exploration of this connection.

3   Although Bion does not explicitly address nascent factors in the infant that interact with the internalization of a thinking mother/infant couple to build α function in the baby, he does nevertheless speak of an inborn tendency to either avoid or modify frustration (Bion, 1962a). This is the same factor that Freud (1911) links to the development of a capacity for thinking. Thus, it is implicit in Bion's view that the internalization of a containing–transforming interaction with the mother builds upon and fosters constitutional proclivities. In addition, the further internalization of the "thinking" Oedipal (Bion, 1963; Britton, 1989; Brown, 2002, 2005; Gooch, 2002; Herzog, 2001) or "dreaming couple" (Grotstein, 2000) augments and strengthens this process.

4   Like with Jason in Chapter 5, this artwork seemed to enable some initial steps toward representing (giving "figurability," transforming, mentalizing) experiences that had never been, or only partially, represented.

5   It is a seeming paradox that a destructive superego emerged as Julie's functioning grew less fragmented. Bion (1992) notes that one reason for the reversal of α function is to forestall the increased integration of the depressive position, which brings a sadistic superego, previously split off, into the now amalgamated psyche. He states: "This breakdown [of α function] is due to the need to prevent the synthesis, in the depressive position, of a frightening super-ego" (p. 59). (See also Britton, 2003.)

6   The same complaint spoken by Ms. B. in Chapter 6, which I have observed in other patients whose thinking is concrete. The words "as if" are experienced as an attack on their perception rather than as one's offering another point of view.

8

The triadic intersubjective matrix in supervision[1]

In this chapter we explore the notion of a *triadic intersubjective matrix* that Miller and I introduced (Brown & Miller, 2002). This phenomenon refers to the unconscious co-creation by the patient, analyst, and supervisor of a resistance against painful affects that permeate the supervisory field. The painful affect is experienced idiosyncratically by each individual and represents each participant's unique unconscious interpretation of the unidentified emotion that suffuses the field. We found that an open attitude of self-disclosure in the supervisory relationship, though unnecessary in the analytic dyad, was an important key to unlocking the *bastion* (Baranger & Baranger, 1961–62) or *impasse* that paralyzed the entire supervisory field. Paraphrasing Cassorla (2005, 2009), this stalemate could be described as *non-dreams-for-three*, which is characterized by a sense of despair or defeat shared by analysand, supervisor, and analyst. In this situation, supervision may be reduced to default-position "explanations," such as "the problem is the patient's resistance," rather than the supervisor and analyst examining the triadic matrix.

We have been tracing the evolution of intersubjective concepts in the analytic relationship which has developed over the last century from an initial "one-person" emphasis to a "two-person" focus and finally to an appreciation of the intersubjective field. Despite this progression in conceptualizing the analytic dyad, change has been slower to develop in our thinking about the supervisory relationship. It is only recently that analysts have begun to address the triadic dimensions of supervision (Berman, 2000; Brown & Miller, 2002); however, these contributions ignore the idea of a jointly constructed unconscious emotional field that draws from the psychologies of the analyst, the patient, and the supervisor. Instead, they discuss the various dyadic combinations that may be formed from the threesome – that is, patient/analyst, analyst/supervisor, and patient/supervisor. We will now review some of this literature from the angle of how various authors have considered the three subjectivities in the supervisory relationship.

In his writings on technique, Freud (1912, 1915a) introduced a dilemma regarding the value of the analyst's subjective feelings toward his or her patient. We have seen that he encouraged the analyst to direct his or her unconscious as a "receptive organ towards the transmitting unconscious of the patient" (1912, p. 115), and through that stance the "doctor's unconscious is able . . . to construct that unconscious, which has determined the patient's free associations" (p. 116). Yet, on the other hand, he also admonished the practitioner to adopt the surgeon's dispassionate posture of "emotional coldness." Later, in the paper on transference love (Freud, 1915a), he cited the need for some patients to fall in love with the analyst and also cautioned the analyst to guard against the countertransference feelings this may engender. Thus, Freud promoted an ambivalent attitude toward the analyst's subjectivity: it was only by allowing one's unconscious to be impacted by the patient's communications that the analyst could decipher the patient's unconscious; however, the practitioner was required to remain opaquely aloof and mindful of the pitfalls that may result from losing one's objectivity. This tension between the experiencing analyst and the objective analyst has framed a central discussion about supervision that has evolved over the last eighty-five years.

As discussed in Chapters 2 and 3, a growing recognition of the importance of the analyst's subjectivity led to a broadened understanding of the inseparability of transference and countertransference and also to how the analyst employs his subjectivity as an "instrument of the analysis" to understand the analysand. Fliess's (1942) exploration of the analyst's "metapsychology" introduced the importance of the analyst's (trial) identifications by which he may empathically grasp the analysand's struggles by placing himself in the patient's shoes. Klein's (1946) introduction of projective identification provided an additional tool with which to employ the analyst's subjective feelings as a means to better grasp the patient's psychic reality that her followers (e.g., Heimann, 1950) used to assert that all of the analyst's reactions are of potential benefit in understanding the patient's subjective world. Racker's (1968) seminal contributions advanced our understanding of the subtle interplay of introjective and projective processes in the analytic setting and described the variety of identifications that the analyst encounters and their relationship to the patient's object world. These influences have led to a greater emphasis on the here-and-now aspects of the treatment relationship, established the inextricable link between the patient's and the analyst's subjective experiences of the analysis, and underscored the vital use to which the clinician's reactions may be put to further comprehend the patient.

These trends, however, have not had a significant impact upon the traditional theory and practice of psychoanalytic supervision. The supervision of psychoanalytic cases has always been, first and foremost, primarily an arena in which "experiential learning" (Fleming & Benedek, 1966) occurs. In the classical tradition, the supervisory relationship was viewed as a teacher/student arrangement in which the exclusive focus was on the student analyst's relationship with his patient. The relationship of the supervisor and the analyst remained quietly in the background of the supervisory meetings. In addition to imparting technical knowledge, the supervisor was used by the student analyst as a model with whom to identify in order to increase the pupil's capacity for self-observation, bolster his "analytic superego," and strengthen his "analyzing instrument" (Windholz, 1970). This "experiential learning" occurs in both the analyst in training and the supervisor; however, "The attention of both the student and supervisor is focused on the patient, *with minimal concern for their interrelationship*" (Windholz, 1970, p. 402, italics in original).

Searles (1955) pioneered a radically different view of supervision when he identified a "reflective process" in which unverbalized conflicts in the patient are enacted in the analytic relationship and the treating analyst, in turn, behaves similarly with his or her supervisor. This perspective pointed to the necessity of paying attention to the subjective experiences of patient, analyst, and supervisor because each acted as antennae to unverbalized conflicts that imperiled the treatment if ignored. Sachs and Shapiro (1976) described situations in which the therapist, having unconsciously identified with the patient during treatment dilemmas, conducts him/herself with the supervisor in the same manner as the patient does with the treating analyst. They viewed this correspondence between the supervisory and treatment relationships as mainly arising in the beginning analyst. Doehrman's

(1976) classic study of parallel processes advanced this issue in two important ways. First, she demonstrated that the direction of influence proceeds not only from the patient to the analyst to the supervisor, but also from the supervisor to the analyst to the patient. A ubiquitous phenomenon in all the treatments she examined was the analysts acting in either the same or the opposite manner with their patients as they experienced their supervisor behaving with them. Secondly, Doehrman emphasized that these parallel processes *were not symptomatic of difficulties in either the analytic or supervisory relationships, but, rather, were an expectable part of every supervised treatment.* Stimmel (1995) has offered a note of caution by counseling the supervisor to be aware of the possibility of hiding his actual transference to the supervisee under the guise of the parallel process, but this caveat also introduced the potential role that the supervisor's transference plays in the process of supervision.

Gediman and Wolkenfeld (1980) conceptualized the supervisory relationship as a "triadic system" in which influence does not run along a one-dimensional path, originating in either the patient or the supervisor, but is a "complex multidirectional network" (p. 236). They asserted that an enactment in the supervisory relationship may reflect not only what is occurring unconsciously between the analyst and his or her patient, but may additionally signal an unconscious identification of the analyst with an aspect of the patient. Thus, it is this composite of the patient's difficulty, fused with similar issues in the analyst, that is enacted in supervision. Furthermore, the enactments that the treating analyst bring to supervision may find a resonance in the supervisor, and distortions in technique may follow from "These unrecognized sectors of the analyst's and the supervisor's personalities . . ." (p. 240). Our emphasis, however, in this chapter is that the multitude of resonances, identifications, and projective identifications that occur in the supervisory relationship are not, in and of themselves, reflective of unresolved conflict in the analyst or the supervisor – although this cannot be ruled out – *but are more importantly part of the clinical data that are investigated in the process of supervision.*

This approach is in keeping with the communicative aspects of countertransference and with the view of the supervisory relationship as providing a container (Ungar & Ahumada, 2001) for the affects of the triad to be transformed. If the supervisor and the treating analyst regard an essential part of their work together as creating *a space for thinking* (Mollon, 1989) that promotes "reflection with a tolerance for not knowing and not understanding" (p. 120), then a framework exists for allowing a wide range of clinical data to be considered as possibly relevant to the treatment process. Furthermore, if the supervisor and treating analyst consider all phenomena that occur in the supervisory mutual space for thinking as possible important communications about the treatment process, then all thoughts, feelings, transient "irrelevant" notions, enactments, etc. that arise in the course of the supervisory hours may be viewed as potentially meaningful (Ogden, 1994a, 1994b, 1996). This does not ignore either the supervisor's or the analyst's individual idiosyncrasies or neurotic tendencies, but regards the appearance of such personal issues as having meaning within an intersubjective context. These perspectives were developed by reflection on the dyadic milieu of patient and analyst, and we suggest extending them to the supervisory situation such that we see a *triadic intersubjective matrix* created in supervision in which the personalities of the patient, treating analyst, and supervisor intersect. Gediman and Wolkenfeld (1980) also viewed the supervisory relationship as a "triadic system" in a way similar to Berman's (2000) recent contribution: that there are three sets of dyads in supervisory field – the analyst/patient, the supervisor/analyst, and the supervisor/ patient. However, our approach differs in that we focus on the "point of interaction" (Brown, 2004), which is at the confluence of the interlocking unconscious processes of the patient, analyst, and supervisor, that co-creates the shared unconscious phantasy (Baranger, 1961–62; Ferro, 2005) of the supervisory field rather than of the three dyads. This becomes the content of what is explored in the supervisory "space for thinking."

When the supervisory relationship is seen as a triadic intersubjective matrix, some important questions arise regarding the conduct of the supervision. Does this approach blur the boundaries between supervision and the candidate's personal analysis? How comfortable are the analyst and the supervisor with talking about what occurs between them? When is self-disclosure on the part of the supervisor indicated? The theory of treatment to which the supervisor and student analyst subscribe is an important dimension to these questions. If there is an implicit understanding that the analyst's subjective experiences with the patient have a vital relevance to understanding and helping his or her patient, then it is a small, but significant, step to expand this to the supervisory relationship. This orientation to treatment comprises a cognitive side to the *supervisory alliance* (Fleming &

Benedek, 1966), which complements the emotional bonds of trust, mutual respect, and, often, friendship that develops between the supervisor and the treating analyst over the course of the treatment. Initially, particularly with novice analysts, the supervisee's self-esteem may need careful attention (Ricci, 1995); however, as the supervisee matures as an analyst, he or she cultivates a capacity to supervise him/herself such that "supervision should develop into a dialogue between the external supervisor and the internal supervisor" (Casement, 1991, p. 32). When the supervisory alliance has sufficiently matured and the candidate's self-esteem as an analyst is more solidified so that he or she has a "mind of one's own" (Caper, 1997), then he or she is better able to engage in a less defensive examination of experiences in the supervisory relationship within the theoretical framework of the triadic intersubjective matrix.

Regarding the question of the boundary between treatment and supervision, this has been discussed by Lewin and Ross (1960) as a "syncretic dilemma" between the goals of treatment and those of supervision. They recommended a sharp delineation between the pedagogical teaching of supervision and the affective experiences in the candidate's personal analysis. Windholz (1970) recognized the existence of similar processes in the supervisory and treatment relationships, but suggested that the relationship between the supervisor and supervisee remain unexamined in order to keep a clear distinction between supervision and treatment. However, if a model of treatment that places primary importance on the interaction of the subjectivities of analyst, patient, and supervisor is adopted as a strategy for supervision – that is, the triadic intersubjective matrix – then there is a danger of losing the clear border between treatment and supervision. This potential pitfall has generally been avoided by keeping the focus on how the analyst's or supervisor's subjective feelings are a kind of commentary on the treatment relationship. For example, Robertson and Yack (1993) discuss a candidate who presented in supervision a dream about her patient. The supervisor and analyst reached an agreement that the candidate would offer associations to her dream as seemed related to better understanding her countertransference and that the supervisor would avoid offering interpretations that crossed into treatment issues. Quinodoz (1994) described the guilty feelings a supervisee evoked in him and his struggle to find a way to bring these up in the supervisory relationship that did not injure the candidate but served to enhance her recognition of countertransference feelings of guilt. This required the supervisor to "contain" his feelings until the propitious moment arrived in the supervision when, in his judgment, the candidate was "ready" to hear his intervention. This led to the candidate's appreciation of how her patient evoked in her strong feelings of guilt and thereby opened up this issue for exploration in the analysis.

Quinodoz, as the supervisor, initiated the disclosure by sharing his subjective reactions; Pergeron (1996), writing from the perspective of the supervisee, reported a case in which he began an exploration of feelings toward his supervisor that permitted the recognition of issues in the analysis of his patient that had remained unappreciated. The supervisor had created an atmosphere in which self-disclosure was valued, and the discussion in supervision addressed those aspects of the candidate's countertransference that were relevant to the patient's treatment. However, Pergeron noted that "supervision can be an effective stimulus for self-analysis and continued work on one's own analysis" (p. 701). Coburn (1997) has emphasized that it is incumbent upon the supervisor to create the ambience of self-disclosure, which fosters the open discussion by the supervisor and treating analyst of their respective subjective experiences of the patient and the supervision. Nondisclosure on the part of the supervisor may result in a stale supervision that can negatively impact on the analysis. When used meaningfully, appropriate self-disclosure on the part of the supervisor can nurture a greater openness in the candidate to his or her counter-transferences and thereby help the analyst "take a broader, empathic step into the subjective world of the patient" (p. 491).

None of the preceding studies explored in depth the interaction between the personal meanings the supervisor, the analyst, and the patient attach to interactions arising in supervision, and the literature has dealt exclusively with emotional reactions *evoked* in the each participant by the clinical material. This is in marked contrast to some of the literature on countertransference (Jacobs, 1991; Ogden, 1994a) in which there has been detailed discussion regarding the interplay between what is evoked in the analyst and the analyst's current and past life experiences. Quinodoz (1994) discussed the induced feelings of guilt that were evoked by his supervisee's handling of his bill to her, but there was no reference to the personal meanings in his life that the candidate's behavior elicited. In Coburn's (1997) study of self-disclosure in supervision, the supervisor's impatience and sense of constriction toward her supervisee was highlighted, but with no reference to what this meant for her personally. Coburn remarked that the supervisor's reactions were "due in part to her own transference organization" (p. 491), but this was left unexplored. In the vignette in the next section, case material is presented from the termination phase in an adolescent analysis in which there was resistance in all participants (supervisor, analyst, patient) to deal with the painful affects associated with separation. Our thinking is close to Berman's (2000) advocating an open dialogue between the supervisor and supervisee, which even includes self-disclosure of some personal associations to the analytic material. A dream by the supervisor, Dr. Miller, about me (the analyst), which he disclosed, seemed to prompt a dream in response by me, which was also discussed. This dialogue led to a consideration not just of parallel processes, but to an exploration of the coalescence of the psychologies of each of the three participants into a trialogue. Approaching the material from this vantage point, the triadic intersubjective matrix permitted us to overcome the resistance to dealing with termination in which we all participated. This collective resistance, which occurred on a triadic level, is reminiscent of Freud's (1910a) caveat about the analyst's contribution to the patient's resistance: "... no psycho-analyst goes further than his own complexes and internal resistances permit" (p. 145). We will argue that *our appreciation of the evoked meanings, together with our attention to the personal meanings, permitted a deeper understanding of the complex shared unconscious phantasy that permeated the triadic intersubjective matrix* and created a situation that might be called "resistance," "bastion," or "non-dreams-for-three."

Clinical material: three amigos coming of age

Jon was nearly 13 years old when he began twice-weekly psychotherapy with me. He was a passive and demoralized boy who comported himself with a befuddled clumsiness. His parents brought him because of his poor school performance, lack of friends, and the sense that he had bottled many troubling feelings within him. Jon's family had been shattered by the revelation that his two older sisters had been sexually abused by his father. As a result, his parents had divorced, but his father continued to live nearby. Jon's mother was extremely depressed and had little to offer him emotionally. He lived with his two sisters and mother and saw his father regularly on weekends. His father was a narcissistic and extremely controlling man who would actively attempt to "help" Jon express his feelings about the family situation by sitting opposite him, knee to knee, and exhort him to emote. The father initiated their wrestling, which was intended to encourage Jon to express his pent-up aggressive feelings. Jon responded to his father's "invitations" by becoming increasing flaccid and helpless, while developing a provocative style of asking absurd questions of male authority figures that was designed to disarm and make them appear foolish.

The analysis, which was my first child analytic case, was started when Jon was 15 and continued for the next four and a half years. Analysis was recommended because of Jon's significant inhibitions, passivity, and poor school performance that had not improved in over two years of psychotherapy. His symptoms notwithstanding, he also demonstrated considerable ego strengths and an excellent capacity for self-reflection. Initially his father was extremely resistant and actually interrupted the analytic work for a period. Jon's resistances blossomed in full force when the analysis resumed and were expressed through many missed sessions and a transference pattern that wooed me into being a powerful male to provide much desired guidance, yet whose authority he simultaneously sought to invalidate. He had discovered that the only way he could feel powerful was to create a mess of his life that also thwarted my efforts to be helpful. Not surprisingly, Jon stirred strong countertransference feelings. Dr. Miller's advice was to stay the course because this was the way the analysis had to unfold. In order to support me through this difficult phase, Dr. Miller chose to disclose aspects of the near-impossible analyses that he had conducted with adolescents. He was empathically attuned to the struggle that I was having and tried to communicate that such feelings were present for all of us who did this work.

My style was to arrive at the supervisory meetings with detailed descriptions of the interactions between Jon and me that permitted Dr. Miller to appreciate fully the extent of the transference/countertransference patterns. The analysis, although arduous and trying, progressed well, as the supervisory meetings focused on the many transference enactments in a playful atmosphere between Dr. Miller and me. We wonder whether the optimism that was present because of the positive supervisory resonance can be an additional measure of progress in the analysis.

The continued exploration of the transference enactments, which stirred considerable anger in me, revealed, in addition to his attempting to disarm me, Jon's wish to be punished. As this wish for punishment was analyzed further, Jon recovered guilty memories of having sexual intercourse with his next-older sister when he was about 5 years old. This working-through of past trauma was linked with Jon's developing a healthy sexual relationship with his girlfriend. He and I were able to work through paternal and maternal transferences that were connected to his passivity and consequent learning difficulties. He often conveyed a bewildered sense of not understanding what seemed to be simple school material, and this "confusion" enlisted my "helpful" efforts. Inevitably my assistance was inadequate, and the analytic examination of this pattern brought to light Jon's deep, but conflicted, longings for parental guidance and his homosexual fears. His academic performance improved significantly, and Jon was on the honor roll for his Senior year.

Jon decided to go away to college, an appropriate decision, and I brought up the reality of the analytic relationship coming to a close. Jon's first reaction was dismissive, and he asserted that he would bring me along as a "shrink on call." He used his capacity for humor to defend against the experience of his sad and anxious feelings about termination. I interpreted this familiar defense regularly; however, although saying good-bye was discussed, Jon managed to avoid feeling the depth of his emotions. About four months prior to actual termination, he began again to miss many sessions. This behavior was confronted and interpreted in many of its defensive and transference implications, particularly as a return to earlier modes of interacting in the face of ambivalence about termination, but Jon continued not to show for many sessions. In the supervision hours, Dr. Miller and I considered the multitude of meanings to Jon's acting out and discussed various technical approaches. In retrospect, there was a mild sense of resignation in the supervision in the face of Jon's resistances that was expressed through a joint acquiescence to "Jon's just being Jon." The impact that Jon's termination would have on the relationship of the supervisor and supervisee was not addressed.

At the height of Jon's avoidance of termination feelings, Dr. Miller began a supervisory hour by saying that he had a dream about me a few nights before. In the dream, *I was giving Dr. Miller a haircut and there was some anxiety connected with the dream*. True to the open tenor of the supervision, Dr. Miller offered some associations to his dream and said he thought it was about "coming of age." It was dreamed on the night of a Progressions Committee meeting of the Child Analysis Program in which my nearing graduation was discussed, and Dr. Miller said the dream must reflect anxious feelings about the younger generation taking over; hence, the haircut in the dream represented loss of strength. He also said that it might have to do with his son reaching Oedipal age, and a clear theme emerged of Oedipal rivalry and threats of loss of power. Dr. Miller was also struggling with the decision to apply to become an adult supervising and training analyst, although at the time he did not mention it to me. (He began this process a few months later.) This dream was not discussed further in terms of its possible relationship to Jon's analysis, but it is interesting that Dr. Miller's supervisory note to the Progressions Committee included the statement: "It feels as if Dr. Brown and Jon and I are all working together."

About ten days later, I had the following dream:

I'm watching John Travolta who is sitting somewhat slouched in a plain, black straight chair. He's wearing a gray, full-body work suit with a zipper or buttons down the front. It has short sleeves. There's a man behind him who I can't make out. He has an electric razor and is going to shave him. He starts to shave the back of the neck and upper shoulders. It is pleasurable to J. T., and I can identify with the pleasure. The work suit is loosely fitting and the man puts his hand through the right arm opening and starts to shave J. T.'s chest from under the garment. An uneasy feeling starts to develop. He moves the shaver around his chest and then removes his hand. I notice a round hole in the garment around J. T.'s crotch. I start to feel increased anxiety as he moves his hand toward this hole with the shaver buzzing. I awaken feeling scared.

My first association was to Dr. Miller's dream of the haircut. It was dreamed the night of the yearly graduation party at Boston Psychoanalytic Institute, and Dr. Miller and his wife were there. In addition, my wife and I sat just in front of my former analyst and his wife, and we had a comfortable four-way conversation about summer vacation plans. I was surprised by the relative absence of anxiety in talking with my analyst and his spouse. My further associations led to guilty feelings about wearing a nicer suit than my analyst and then to the gray work suit in the dream which conjured images of prison attire. Associations to John Travolta were to the patient, Jon, and also to Travolta having matured from his early career as a high school goof-off into a serious actor. In this connection, my associations were to the pleasures and dividends of maturing, but also to the Oedipal guilt of overstepping one's bounds, and the anxiety of retribution/castration. Thus, my dream seemed to take Dr. Miller's as a day residue and further transform the "coming-of-age" conflicts to express the deeply frightening elements graphically. In this regard, Dr. Miller and I were engaged in representing the O of an unconscious phantasy that defined the triadic intersubjective matrix.

The anxieties in both Dr. Miller's and my dreams gave an Oedipal cast to the "coming-of-age" issues that permeated the supervisory atmosphere and provided important data as to the nature of what had been stalling the analysis and had created a bastion to which Dr, Miller's and my conflicts about "coming of age" had contributed. This new perspective led Dr. Miller and me to reflect on themes of dangerous rivalry and competition as they appeared in the supervision and the analysis. This reflection was done in a playful manner: when Dr. Miller shared his dream of my cutting his hair, he bent forward to show his bald spot, joking that the "evidence" was clear of my having injured him. I responded by revealing my own less advanced bald spot in order to "reassure" Dr. Miller. Thus, anxiety-provoking affects associated with "coming-of-age" conflicts were made less terrifying through our spontaneous play in the supervision.

Up to this point, my interpretations had been addressing Jon's defenses against sadness and loss but had not dealt with the frightening aspects connected with graduating as his own man (his dangerous rivalrous and competitive feelings). This discussion in supervision led me to focus additionally on Jon's dread of growing up and resulted in his having some terror-filled dreams. Jon dreamed *that he was sad to say good-bye to his best friend, A., and learned that A. was dying of AIDS. This sadness turned to terror as Jon discovered in the dream that he too had AIDS, having contracted it from A. A. explained that they had anal intercourse in childhood, that A.'s living cells remained inside Jon, and that these cells had become infected with the AIDS virus.* Discussion of this disturbing dream led to more exploration of some homosexual anxieties, as Jon questioned what aspects of me would stay inside him as separation approached. He could link this with both his wishes and his fears related to molestation. He was also worried about what would remain inside him of his father; whether he would end up with a lethal sexual perversion. Jon was able to confront with considerable affect the fact that his father had not only been sexual with his sisters, but had been intrusive, and therefore psychologically abusive, with him. Finally he could see that his behavior with me in the past had invited intrusiveness in the transference. The sessions became more emotionally vibrant, and Jon did not miss another appointment for the last two months of the analysis.

Discussion

Windholz (1970) pointed to the analyst's resistance to deal with termination in some supervised analyses stemming from the reluctance to separate from the supervisor, and we believe that that was occurring in my analysis of Jon. Dr. Miller and I enjoyed a close working relationship that was gratifying to both of us, and there was, to some extent, an unconscious collusion to deny the reality of that termination. This dovetailed with Jon's avoidance of separation from me; thus, there were parallel processes occurring (Searles, 1955). From this perspective, I was identified with Jon's resistance, and/or, stated in another way, I had unconsciously become the container for Jon's projected anxieties (Bion, 1962a; Joseph, 1987). In this manner, there was an "upward" movement of the resistance from the patient/analyst couple that was enacted in the supervisor/analyst pair (Marshall, 1997). It may also be said that a significant share of the resistance emanated from the supervisory relationship and was displaced "downward" into the patient/analyst dyad (Doehrman, 1976). In this connection, Stimmel's (1995) remarks about the supervisor's unappreciated transference to the supervisee appear relevant; however, her notion of transference seems rooted in a one-person psychology, which gives scant attention to the many complex layers of interaction that we have tried to emphasize. In our view, the interactional situation was actually quite complex and may be more fruitfully considered from the framework of the *triadic intersubjective matrix*. All three participants contributed to the affective disavowal of termination, and that reluctance occurred at the intersection of the personalities of each party around deeper anxieties that had remained the unrepresented unconscious phantasy of the field (Baranger & Baranger, 1961–62).

Dr. Miller, Jon, and I each were dealing with "coming-of-age" conflicts in our respective lives, and the full appreciation of the associated powerful affects was realized through the transformational dreams of Dr. Miller, me, and, finally, Jon. These provided a window for the gradual, evolving recognition of the unrepresented O that had been simplistically mislabeled as "separation anxiety." What processes were at work that permitted the eventual emergence of a deeper affective understanding? While it was true that termination appeared to trigger the so-called resistance, the more powerful and daunting emotional truth (Bion, 1970; Grotstein, 2004) had to do with terrors about "coming of age" that the three of us had unconsciously colluded to banish to an unmentalized realm of the triadic intersubjective matrix. Each of us had to "become" our own version of the collective O, thereby narrating the shared communal fear for the supervisory field as well as for our own psyches.

We also believe that not only is the intersubjective field, whether dyadic or triadic, an arena in which the subjectivities of the participants interact, but, in keeping with the Barangers' (1961–62) and Ogden's (1994a, 1994b, 1996) observations, the interactions of the subjectivities create a new superordinate subjectivity that has a life of its own in the intersubjective field, manifest by a shared unconscious phantasy. Ogden asserts that in the patient/analyst pair there is the expected intermingling of the subjective experiences of both – for example, the analyst may have a phantasy that is a compilation of what the patient has evoked and the personal meaning the analyst attaches to that which is evoked. It is this created third area, to which both patient and analyst contribute, that Ogden terms the "analytic third." However, the shared unconscious phantasy of the analytic third is not merely a static condition but, rather, takes on important significance by having an effect upon the unfolding psychoanalytic process. Thus, a phantasy that the analyst experiences, an example of the analytic third, will lead him or her to a new view of what is occurring in the analysis, and that new view, in turn, will affect his or her interventions. In this fashion, there is a constant ongoing dialectic between the subjectivities of the analyst, the patient, and the area of a shared subjectivity. Within this framework, according to Ogden (1996),

> As an analyst and analysand generate a third subject, the analysand's experience of dreaming is no longer adequately described as being generated in a mental space that is exclusively that of the analysand . . . and might therefore be thought of as a dream of the analytic third.
>
> (pp. 892–893)

Berman (2000), also advocating an exploration of personal meanings associated with the clinical material in supervision, has applied Ogden's notion of the "analytic third" to the supervisory relationship as well and suggests that:

The inner freedom achieved may allow a supervision with an inter-subjective focus to *evolve into a transitional space, within which the dyad generates new meanings* not accessible by the intrapsychic work of each partner in isolation.

(p. 285)

However, we have emphasized the development of meanings that are formed at the *triadic* point of interaction where the unconscious processes of patient, analyst, and supervisor meet, become inter-twined, and generate meanings that are unique to the *triadic intersubjec-tive matrix* of the moment. If we extend this idea of an analytic third to the supervisory relationship, we may view the dreams by Dr. Miller, me, and then Jon as products of a new combined area of experience – one might call it a *supervisory fourth* – to which the subjectivities of each contributed. Prior to Dr. Miller's dream, the termination was being talked about, but the depth of the associated affects was defended against. Dr. Miller's dream, considered as a product of the triadic intersubjective matrix, was the initial signal that there were "coming-of-age" issues that had an as yet untransformed frightening meaning. This dream, having been shared with me, then became an instigating force, a supervisory fourth, so to speak, which had a rip-pling effect in the three-person intersubjective field, one aspect of which was the instigating of my dream. In a way, my dream was an expression of my unconscious of having received (Freud, 1912) Dr. Miller's unconscious communication and also elaborating further on it. It was as though my dream was saying, "You are right Dr. Miller, there *is* something frightening here – this is what I see." This dream having been shared and discussed in the supervisory meeting helped to transform the evolving terrifying O that we had unconsciously colluded to leave unrepresented and *also brought about a shift in the triadic intersubjective matrix*. Just as Dr. Miller's disclosure of his dream and his associations to it altered the shared three-way intersubjective field, so too did the revelation of my dream have the same effect. The most important aspect of this shift was the change in emphasis of my interventions with Jon that resulted, several days later, in Jon's dream.

192

Jon's unconscious, attuned to and part of the triadic intersubjective matrix, responded in kind, as though saying, "Yes, I hear what you guys are telling me – here's what it's like for me." In this complex reciprocal manner the termination phase of Jon's analysis moved from emotional staleness to affective aliveness.

We believe that the complexity of the interactions described in the supervision of Jon's analysis occur in every supervised treatment. The unconscious of each of the three participants is constantly contributing to the creation of, and taking signals from, a combined supervisory fourth. To the extent that an atmosphere of self-disclosure is an element of the supervision, these processes may be brought into conscious discourse. Of course, the development of such self-disclosure depends upon the level of comfort the supervisor and the treating analyst are able to establish over time. Indeed, with respect to the issue of time, it is important to note that Dr. Miller's disclosure of his dream occurred at the end of a long treatment. The value of the revealing of such disclosures earlier in the supervisory relationship remains an open question and likely depends upon the supervisor's "read" of how relevant his or her private reactions are to the clinical material, as well as the status of the supervisory alliance at that moment. However, to the extent that this can be fostered, an increased appreciation of the triadic intersubjective supervisory field will result in attendant benefits for the patient's analysis, itself embedded in a field that includes emotional growth in the treating analyst and the supervisor.

We have also been considering the various components of intersubjectivity, one of which is that there is growth in both the analyst and patient in analysis. Tronick (2005, 2007) has addressed the *dyadic expansion of consciousness* in the mother/infant pair as emotional development unfolds, and I suggest that successful analysis also involves a commensurate expansion of *unconsciousness* in both partners. Furthermore, with regard to supervision, we may similarly observe a three-way process of reciprocal affective enrichment that leads to each member re-narrating aspects of himself that had been unconsciously joined for a period of time in the formation of an ephemeral supervisory fourth. For a portion of our combined analytic endeavor, Dr. Miller, Jon, and I were "joined at the hip," so to speak, by an unconscious shared phantasy crafted from the fearful associations each of us had about "coming of age." Ogden (2005) has written that in supervision the analyst and supervisor dream the patient into existence, and I suggest we broaden this statement to include the notion that each member of the triad, by virtue of re-narrating an aspect of himself, is also dreamed into existence. Thus, Jon went off to college, Dr. Miller and his son successfully navigated their Oedipal situation, and I went on to graduate as a child analyst. We all survived the analysis, grew individually as a result, and, as far as I know, are continuing to thrive.

We have described how the analysis of my countertransference dreams in Chapters 3 (Ms. C.) and 6 (Ms. B.), and in this chapter Dr. Miller's, my, and Jon's dreams, helped to illuminate and transform the shared unconscious phantasies of the field. We turn now in Chapter 9 to a more detailed exploration of countertransference dreams, their similarities and differences from unconscious waking thought (Arlow, 1969a, 1969b; Bion, 1962a, 1992; Reik, 1948). We will also briefly revisit the supervisory relationship Dr. Miller, Jon, and I shared from the perspective of countertransference dreams.

Note

1. This is an expanded version of L. Brown & M. Miller (2002), "The Triadic Intersubjective Matrix in Supervision: The Use of Disclosure to Work Through Painful Affects," *International Journal of Psychoanalysis*, 83: 811–823.

9

On dreaming one's patient: reflections on an aspect of countertransference dreams[1]

In this chapter, we explore the phenomenon of the countertransference dream. Until very recently, such dreams have tended to be seen as either reflecting unanalyzed difficulties in the analyst or unexamined conflicts in the analytic relationship. However, as we have seen in previous chapters, the countertransference dream may be a window into the shared unconscious phantasy of the analytic couple and is therefore a product of the intersubjective field. So while the analyst's dream of his or her patient may represent problems in the analytic relationship, these dreams may additionally indicate the ways in which the analyst comes to know his patient on a deep unconscious level by processing the patient's communicative projective identifications. In my view, the countertransference dream is embedded in an ongoing unconscious process of the analyst coming to know the analysand experientially by becoming in his own experience something similar to what the patient is unable to feel (transformation in O). Finally, we will revisit the question of how the countertransference dream may be put to use in supervision and take a second look at the dreams Dr. Miller and I had that were discussed in Chapter 8.

Mr. A., a man several years older than I, began analysis to deal with a chronic sense of stumbling into his life, especially with regard to relationships with women. Although successful in business, he found it very difficult to be firm with others when necessary and preferred instead to be patient and understanding, a quality that we came to diagnose as "chronically nice." In our initial discussions about what he hoped to gain from analytic work, Mr. A. quipped that he wished for some "magical injection," which led me to inquire as to the nature of the substance that would be injected. "Essence of balls," he joked, and though we both appreciated that this was no laughing matter, his joke seemed to disguise what were surely more painful feelings while simultaneously inviting me to make light of his deep distress.

Mr. A. began the tenth analytic session, the last of the week, by saying he would like a nap. His thoughts turned to the new apartment he was moving into, his daughter getting stomachaches as a child on Sunday nights before school the next day, to the fact that his brother had been in treatment for ten years, and his nostalgia for the woman from whom he recently separated after a long relationship. I commented about the end of our analytic week together and linked it to the themes of loss and separation. He began to speak with considerable feeling about how looks can be deceiving, especially with tall men who dress well, like Mr. A., and that "I'd walk into a room and people would think I'm an ambassador or something." I remarked that yesterday he was dressed in a formal-looking suit and indeed looked rather ambassadorial, yet today he seemed to want me to know that looks can be deceiving and that he was lonely with the weekend approaching. He went on to elaborate more deeply his melancholy feelings.

That night I had the following dream:

> I bumped into Mr. A. somewhere, a casual place, like a beach or movies. We started talking in a friendly way; I think he was with someone else, perhaps his brother, F. [who had been in treatment for 10 years]. I was friendly and animated and then realized that a good part of the afternoon had gone by. One of us asked the other about what to do next, and he might have invited me to go to the beach. For some reason I had to go somewhere and was driving my car on a beautiful New England road in fall, with the leaves fiery red, yellow, and orange. The road was going downhill to a lake, and as I was driving down the road I thought Mr. A. would like to see this, as though he were an out-of-town guest I was hosting. I turned around and went back to where I left him; perhaps I was with my wife. When I got to that place, he and whomever he was with were preparing to go to the beach. He was in shorts and I noticed he had well-muscled, thickly hairy legs which made me feel somewhat inferior, thinking that although he's older than I am he probably looks better on the beach.

196

My first association to the dream was to my consciously friendly feelings for Mr. A. which led me to wonder whether the dream was alerting me to some kind of collusion to avoid painful emotions by allowing "a good part of the [analytic] afternoon" to go by. I also associated to the obvious competitive themes, and this brought to mind an older cousin (with the same name as Mr. A.'s brother), whose strength I admired and whose presence I sometimes resented, who lived with my family for some time during my adolescence. Thus, I wondered whether the affable analytic mood, in addition to resisting painful emotions, might belie underlying adversarial feelings. I was also aware of feeling protective of him, an emotion that was connected to the beautiful fall road, which seemed to be a wish to show him that there are special pleasures to be had in approaching the autumn of one's life that differed from the fun of being a beachboy. But was that wish also an evasion of his invitation to the beach, and the possibility of kicking analytic sand into the other's face, when I instead sought out the bucolic New England scenery? There was something about looking like an ambassador that seemed to stick in my mind, though I could not connect that to the dream imagery. Was I competitively turning the ambassador (the ambivalently valued older cousin from another family) into a beachboy to undo my feeling inferior? These thoughts, centering largely around rivalry and status, swirled about my mind, and I was left with the sense that the meaning of this dream escaped me; thus, the dream was placed on the proverbial "back burner" to wait for further elaboration as the analysis unfolded.

A dream of one's patient can be an unsettling event, filling the psychoanalyst with doubts and uncertainties as to its meaning. Quite often one has the sense of having trespassed an ill-defined boundary by bringing the analysand into that most private of places, the uniquely personal realm of dream life. At other times, the analyst may feel that the patient's appearance in his dream is an unwelcome intrusion that may mirror his waking experience of the analysand. In such situations, the analyst is inevitably left with the feeling of having shared an intimate exchange with his patient, despite the analysand's absence of awareness. And upon seeing the patient the morning after dreaming of him or her, we may feel awkward, as though we have gained secret knowledge of our patient and cannot reveal it. Thus, the analyst may feel alone with a sense of the patient that may seem like an ill-gotten gain that he is loath to share with colleagues, a hesitation that has at least a hint of shame and a measure of guilt that might require some act of analytic contrition, such as going back into analysis.

Indeed, encouraging the analyst who has dreamed of his patient to return to analysis was regularly suggested in the years prior to our more current view of countertransference in its various manifest-ations. In our contemporary literature, a clinical report that does not include both the *yin* of the patient's transference and the correspond-ing *yang* of the analyst's experience is considered incomplete. It is interesting that while the shift toward an intersubjective psychology has had the effect of providing the analyst the freedom to openly explore his subjective reactions to his analysand, the phenomenon of the countertransference dream has until very recently remained in a kind of time warp in which dreams of one's patient tended to be viewed as problematic. We will be examining the psychoanalytic understanding of countertransference dreams in this chapter and offering an additional point of view on this subject. My primary hypothesis is that while dreams of one's patient may reflect problems in the analyst or in the analysis, they also represent a means by which the analyst is coming to unconsciously know his analysand. This unconsciously registered knowledge must be "unwrapped," so to speak, through the analyst's self-analytic work; consequently, we may find that what we have unwrapped contains important information about the analysand's emotional world or, perhaps, is a misrecognition that discloses more about the analyst that is useful in his or her self-analysis. Finally, the analyst's unconscious misrecognition of his patient may be an obstacle to allowing the patient's transference to fully develop.

But what does it mean to say we know a patient? To paraphrase Elizabeth Barrett Browning's poem that begins with "How do I love thee? Let me count the ways," there are different ways in which we "know" our analysand. There are the facts of his or her life that include family members, births, deaths, place among siblings, etc. To these data we add the emotional meaning that the events of the patient's life have upon him. Our analysands relate the sadness, dread, joy, anxiety, terror, and passions to us and, depending upon one's theory, we share, sometimes very deeply, in their emotions through processes we call empathic immersion, projective identification, reverie, trial identification, and so on and so forth. This emotional "knowing" brings color to the black and white of our factual "knowing," both of which occur largely on a conscious or a pre-conscious level. Bion (1965) has designated this kind of accumulation of "knowing" the patient as a *transformation in K* where K ("know-ledge," abbreviated by "K") represents a link between the analytic couple in which the analyst is in the process of getting to *know about* the analysand. However, Bion states that this gaining of information "does not produce growth, only permits accretions of knowledge about growth" (p. 156).

There is also another layer of "knowing" a patient that occurs on an unconscious basis, a knowing that only very slowly begins to dawn on the analyst, a knowing that derives from the patient having found or been given a place in the analyst's mind. This deep unconscious "knowing" is an underground current of meaning, the detection of which may be glimpsed by the analyst's slips of tongue, other parapraxes, or barely noticed fleeting reveries in relation to his patient. Then, often with a sense of surprise, the analyst, quite literally caught unaware, has the realization that he "knows" the patient in a particular way that may or may not be accurate. This is a manner of "knowing" that Bion (1965, 1970) terms *transformation in O* where "O" represents the slow evolution by which the "ultimate reality of [emotional] truth" (1965, p. 140), itself essentially ineffable and only approached asymptotically, is gradually apprehended. Mitrani (2001) describes how the analyst establishes contact with the patient's O through

> the introjection by the analyst of certain aspects of the patient's inner world and experience, and a resonance with those elements of the analyst's own inner world and experience, such that the latter is able to feel herself [the analyst] to actually be that unwanted part of the patient's self or that unbearable object that has previ-ously been introjectively identified with.
>
> (p. 1094)

It is this last kind of knowing – the deeply unconscious *transformation in O* – that I believe is a central feature of the countertransference dream. The analyst is constantly taking in information about his patient through the channels of knowing about (transformation in K) and knowing through experience (transformation in O). Technically speaking, what Betty Joseph (1985) describes as "real contact" between patient and analyst appears to dovetail with the prominence that Bion accords to transformations in O. In order to truly reach the heart of the analysand's suffering, the analyst must avoid offering "interpretations dealing only with the individual associations" (Joseph, 1985/1989, p. 159) (Bion's K) and instead focus on "the pressures brought to bear on the analyst" (p. 159) (Bion's O). Although Bion is clear that transformations in K do not produce emotional growth, this accumulation of knowledge is central in guiding the analyst to areas that yield deeper emotional understanding. Grotstein (2004) reminds us of Bion's (1970) statement that O is also an intersubjective event and that there is a shared O of the analytic hour that is the emotional truth about the analytic field unconsciously constructed by the patient and the analyst.

Returning to Mr. A., my dream about him may be approached from multiple perspectives, one of which is that the dream reveals the analyst's diminished sense of competence, a view that derives from discussions of Freud's famous dream of Irma's injection (Freud, 1900; see also Erikson, 1954; Zwiebel, 1985). Freud's treatment of Irma left him feeling inadequate, and he dreamed that her poor response was due to someone else's failure. He concluded that the dream '. . . was a sign that I was not responsible for the persistence of Irma's pains, but that Otto was" (1900, p. 118). While my dream of Mr. A. expressed similar themes of threatened competence, there was an additional component in which I resonated with his anxiety that though he appeared ambassadorial, he actually felt insecure. From this perspective, the dream also reflected my unconscious identification with (or *becoming)* the depth of Mr. A.'s feeling inadequate, an unconscious communication that was transformed by my dream work into the fabric of the countertransference dream by stitching together elements from Mr. A.'s story with associated aspects of my own life. This is what Freud meant by the analyst using his unconscious as "an instrument of the analysis" (1912) by which the patient conveys affects through projective identification (Brown, 2004; Zwiebel, 1985) for the analyst to absorb, give unconscious meaning, and then decode through self-analytic work.

There is, however, another level of meaning, one informed by an ongoing process of transformations of O, having to do with coming to unconsciously know our analysands more deeply, a knowledge stored in our unconscious which we do not know that we know. My initial associations to the countertransference dream about Mr. A. had to do largely with concerns around competition and feelings of inferiority.

200

These ideas led me to be on the lookout for such themes; however, neither Mr. A.'s thoughts nor my private reactions confirmed these speculations. Instead, he spoke about his sense of finding himself in this or that situation, wondering how to "tap dance my way out of it." My suggestions that this pattern might be a retreat from more active, competitive strivings yielded little emotionally significant associations. I found that the word "ambassador" kept reappearing in my mind, though I could attach no particular significance to it other than the matters of status. Then, one day I suddenly remembered that my father once bought a new AMC Ambassador, an automobile I was very proud to drive. I was surprised at not having made the connection previously, and this revelation led once more to further associations of my older cousin who spent time with my father tinkering with cars, an activity that excluded me. This association led to my awareness of affects tied to missing my father, and it permitted a shift in attention to Mr. A.'s yearning for his father's counsel (the "magical injection" of "essence of balls"), without which he felt adrift, and its appearance in the transference.

The surprising connection to the Ambassador automobile signaled a knowledge that I had of Mr. A. yet did not know that I possessed, a knowledge that was masked by my focusing on issues of competition and inferiority instead. Was this inattention to the latent father transference an expression of my resistance based upon my identification with the patient (Favero & Ross, 2002; Rudge, 1998)? Probably yes. But what I wish to emphasize here is the process by which I was coming to know Mr. A. on a deep unconscious level. It can be said that we come to know another person by attributing to him (through projective identification) aspects of our own inner object worlds and that we unconsciously scan their reactions to see how they conform or not to these unconscious perceptions. In this process we learn something about them and something about ourselves (Caper, 1996), a process in which we are always in the course of *coming to know* our patient, and ourselves, by successive accretions in the transformation of O (Bion, 1965; Grotstein, 2004; Ogden, 2003b). In the case of Mr. A., my initial interpretation of the countertransference dream, based upon themes of rivalry and inadequacy, was a misrecognition of him at that point in time that was corrected by my later realization. This realization — that I had introjected and identified with Mr. A.'s longings for an unavailable father's guidance (Mr. A.'s unacceptable O) – afforded me a level of knowing him; therefore, my countertransference dream was expressive of my unconscious working attempts to transform the evolving O of Mr. A. I also believe that my inability to recognize the paternal transference was linked to my anxieties in *recognizing my own* disavowed paternal longings because of their homoerotic associations (Mr. A.'s "muscled, thickly hairy legs"). Thus, this resistance was a joint endeavor that was intersubjectively constructed at the place where Mr. A.'s anxieties meshed with analogous conflicts in me (Smith, 1997) – or a *concordant* identification, in Racker's (1968) terms.

Ogden (2005) writes about how the supervisory process involves "dreaming a patient into existence" through the collaborative imaginative work done by the analyst and the supervisor. I view the countertransference dream as revealing the deep unconscious way the analyst is *dreaming the patient into existence* – that is, introjecting the patient's projections and finding common ground with them through analogous experiences of his own in order to get some sense of who the patient is and who he is not. When a psychoanalyst has a dream in which his patient appears, *he is both dreaming about, and dreaming into existence, the analysand*. To *dream about* a patient implies that he figures as a character in the dream, perhaps representing himself, standing in for someone else in the analyst's life or possibly embodying an aspect of the analyst. In this connection, *dreaming about* the patient is an aspect of a transformation in K. By contrast, *dreaming the patient into existence* is an unconscious mental activity by which the analysand gradually comes emotionally alive in the analyst's mind. Thus, *dreaming the patient into existence* is a component of a transformation in O.

The distinction being drawn here between *dreaming about* and *dreaming the patient into existence* relates to Bion's (1962a, 1992) views of why we dream, which I will now briefly review. He believes that there is a function within the mind (α function) that transforms raw emotional experience into thoughts and images that may be combined together to form the elements of a dream that upon analysis yield their latent content. Bion asserts that this process occurs when we are technically asleep and also in the unconscious waking state, meaning that the psyche is constantly engaged in a course of emotional alchemy by which unrefined affects are processed. When a patient is unable to dream, he is incapable of absorbing new affective experience and therefore cannot grow psychologically; however, the capacity to dream, as Bion understands it, permits a broadening of emotional life that fosters learning from one's experiences. Thus, *dreaming one's patient into existence* (while awake or asleep) is the means by which the analysand gradually and unconsciously comes into being as an alive and sentient individual in the analyst's mind (Grotstein, 2000, 2004; Ogden 2003b, 2004b) – that is, a step in the process by which the analyst transforms the O of his patient, which inevitably involves some emotional reworking of the analyst's conflicts because transformation of the analysand's O requires contact with an analogous aspect of the analyst's unmetabolized O.

The dream of Mr. A., dreamed after the tenth analytic session, thus represented my unconscious attempt to get to know him at the outset of analysis by introjecting his unacceptable[2] O (his longing for a father) that had been transmitted to my receptive unconscious through projective identification. Having taken in this unconscious transmission, I "dreamed" Mr. A.'s O by linking it with corresponding emotional trends in myself (the "ambassador" that, when analyzed, yielded the underlying yearning for a father and anxieties about such wishes). Ogden (1996) has stated that we should consider an analysand's dream as "no longer simply the 'patient's dream'" (p. 892) but, rather, as a product of the interaction between the analyst's and analysand's subjectivities. It seems likely that this assertion would also apply to a dream by the analyst. However, one might object that since my dream of Mr. A. occurred so early in the analysis it had more to do with the analyst than the patient and that, therefore, linking it to the analysand's life is rather spurious. This appears to be a valid objection and should be a caveat to the analyst not to jump to conclusions too quickly about the workings of a patient's mind. Smith (1997) has similarly cautioned the analyst and emphasizes the commitment to self-analysis to sort out the patient's dynamics from those of the analyst, and the interaction between the two, and to be aware that this self-analysis is multilayered and evolving. With regard to Mr. A., I thought I knew something about him when my initial dream associations led in the direction of competitive conflicts, but *his* associations did not. More importantly, I was *dreaming him into existence*, trying to unconsciously sense who he was and who he was not. In this connection, and more to the point for this discussion, my dream was a beginning step in a continuous unconscious process (transformation in O) of my coming to know Mr. A.

A countertransference dream from the end of an analysis

Ms. D. was in a long analysis that was very helpful to her, although it required struggling with wrenching feelings of being excluded from an archaically organized Oedipal couple (Brown, 2002). In particular, her transference, to which she clung for several years, was characterized by phantasies of my wife draining me of energy by imagined endless sexual demands. She hated any other female patient, whom she experienced as similarly bent on starving her by stealing my attention and affection away. Ms. D.'s marriage was also plagued by the same conflicts, in which the connection to her husband was based on the model of a "feeding couple." Consequently, their partnership was simply that: a sexless collaboration centered around providing for their children but with no joy, conjugal or otherwise, between them. Through her analysis, Ms. D. was able to work through her traumatic past in the transference, which enabled her to have a considerably more satisfying marriage. Termination was very painful for her, stirring once again the old feelings of being tossed away to starve by a couple who loved and cared only for themselves.

After terminating her analytic treatment, Ms. D. continued in weekly psychotherapy because she felt my ongoing assistance would be useful, especially to help her with her son who was experiencing substantial anxiety at that time. While pleased to offer help in psychotherapy, I was also aware of not wanting to completely say good-bye to her. I also questioned whether I had agreed too quickly to terminate, even though we had dealt with her leaving for well over a year. Then one night, several weeks after ending analysis, I had the following dream:

> I am laying in bed, but perhaps not under the covers, on my back, and Ms. D. is there to my left. We had been talking about something, perhaps her concerns about her son, and then she comes over to me. She is standing at the end of my bed where my head is and leans over and kisses me gently, I think first on the forehead and then lightly on the mouth. I say that that feels very good. She agrees and says it would feel even better to make love. I find myself getting analytic and starting to say something like "What do you think that would be like," but instead say "Yes, that would be nice." At this point, my wife walked in, and Ms. D. quickly went to a corner of the room. My wife, seeing her, asked insistently "What is she doing here?" and emphatically said that Ms. D. had to leave. She left the

204

bedroom, and I felt a sigh of relief that my wife had intervened in such a direct manner.

This was a compelling emotional dream with many layers of meaning in my life, and I will only address those features that are relevant to Ms. D.'s analysis. One point of view is that this reflects my uncertainty over agreeing to end analysis too readily; therefore, it expresses doubts about analytic competence. Furthermore, a powerful sense of seductiveness was the central affect in this dream, and I wondered whether my getting analytic at that juncture in the dream might have been defending against the strong sexual feelings. Ms. D.'s treatment was highly eroticized, with an intense transference and countertransference, but this segment of our work had more to do with mourning the analysis and other losses in her life, especially her children growing up and leaving home. I also remembered that Ms. D. frequently transmitted her dependent longings in sexual language, an association that led to doubts about whether I was unresponsive to such longings following the end of analysis. It seemed that my wife was brought into the dream to represent the other side of my ambivalence about letting go of Ms. D.: she would be to blame if my patient was pushed out the door, just as Otto was at fault for Irma's lack of treatment progress in Freud's dream.

These associations felt relevant to my dream, yet there was a lingering sense that something important remained unappreciated. The associations regarding my ambivalence about termination, the seductive sexual atmosphere that expressed Ms. D.'s yearning for closeness, and giving my wife the task of sending my patient away all seemed obvious. A comment of Freud's (1900; see also Scalzone & Zontini, 2001) seemed especially applicable at this point: "There is often a passage in the most thoroughly interpreted dream which has to be left obscure .... This is the dream's navel, the spot where it reached down into the unknown" (p. 525). Some days later I realized that Ms. D. had been placed in the position of a psychoanalyst: in the dream, I was lying down and she was behind me and slightly to my left, just as I was in relation to her during analysis. She offered to comfort me, and I struggled with my wish for that versus being her analyst. Thus, my *dreaming her* as a former Oedipal partner – a necessary aspect of the termination that I give to my wife – appeared to cover a deeper level of the dream symbolized by *dreaming her* as my analyst.

While I was mulling these thoughts over in my mind, Ms. D.

continued to express her concerns about her son's intense anxiety, which led to my asking if she were worried about how I was affected by the end of our analytic work. She immediately said that my income had just dropped considerably and joked about how I was managing the loss of income. I commented that her humor seemed to be a way of clouding her fear that, like her son, I needed her comfort in order to manage being on my own. I also began to question whether there might be some accuracy to her concerns about my emotional well-being, and this brought my training analysis to mind. My analyst had to interrupt the analysis for a while, and we spent considerable time questioning whether I was "ready" to end treatment. This realization permitted me to see how I had likely identified with her anxious son whose mother/analyst was leaving. This piece of self-analysis allowed me to feel more at ease with the decision to terminate, and, in a parallel manner, Ms. D.'s anxiety about her son substantially diminished.

This countertransference dream reflected my conscious anxiety about making a competent decision in agreeing to Ms. D.'s termination. Furthermore, the fact that the venue was my bedroom came as no surprise and served to highlight the strong Oedipal atmosphere to the end of analysis. Additionally, casting my wife as a spokesperson for one side of my ambivalence also appeared to be self-evident. These "insights" from the dream added nothing new and did little to illuminate the nature of Ms. D.'s immediate concerns about her son, which constituted the ostensible reason for continuing in weekly psychotherapy. Indeed, I thought her telling me about her son's anxiety was more a communication about how panicked *she* was feeling. On the contrary, if we consider my dream as an attempt to unconsciously transform an emotional experience evoked in me by Ms. D. (her objectionable O conveyed through projective identification for me to "dream"), then we might wonder what had been unconsciously communicated to me that I could not yet find the symbols for in order to know that I knew it. When I later realized she was dreamed as my analyst, Ms. D.'s concerns about her son took on new meaning: that she was accurately experiencing me as having been made anxious by her termination (my identification with her anxious son as well as with Ms. D., whose analyst might have been letting go of her before she was ready) and therefore required her soothing. This realization led to my bringing up Ms. D.'s fears about the effects of termination on me, which, in turn, significantly enlivened the hours because my anxiety was considerably lessened, thereby freeing her to experience her own very deeply felt terror of leaving and her near conviction that someone would die as a result. Thus, while it was true that I was consciously anxious about the wisdom of termination, continued analysis of the dream clarified the more frightening and unconscious determinants of my anxiety, which reached down toward the navel of the dream that was receptively connected to the O of Ms. D.'s transmitting unconscious that had found common cause and resonance with similar unprocessed feelings in me.

Discussion

The dreams of Mr. A. and Ms. D., like other countertransference dreams, are complex products that may be understood on multiple levels. Zwiebel (1985), for example, states that such dreams are "the sign of a disturbance in the analytic relationship in which both partners take place" (p. 87), involving a perceived threat to the analyst's competence. Myers (1987) similarly emphasizes that dreams of one's patient occur within the context of a "countertransference bind" that may be deciphered through the analyst's self-analysis. These points of view surely apply to aspects of my dreams of Mr. A. and Ms. D. Themes of analytic competence were evident in both instances and formed one vertex of the dreams' meaning. However, especially with Mr. A., my dream did not seem to be a response to a countertransference bind. Rather, it was dreamed in the context of getting to know my patient, and neither Mr. A. nor I was experiencing any difficulties in getting our analytic work underway. The dream of Ms. D. was more intensely charged with emotion and surfaced in the context of my conscious anxiety around whether termination was perhaps premature. It did not seem to express a particular quandary in which we were stuck as much as it suggested the way in which my unconscious represented her fears and had captured Ms. D.'s anxieties about how I had been affected by the termination and how her accurate unconscious perception that I was anxious tied to experiences in my training analysis.

There is another axis – that of unconscious communication – from which the countertransference dream may be appreciated. Zwiebel states that the analyst's dream of a patient occurs when there is intense projective identification that evokes powerful feelings in the analyst that he is unable to manage and which tax his capacity to cognitively handle. He uses projective identification in the evacuative sense as a means of the patient unburdening himself of unbearable emotions and ignores the communicative aspects of projective identification (Bion, 1959) or what Grotstein (2005) calls projective transidentification. Rudge (1998) more accurately states that "The countertransference dream warns the analyst that some symbolic elaboration is necessary" (p. 110). Favero and Ross (2002) also adopt this view and emphasize that the countertransference dream is the analyst's attempt to mentally digest what the patient has unconsciously communicated through projective identification. Unlike Zwiebel and Myers, they do not see the analyst's dream as embedded in conflict or signifying a treatment difficulty. Indeed, they stress that the countertransference dream, once understood through self-analysis, may assist the analyst in becoming aware of his resistance to accepting the patient's transference. This was certainly the case with my initial assessment of the dream about Mr. A., in which my focus on themes of competition and rivalry served as a resistance to accepting the paternal transference.

Yet another dimension of the countertransference dream derives from Bion's (1992) statement that "the origin [of a dream] is an emotional experience . . . and that this is worked on to produce the dream" (p. 135). As we have discussed in previous chapters, Freud taught us that the unconscious of the patient transmits to the analyst's unconscious and that we should use our unconscious as an instrument of the analysis (1912); however, he did not instruct us as to how this is done (Brown, 2004). If we put Freud's notion of the transmitting unconscious together with Bion's concepts, then we may conclude that the patient transmits an unprocessed emotional experience through projective identification to the analyst's receiving unconscious. It is then up to the analyst to "dream the analysis," meaning that he discovers within himself symbols that represent the formerly untransformed emotional experience of the analysand. Thus, Bion (1992) concludes somewhat wryly that the analyst "must be able to dream the analysis as it is taking place, but of course he must not go to sleep" (p. 216).

Needless to say, the analyst does literally go to sleep at night and constructs his dreams around a day residue, just as a pearl is formed around a grain of sand. At the heart of a day residue is an emotional experience that initiates a transformation of unrefined emotion into the dream symbols from which the dream narrative is fashioned. In the case of a countertransference dream, the day residue is an emotional experience that emanates from the analyst's encounter with his patient. This may be a troubling engagement that threatens the analyst's sense of competence, or perhaps it is an emotional experience that has been forcefully evoked in the analyst by the patient's powerful projective identification. Alternatively, the day residue around which the analyst's dream of his analysand forms may be the result of an ordinary process of unconscious communication that is the expression of the patient's wish to be known by an analyst interested in knowing him or her.

In this connection, the analyst is constantly engaged in finding a place for the analysand in his mind by coming to know the patient both consciously and unconsciously, a knowledge that is shared with the patient (through interpretation), who deeply desires to be known. While much of the analyst's activity may be categorized as transformations in K, the countertransference dream is a component of "Transformations in O [which] are related to becoming or being O" (Bion, 1965, p. 163). This "becoming or being O" is accomplished by the analyst being receptive to the analysand's projected unmentalized emotional truths (Grotstein, 2004) and identifying with them. This is a trial identification (Fliess, 1942) that is perhaps the most difficult aspect of what has been called "taking the transference" (Mitrani, 2001), realized through the analyst "dreaming the analysis" while he is awake in the consulting room; the more deeply unconscious aspect of this process has been called by Ogden (2003b, 2004b, 2005) *dreaming the patient into existence*. The countertransference dream is a special instance of coming to know the patient while the analyst is technically asleep, and it requires a significant amount of self-analysis to discern which elements relate to the patient and which to the analyst. Thus, we must proceed with significant respect for what we do not know and stay mindful of Bion's (1992) caveat that "We use our knowledge and experience to gain more knowledge and experience" (p. 183).

While it is surely true that the countertransference dream is a product of what Ogden (1994a, 1994b) calls the "intersubjective analytic third," or the Barangers (1961–62) term the unconscious phantasy of the couple, my experience leads me to conclude that there is a qualitative difference between the analyst's reveries while technically awake during an analytic hour and his dream of the patient while technically asleep at night. Both may provide access to the evolving O of the analytic relationship; however, the analyst's waking reveries, when he becomes aware of being in such a state, can be contextualized in the ongoing give and take between the analyst and patient in the analytic hour. Thus, the connection between the reverie and the analysand's associations is more readily established. The situation with the analyst's dream of his patient is more complicated. On the one hand, the countertransference dream may indicate a delayed transformation of an emotional experience from the session that was too powerful for the analyst's reverie to manage,[3] a point that Ferro (2005) appears to support from a slightly different perspective by stating that night dreams consolidate what has not been fully processed during the day. On the other hand, in all likelihood there have been many intervening events in the interim between the analytic session and the countertransference dream, and so the connection between the day's session and the analyst's dream may be more difficult to discern. Heenen-Wolf (2005) appears to reach a similar conclusion:

> Now the night dream represents a mode of psychic functioning that is much more under the sway of the primary process of the subject (the analyst) than the analyst's "reverie" during the session, which remains more colored by secondary processes. Furthermore, the night dream is temporally deferred in relation to the session. The content of a session or other elements arising from the analytic situation are thus in danger of being taken up and "used" for the analyst's own psychic purposes.
>
> (p. 1545)

In this regard, the dangers of the analyst gaining knowledge of the analysand that is really a misrecognition appear greater with the countertransference dream.

Consequently, it is difficult for the analyst to know what to do with such "evidence" about the analysand gleaned from dreams in which his patient appears. Bion (1965) viewed the countertransference dream as an important event, but was cautious about the use to which it could be put:

> ... the analyst should be cognizant of dreams in which patients

210

appear, though his interpretation of the significance of their appearance will relate more to their characteristics as column 2 phenomena[4] than to their significance of his own psychopathology.

(p. 50)

Later, Bion (1967) cautioned the analyst to eschew "knowledge" that only he possesses, because this may distract him from the more important mission of attending to what is not known in the analytic hour. The analyst may delude himself into believing he understands the patient by virtue of having dreamed about him or her, but this supposed "knowledge" may be a resistance to comprehend the deeper, initially unmentalized, resonance with the O of his analysand. Indeed, Bion (1965) defines *resistance* as an anxiety-based reluctance to transform K→O, meaning that the patient (or analyst) finds it less discomfiting to *know about* some difficult-to-bear emotional truth than to *experience* that truth through a "trial identification" (Fliess, 1942) or being at "one-ment" (Bion, 1970) with the analysand's projection. I believe this occurred in my dream about Mr. A. when my focus on the competitive aspects served to distract my attention away from experiencing myself as the transferential father, including its erotic aspects. This also transpired in my dream of Ms. B. when I found it more familiar to *know about* the Oedipal issues in the termination than to *experience* her profound anxiety about my being able to survive without her and how that was linked with uncertainties in the termination of my analysis.

The countertransference dream in supervision

Just as the countertransference dream was initially viewed as problematic, so there has been a parallel tendency to consider countertransference dreams discussed in supervision as reflective of treatment difficulties. Langs (1982) did not discuss the countertransference dream per se but offered the view that any dreams reported by a supervisee during supervision represented a "supervisory crisis."[5] It seems likely that he would also deem dreams of one's patient as illuminating a problem in the supervising relationship or the treatment. Such dreams convey the supervisee's unconscious perceptions of the supervision:

211

. . . supervisees report dreams to their supervisors as a means of conveying highly significant perceptions and fantasies that are either entirely repressed within the supervisee, or too dangerous to communicate directly in supervision.

(p. 594)

Although I believe Langs was too narrow in his exclusive emphasis on the dream expressing a crisis in the supervision, he does implicitly favor the communicative importance of the dream shared in supervision. In addition, his description of the dream encoding something "too dangerous" to discuss in supervision underscores the importance of the supervisee feeling safe to experience the "emotional truth" (Bion, 1965; Grotstein, 2004) of what is happening in the treatment and/or in supervision. Unfortunately, Langs's perspective that dreams reported in supervision indicate a crisis would probably lead to an atmosphere in supervision that would restrict the supervisee's freedom to speak freely and candidly, not to mention dream with a sense of abandon.

Instead, the supervisory experience ought to provide what Mollon (1989) calls a "space for thinking" that would have the welcome mat out for a variety of experiences, including the freedom to report dreams of one's patient. This view of supervision aims at assisting the supervisee to enlarge the "material" that is considered relevant to his work with the analysand and emphasizes an examination of the conscious and unconscious processes between the analyst and the patient and between the analyst and the supervisor, as well as the multitude of influences between the three.[6] This approach accesses different channels of learning and discovery that enable the treating analyst and supervisor to simultaneously *know about* (transformation in K) the analysis and to *experientially become* the analysis (transformation in O). Ogden (2005) has characterized this latter approach as "dreaming up the analysand in the supervisory setting" (p. 1267) and observes that

creating the patient as a fiction – "dreaming up the patient" – in the supervisory setting represents the combined effort of the analyst and supervisor to bring to life in the supervision what is true to the analyst's experience of what is occurring at a conscious, preconscious and unconscious level in the analytic relationship.

(p. 1268)

I would add that in addition to "dreaming the patient into existence" (p. 1269) through the mutual reveries of the analyst and supervisor, the countertransference dream, when shared in supervision, may constitute yet another channel tuned into the unconscious resonances streaming between the analysand, the analyst, and the supervisor.

Supervision, especially of long analyses, may become stale when it primarily centers on extracting meaning from the verbal "material," and the situation may arise in which patient, analyst, and supervisor collude in a faux analysis and supervisory relationship. This is associated with the kind of resistance that Bion (1965) mentions in which there is no transformation from K→O. In this regard, I want to revisit a paper – one of the few papers discussing the use of countertransference dreams in supervision – that Martin Miller and I (Brown & Miller, 2002 – see Chapter 8, this volume) published and offer an additional perspective on what we had earlier discussed. This was my treatment of Jon, during the termination phase of an adolescent analysis in which Dr. Miller (the supervisor) and I (the analyst) had implicitly acquiesced to the Jon's avoidance of emotion. There was a tacit assumption that he was avoiding dealing with separation, and my interpretations addressed the analysand's "defenses against separation feelings." In the midst of this atmosphere of resignation, Dr. Miller reported a dream he had dreamed about me the previous night, a dream filled with much anxiety. He offered some associations that had to do with my nearing graduation from the Child Analysis Program and also about his own son having reached an Oedipal age.

Several days later I had a very frightening dream of someone also named Jon (but spelled John), and my associations were to scary themes of castration and guilt related to maturing into manhood. There were many overlapping elements in Dr. Miller's and my dreams in which the two seemed to be elaborating a previously unconscious anxiety shared by us – that is, our respective unconscious perceptions of the O of the supervisory field. Thus, my dream appeared to be an elaboration of Dr. Miller's dream about me. As this was discussed in supervision, the understanding of the patient's "resistance" shifted from resistance to experiencing separation feelings to resistance against feeling terrifying "coming-of-age" anxieties. This animated the supervisory hours, and I began to shift the interpretive focus to the analysand's very intense anxiety about what "coming of age" unconsciously meant for him. This change in my interventions prompted a dream by Jon that graphically depicted the terrors he connected to the "coming-of-age" theme that permeated the total atmosphere of the supervision and treatment. We concluded that

> All three participants contributed to the affective disavowal of termination, and that reluctance occurred at the intersection of the personalities of each party.
>
> (p. 190, this volume)

Dr. Miller and I referred to the interactive meshing of emotional vectors from the patient, the analyst, and the supervisor as the "triadic intersubjective matrix." For the purposes of this discussion, I want to underline the process we described in which we literally "dream up" (while we were asleep, and not through unconscious waking thought of a reverie) the patient (Ogden, 2005) and, perhaps more importantly, dream the "field" (Baranger, Baranger, & Mom, 1983; Ferro, 2002, 2005) out of which the collective resistance emerged. Ferro (2005) notes that "the presence and constellation of defenses in the analyst 'costructures' the field together with the patient" (p. 10), to which I would add, in the case of supervision, the defenses of the supervisor. Thus, the triadically composed field of resistance that we adumbrated in which the treatment and supervision was mired may be characterized by the communal inability to transform the field from K→O. It was only by a succession of dreams, initiated by Dr. Miller's revelation, that the triadic intersubjective matrix could evolve beyond the relative comfort of the familiar K (resistance to separation anxieties) to confront the intensely anxiety-laden and shared unknown O (terrors associated with "coming of age") of the analytic threesome.

Taken from another angle, Dr. Miller, my patient, and I were also engaged in a process of mutual unconscious communication that gradually transformed the "coming-of-age" anxieties into a more manageable form for all of us. Dr. Miller, my analysand, and I ran aground on the shoals of a shared resistance, in which each of us participated in our own unique way, that required analysis to overcome. However, this was not a collective resistance that had to be merely "overcome" by virtue of sweeping away the defensive forces blocking its appearance, but one that required a mutual process of containment and transformation (Ungar & Ahumada, 2001) that enabled that which was resisted to be represented/mentalized. Dr. Miller and I had unknowingly surrendered to a sense that my patient was just being his typical passive self, an impression from which we were suddenly awoken by Dr. Miller's surprise dream. Smith (1995)[7] links the appearance of such surprises in individual analysis to a sudden shift in the resistance that is a compromise formation between intersecting conflictual areas in the patient and analyst:

> Surprise may then reflect a momentary reorganization of those compromises, a shift in forces as the analyst allows himself to overcome an internal resistance and to see something "new" in the patient because he has gained or regained access to something he has been fending off in himself.
>
> (p. 71)

The same may be said of resistances in supervision that stem from the failure to contain and transform unformulated anxieties resulting from a compromise formation that draws from the unconscious anxieties of the patient, the analyst, and the supervisor – resistances that seem to await the arrival of a surprise (waking or sleeping) dream to free the analysis to take its course.

Conclusion

Like any other dream, the countertransference dream has at its core an emotional experience that is worked on to produce the dream. In the case of the countertransference dream, the stimulus is an emotional reaction the analyst has in response to his patient. The dream may have little to do directly with the patient, whose appearance in it may be as a stand-in for someone else in the analyst's life. However, the appearance of a patient in the analyst's dream may also be stimulated by the transmitting unconscious of the patient making contact (through projective identification or projective transidentification) with the analyst's receptive unconscious in order for the analyst to contain and transform (or "dream") some mental content that is as yet "undreamable" (Ogden, 2004b) by the patient. I suggest that this aspect of the countertransference dream may enable the analyst to become aware of how his psyche is experiencing the patient or, put another way, dreaming the patient into existence. This opens the possibility of gaining knowledge about the patient that Bion (1965) refers to as a transformation in O – that is, the analyst "becoming"

(through introjection) the unacceptable part of the patient and finding symbols within himself to represent what the analysand has been
unable to mentalize for himself. I have tried to demonstrate this process by the analysis of two of my countertransference dreams and also
by a discussion of how these issues apply to analytic supervision.

Notes

1   This is an expanded version of L. Brown (2007), "On Dreaming One's
    Patient: Reflections on an Aspect of Countertransference Dreams,"
    Psychoanalytic Quarterly, 76: 835–861.
2   One would assume that there also exists an "acceptable O" – perhaps
    something akin to Freud's reference to the "ordinary unhappiness of
    everyday life" – that the patient is fully capable of transforming on his
    own. However, patients seek us out to help them bear and transform
    emotional experience that is too powerful for them to manage
    ("unacceptable O") and for which they require our services to "dream
    undreamt dreams" (Ogden, 2004b).
3   I am indebted to members of the Klein/Bion Study Group of the
    Massachusetts Institute for Psychoanalysis for this observation.
4   "Column 2" of Bion's (1977b) Grid refers to phenomena that are the
    stuff from which lies and deceptions may be constructed. These occur-
    rences exist solely in the mind of the patient or analyst, without any
    corroboration from the other. Column 2 phenomena may pass for the
    truth but may actually be falsehoods. Thus, the analyst must be cautious
    about the use to which he puts the countertransference dream because it
    is a potential lie (or misrecognition) about the patient that has a life only
    in the analyst's mind.
5   Interestingly, when I gave this paper at the Boston Psychoanalytic Insti-
    tute, one of the discussants was a candidate who experienced her first
    countertransference dream the night of reading this paper. The candi-
    date described a sense of "permission" to dream about a patient that
    reading this report by a senior analyst seemed to grant. I have sub-
    sequently spoken with other candidates who express a reluctance to talk
    about countertransference dreams in supervision because of some sense
    that these are inappropriate.
6   The broad literature available on this subject was addressed in Chapter 8.
7   See also Theodor Reik's (1937) book, *Surprise and the Psycho-Analyst*.

10

Final reflections: dreaming the future

The task of psychoanalysis is, via repetition, to enable an unblocking of a present frozen in the past onto a possible future of open possibilities.

(Birksted-Breen, 2009, p. 39)

We could say that today is the future's gift to the past – "offering," one might say, the present moment as an opportunity to relive and rework that past, perhaps also an opening for reparation and new beginnings. Thus far we have largely been attending to the past and the present – the *theoretical* development of the concept of intersubjectivity from Freud's thought to contemporary notions, and the *clinical* admixtures of the patient's and analyst's histories in the co-created narratives of the present – and in this final chapter I wish to redirect our attention to the future. We are constantly imagining the future, partly on the basis of what has already occurred, but always a future that is conceived in the present moment. How does the future grow out of the past, or, put another way, what are the intersubjective dimensions of an analyst and analysand working together that "enable an unblocking of a present frozen in the past onto a possible future of open possibilities?"

But first . . .

Salvador Dali's painting, *Discovery of America by Christopher Columbus,* freezes a critical moment in time and creates a feeling more of invasion than one of discovery. A youthful Columbus is depicted about to put a foot on the shore, the other still in the ocean, and the painting captures the shadow of his raised foot in the moment before touching ground. His right hand has already planted a large banner in the sand, festooned with a huge image of the Virgin Mary, thereby emphasizing his humility in claiming this new land first for his church before allowing himself admission. Innumerable crucifixes of all sizes and colorful banners flank him on either side, fading into the ocean's border with the sea behind him, and rising from there into a turbulent gray sky toward the heavens. The scene is viewed from somewhere on shore, as though from the perspective of an indigenous American gazing with awe at the majestic spectacle and this splendid young man towing the huge ship unassisted with only his left hand.

The view from the land stirs a sense of foreboding: a future of colonization both in spirit and territory. There is an object on the beach cloaked in shadows that looks like a large sea urchin shell, which could be a symbol of other planets this new world will later explore in the tradition of Columbus. Is this the arrival of a new religion that will free the souls of the inhabitants, or the importation of an old system that will crush the nonbelievers? Dali, a Spaniard, was surely aware of Columbus setting sail simultaneous with the introduction of the Inquisition by Ferdinand and Isabella, who financed his mission, and so leaves us to wonder further about the meaning of the triumphant mood of the painting. It seems there is an air of sadness underneath the pomp and ceremony, as though the artist is expressing a resigned inevitability that the future of this new land is a repetition of the European past of political and religious oppression. Thus, this moment of apparent exuberance and the thrill of newness portrayed by Dali is a palimpsest covering a darker reality: that the future is the past and the past the future. Time has collapsed, and the moment of promise caught in the picture is fleeting.

Dreaming of the future serves an important role in the life of an individual. Even before the birth of a baby, parents imagine their child and anticipate the arrival with hope and sometimes with dread. There are imaginings that reflect parental wishes, both conscious and unconscious, for a new life that fulfills the unrealized longings in the mother and father, not unlike the fantasies of an explorer who approaches an unknown continent with visions of a wished-for paradise. And not infrequently the new child can be the receptacle for unrealized dreams, both deliciously fanciful and horribly fearful, that the parents dare not countenance but look to the child to dream for them. In these instances, the child has a sort of time capsule lying fallow within him or her, a secret agenda to be realized that belongs to a previous generation but awaits the growing child as his or her rendezvous with the future. The generational boundaries have collapsed, as have the future and the past, creating what Bion (1991b) calls a memoir of the future.

Caught in the past: Alice's dream

Life for 8-year-old Alice, as depicted in her analytic play therapy sessions, was full of promise yet proved to be immeasurably cruel. She cast herself as a brilliant student who began university at age 1½ years and soon rocketed into prominence as the college's best student in all subjects. Though clearly younger than her classmates, Alice did her best to befriend the other students but was repaid with contempt. Her roommate, who was also her older sister, committed vile and sadistic acts toward her every night, and Alice was discovered each morning by the dormitory parents in a nearly dead state. The clues that undoubtedly pointed to her sister's culpability were ignored by the adults. Policemen from the surrounding community were summoned to investigate, and they too could not substantiate the small girl's complaints. Her sister offered the flimsiest of excuses to explain away Alice's injuries, and these were readily accepted by the authorities. Undaunted by the scrutiny of the dormitory parents and the police, the sister intensified the ferocity of the attacks: initially these assaults involved pummeling, stabbing, and shooting but evolved into chopping, pureeing, baking, and actually devouring Alice. Her blood was sucked out and the big sister skinned her alive, wearing the younger girl's skin as a garment. These nightmarish experiences continued unabated for months.

Shortly before this long play sequence, which occupied our play for several months, Alice said she had a dream to share with me but would only do so if I promised not to tell her parents. It was a repetitive nightmare, first dreamed when she was about 3 or 4 years old, and it still regularly haunts her nights five years later:

> Me, mom, dad, Claudia [her sister], my friend E., and her mother went to a restaurant where the waiters go around and take the children out of the booth when the parents aren't paying attention. They take the children and pull them over a scanner [as in a supermarket checkout] so it goes beep,

beep, beep. Then the children form lines: one for kids age 10, then 12, and other ages. Then they put the children on the stove and kill them. If people order bone soufflé, it would be children. Then there was a staircase and some kids tried to run up it to escape, to hide up there. Then, when they heard their parent leaving, they ran downstairs after them.

I inquired why Alice did not want me to tell her parents, and she said they get unhappy with her when she whines or bothers them. I said that I knew she always tried to be a good girl who does not trouble her parents and added that, if I had a book about kids' dreams, it would probably say that a girl who had the same scary dream from when she was 3 until 8 years old probably had a very big worry on her mind that had not gone away. Alice did not respond, and I said she might be worried about bothering me like she feels with her parents. She turned around with her back to me and quietly gave me two energetic "thumbs up."

Taken from a classical psychoanalytic perspective, Alice's dream and play narrative are both expressions of an *infantile neurosis*. Freud (1918) gave this subject his greatest attention in the *Wolf Man* case ("From the History of an Infantile Neurosis") where he proposed that his patient's obsessional "neurosis in later life was preceded by a neurosis in early childhood" (p. 54.). Freud and his analysand spent considerable time on the analysis of a dream from the Wolf Man's childhood of wolves perched on a tree outside the boy's window. Freud ultimately came to interpret this dream as a transformation of a forgotten primal-scene memory first witnessed at the age of 18 months. He called this process of re-enlivening the earlier primal scene "deferred action" [*Nachträglichkeit*], and Freud was quite vigorous in his interpretations to the Wolf Man about the meaning of the dream: that it was unquestionably a reworking of the earlier memory that had lain dormant and was then reconfigured in the later dream. Freud was insistent in his interpretations and adamant that at some point the Wolf Man would recover memories of the inferred primal-scene experiences. Years later, the Wolf Man wrote that he had done everything imaginable to "remember" the primal scene Freud had assured him would emerge, yet no such memories surfaced.

I want to highlight the *implicit connection Freud draws between the process of dreaming and the transformation of early experiences into later refashioned narratives*. In Freud's view, the Wolf Man's experience of witnessing parental intercourse at 1½ years of age remained without emotional meaning until it was transformed by the process of "deferred action" (Freud, 1918) or *Nachträglichleit* into a meaningful psychological event. He refutes the argument that such putative early memories are merely fantasies and states that

> It seems to me absolutely equivalent to a recollection, if the memories are replaced (as in the present case) by dreams the analysis of which invariably leads back to the same scene and which reproduce every portion of its content in an inexhaustible variety of new shapes. Indeed, *dreaming is another kind of remembering, though one that is subject to the conditions that rule at night and to the laws of dream formation.*
>
> (p. 51, italics added)

Thus, when Freud asserts that dreaming "is another kind of remembering," he is acknowledging that the Wolf Man's primal scene experience from one and a half years has been revived from its slumber and transmuted "by the laws of dream formation" into the dream of a nearly 5-year-old boy.

Though Freud does not make the point explicitly, there is an implicit assumption that the process of *Nachträglichkeit*, or what French analysts term *après coup* (Faimberg, 2005, 2007), is forged by "the conditions that rule at night and to the laws of dream formation." Faimberg states that *après coup* involves processes of *anticipation* and *retrospection* – that is, that the Wolf Man's primal scene anticipated its later avatar in the dream *and also* that the dream retrospectively (Freud's "deferred action") gave meaning to the earlier experience. I suggest that Bion's (1962a, 1992; Grotstein 2000, 2007, 2009a, 2009b, 2009c) theory of dreaming offers a model by which to understand the processes at work in *Nachträglichkeit* or *après coup*. As we have seen in previous chapters, Bion views dreaming as occurring while one is asleep and awake and is the mind's way of digesting new experiences by giving them emotional meaning. When an affective experience cannot be dreamed, as with the Wolf Man's primal-scene observation, that experience cannot be absorbed in order for emotional growth to proceed (Ogden, 2004a, 2004b).

The Wolf Man was unable to do unconscious mental work (dream) at age 1½ years to transform the primal scene into a meaningful psychological event – that is, convert it from an "undigested fact" (Bion, 1962a) into a memory (like Julie in Chapter 7). It was not until several years later, probably when the Wolf Man's ego had grown in strength, that he was able to dream (both in the Freudian and the Bionian sense) the earlier experience into meaningful psychological existence. Freud also included the importance of the Wolf Man's recent observation of copulating animals as the immediate "day residue" (Freud, 1900) that stimulated the dream. Thus, this initial stimulus instigated the dreaming process in which the day residue (observation of copulating animals) was given affective meaning through creation of the dream (the wolves on the tree), which both *retrospectively* reworked the earlier experience (primal scene) and was *anticipated* by it.

Returning to Alice's treatment, we can see how the dream at 3 or 4 years of age similarly *anticipates* the later play sequence, and, from another perspective, the play sequence *retrospectively* revises the earlier dream. Put another way, these are two dreams. The one dreamed repetitively at night is a nightmare "that need[s] the mind of another person . . . to help him [her] dream the yet to be dreamt aspect of his [her] nightmare" (Ogden, 2004b, p. 861). Alice's nightmare is a traumatic dream (Chapter 7) that has captured and represents some overpowering emotional event and perpetually repeats it, like playing a 78-rpm record from a former age that is stuck in a groove and does not move forward. This kind of dream does not assist the patient into coming alive emotionally: it tells us something about the nature of the trauma but is not "felt as life-promoting . . . [it is] as deficient in life-promoting qualities as a hallucinated breast is felt to be deficient in food" (Bion, 1992, p. 67). Nevertheless, her nightmare alerts us to the horrors that may befall a girl "when the parents aren't paying attention" and also anticipates the later play when she was with me "to help [her] dream the yet to be dreamt aspect of [her] nightmare."

Just as the cruel waiters and waitresses in Alice's dream took the children "when parents aren't paying attention," so in the play she had the parental figures asleep while the older sister brutalized the younger girl at night. This theme was replayed on a daily basis in her analysis for some months, what Bion (1965) calls a *rigid motion transformation*, which involves the wholesale transfer of an organized phantasy from the past onto the present. I often commented on how frightened the little girl must be of the older girl's cruelty and also about how blind the parents were, but Alice continued the play without change, which suggested that my interpretation had not tapped into that aspect of the trauma yet to be dreamed by us as we played together. This led to our discussing the motives for the older girl's sadism, and Alice volunteered that she must be jealous of the younger sister. We had many discussions of this, and one day, seemingly out of the blue, Alice put her finger to her chin and asked "Do you think Claudia could be jealous of me?" We explored this possibility, and she thought it probably true, although Alice denied that she herself possessed even a hint of jealous feelings.

The play began to lose its fixed quality as we talked together about the nature of jealousy. In one session, the older sister ate the small girl and exclaimed how delicious she was, and I wondered privately about the connection between consuming the little girl and jealousy. I suggested that the older one might be so jealous that she wanted to make the younger sister disappear, yet have the special qualities of the younger one inside of her for her very own. It was still a foreign idea that Claudia would have any reason to be jealous of Alice. Around this time I had a meeting with her parents and brought up the question of sibling jealousy, and the parents "remembered" something they had "forgotten" to tell me: at age 6 or 7 months Alice fell down the stairs, and they strongly suspected that Claudia had pushed her. She never accepted Alice's birth and had ridiculed her from the outset. It was remarkable to me that the parents spoke about Claudia's viciousness with an attitude of nonchalance, as though they were helpless to stop her cruelty. I began to understand how Alice's experience (created partly through projection) of Claudia's horrifying sadism was the undreamt mover that drove the relentless repetition of the nightmare, much as the Wolf Man witnessing the primal scene awaited his later dream to bring it to emotional life. The absent parents in the dream, as in reality, allowed the cruelty to continue unabated and also, on another level, represented her sense of missing an internalized *dreaming couple* (Grotstein, 2000) who could internally help Alice to "dream the undreamt dream" on her own. Alice and I were to become that couple as we imaginatively wove together our analytic narrative.

Indeed, it seemed to me that Alice was more at ease with being the victim of sadistic attacks than claiming ownership of her own hostile wishes. One day she brought a new toy dog to the session to show me, and it became part of the play. The younger sister asked parents to get her a guard dog to sleep with her at night in case the "mysterious" attackers attempted to intrude. When I suggested that the dog could protect her by biting the older girl, Alice said with some alarm, "Oh, he would never do anything like that, he's a good dog!" I said that even good dogs could have mad, biting feelings, and, after reflecting for a moment, she said "I guess he could, but *only* in pretend." I went on to say that sometimes a good dog could worry, like a good girl might, that he or she could become bad if he or she had strong angry feelings. She responded by telling me that her dog had pretty fur that was nice to feel, and I said that even though he had pretty fur on the outside he could worry that his angry feelings might make him ugly on the inside. Alice looked sad and glanced away from me, and I added that girls could feel that way too. She sighed and just somberly said, "Yeah, I guess so."

Alice's seemingly endless waking dream in the playroom was now gone, though her repetitive nightmare while asleep continued but with much less frequency. Her depression had lifted, and her parents felt pleased with the return of their formerly happy daughter. However, her mother remained very concerned that Alice's obesity – another reason for the initial referral – had not yet been helped by the analysis. While conflicts around hunger, greed, and envy had been addressed in the play, it seemed that the continuation of her nightmare signaled that additional powerful affects remained unprocessed. In the sessions, Alice became very demanding and insisted that I give her one of the new puppets I brought back from vacation – in, ironically, given her eating conflicts, Hungary. It was a hand puppet of three puppies in a basket, and she said they had been left by their mother to be tended by a nice man who fed them and taught them how to read and write, and instructed the mother in how to help the puppies feel loved. Thinking of my recent vacation, I addressed the puppies' worries that their mother would not return and they would starve, and how lucky they were that this man could help them when their mother did not know how to provide. Alice listened intently and noted a couple of sessions later, when I opened a window, that "your reflection looked like my mother's complexion," adding that my complexion looked sad because it was shadowed in the window.

In thinking about Alice's perception that I appeared sad like her mother, I recalled a piece of mother's history that she related in our first meeting. Her mother had an adopted sister, with whom she felt very close, who was also obese and who ran away as an adolescent, disappearing from her mother's life for many years. This depressed her as a child; thus, she felt her daughter Alice to be her "soul mate" because of Alice's depression. I suspect that Alice was also a surrogate for the mother's unhappy, obese sister and that, on some level, Alice understood the important role she was to play for her mother: that she was to be the overweight child who could be lost and is the source of mother's sadness as well as the cure for that very same melancholy. In this regard, there was what Faimberg (2005) calls the "telescoping of generations," in which the generational firewall that should separate Alice from her mother's troubled sister had dissolved. Put another way, Alice was lending her mind to her mother in order to "help her [mother] dream the yet to be dreamt aspect of her [mother's] nightmare" (Ogden, 2004b, p. 861). In our play, Alice and I became the *dreaming couple* who could teach her mother how to nurture children by repairing the maternal sad complexion and simultaneously heal Alice's funk while, in unconscious phantasy, restoring mother's distraught sister to health.

This *telescoping of generations* became evident in Alice's play narrative of the saga of Harry and Henrietta who meet and fall in love. I was assigned the role of Harry and she was Henrietta, and we discovered that we were twins, now 25 years old, who were separated when we were 10 because of our parents' death. She decided we would marry in order to stay together forever and suggested we get married by the same rabbi who joined our parents in matrimony. However, Alice thought he might get confused because we looked identical to our parents when they were our age. Alice announced that Henrietta had gotten pregnant the day before and would give birth tomorrow at the wedding. Indeed, at the wedding Henrietta gave birth to twins, a boy and a girl, who looked exactly like the same-sexed parent, and Alice added that it was miraculous because we were all born on the same day! I said that would make all of us *very, very* close; whereupon our parents, whom we thought dead, reappeared and we were all reunited.

This play interlaces several important storylines – including denial of loss and separation, Oedipal transference themes, phantasies about birth, etc. – but I want to focus on the negation of intergenerational boundaries. Harry and Henrietta are destined to become identical to their parents: first, by getting married by the same rabbi, and then by confusing him because their appearances exactly match their mother's and father's. Henrietta next gives birth to a twin boy and girl who are replicas of them; thus, the difference between the three generations is eradicated and, moreover, all share the same birthday. I believe this chronicle of Harry and Henrietta also expressed part of

Alice's dilemma that she and I dramatically conjured up together: that, among various themes, her fate incontestably was anchored in her mother's history. Furthermore, this collapse of the generations denotes "In psychic reality a frozen mental state [that] is a 'real' stoppage of time" (Birksted-Breen, 2009, p. 36) that folds together the past, the present, and the future and is simultaneously a denial of the Oedipal implications of generational differences.

How are we to understand this "telescoping of generations?" Faimberg clearly explains the phenomenon in terms of identifications that form between the patient and aspects of the parents and/or with figures from the parents' internal or external object relationships. In my view, there are several kinds of identifications that are a common pathway leading to the telescoping of generations. One is the result of a *forceful projective identification* (Bion, 1959) that effectively press-gangs the receiver into becoming the figure with whom he or she is identified. Alice's mother all but guaranteed that her daughter would become the obese sister of mother's childhood by micromanaging her food intake and by experiencing Alice's depression as an adhesive that glued them together as "soul mates." In such situations, the child's destiny is a rendezvous with a fate that actually belongs to someone else or a "memoir of the future" (Bion, 1991b). The child is thus burdened with having to do the unconscious work the parent was unable to achieve in order to dream/transform the unprocessed painful affects that belong to another era.

A second kind of identification leading to the telescoping of generations results from a process of *communicative projective identification*, in which the parents' unrealized hopes and wishes are expressed as preferences for the child's future, though not as marching orders. For example, a male patient's father had to drop out of medical school because of financial constraints, and the patient himself would have loved to become a physician but could not owing to a physical limitation. He encouraged his children to attend medical school, which they willingly did, and thus they realized ambitions that were clearly theirs as well as fulfilling an aspiration that had remained thwarted for two generations. The unrealized generational hope is experienced as a prompt that ideally meshes with the child's conscious and unconscious intentions for his future, and the child does not feel coerced into becoming a petri dish in which someone else's frustrated visions may be nurtured.

A third kind of identification underlying the telescoping of

226

generations could be termed an *altruistic identification*, which is initiated by a compassionate concern for the individual with whom one is identifying. A young woman in psychotherapy, whose maternal and paternal grandparents are all Holocaust survivors, expressed a high degree of ambivalence about her employment as a childcare worker at an inpatient facility. On the one hand, she thoroughly enjoyed this difficult work and the chance to help the troubled children. In fact, she also noted that she typically is very helpful to others, frequently going overboard to offer a favor to friends and acquaintances. On the other hand, my patient also complained that this behavior is compulsive, that she rarely feels satisfied with her efforts and constantly apologizes for her alleged failure to do enough. In psychotherapy, she expressed a deep love and empathy for her grandparents' suffering during the Holocaust and said, "I wish I could've been there to help them, to take on some of their load, like that song 'He Ain't Heavy, He's My Brother.'" Thus, she willingly and unconsciously identified with their painful burden *altruistically*[1] in order to lighten their misery, as though their future well-being rested partly in her hands.

In Alice's case, the telescoping of generations, so clearly in evidence in the Harry and Henrietta play, was largely a product of *forceful projective identifications* of her mother's untransformed losses and difficulties with eating. For her, eating was "only business": rather than sharing the pleasure of food, she micromanaged her daughter's caloric intake and ensured that Alice would become the split-off hungry self that mother could never integrate. Consequently, Alice's obesity became a "suitable target for externalization" (Volkan, 1976) of her mother's unresolved grief over her own overweight sister, an identification that was foisted upon her. From another vertex, Alice may have also *altruistically identified* with her mother's sister in order unconsciously to try to repair and shoulder some of mother's sadness. She was genuinely moved by seeing my "sad complexion" reflected in the window, which reminded Alice of her mother, and I suspect that one (unconscious) motive for identifying with her mother's lost sister was to ease her mother's burden and transform that sadness. However, she was unable to dream on her own the unprocessed affects that she was recruited across generational lines to carry for her mother, and she was caught, like Harry and Henrietta, in a past that was indistinguishable from a future yet to come. Unlike Harry and Henrietta, in our analytic work Alice and I were a collaborative couple who could re-imagine a future that was truly hers, and it was this creative couple that she internalized to enable her α function to dream her own distinct destiny.

★ ★ ★

The evolution of an intersubjective approach to analytic understanding and technique is also associated with an increased emphasis on the importance of the here-and-now. The prominence accorded to the "present moment" (Stern, 2004) stretches across most contemporary analytic schools, from ego psychology (Busch, 1999; Gray, 1994), to American relational (Greenberg & Mitchell, 2000; Stern et al., 1998), Kleinian (Spillius, 1989), and perhaps reaching its apogee in the contributions of Bion (1967; Ferro 2002, 2005; Grotstein, 2007). However, such innovations, while enhancing the liveliness of the clinical encounter, have sometimes come at the expense of an appreciation of the panoramic historical development of a patient's difficulties. Thus, concepts such as an *infantile neurosis* have tended to be neglected or, worse yet, put out to pasture like the old Stalinist relics that emerged in my reverie during Sally's (Chapter 4) analysis. But do we act too quickly to discard what we deem an outmoded idea and, in so doing, lose sight of how our theories evolve, forgetting the genealogy of our thinking as analysts? In my view, we should approach the evolution of psychoanalytic theory as we would a dream's narrative: just as Alice's experiences with her sister's cruelty created a kernel of affect that required a dream's elaboration, so each analytic concept can be viewed like a day residue that stimulates further theoretical growth and expansion. And just as her mother's cross-generational projections confused Alice as to whose fate she was realizing, so the epigenetic unfolding of psychoanalytic ideas may lead to the question, "Whose idea was it?" (Ogden, 2003a).

Let us reconsider the notion of the *infantile neurosis* in light of the current stress upon the *present moment*. Anna Freud (1970) comments that there is

> a multiple view of the infantile neurosis . . . we regard it as . . .
> psychopathology and realize that in its extensive form it can
> be severe and crippling. . . . Seen from the developmental point
> of view, the infantile neurosis can represent a positive sign of per-
> sonality growth; a progression from primitive to more sophisticated
> reaction patterns . . .
>
> (p. 202)

I suggest that the more "extensive form" of the infantile neurosis may be seen as a psychological structure – akin to pathological (Rosenfeld, 1987; Steiner, 1993) or traumatic (Chapter 7) organizations, a rigid motion transformation in Bion's (1965) terms – that is fixed and beyond the capacity of the individual's mind to dream. It brings structure to a fragile psyche that would otherwise face a greater mental catastrophe (Bion, 1970; Winnicott, 1974), but at the cost of stunted growth. It is a nightmare that cannot be properly dreamed in order for development to proceed, but can only be repeated through enacted repetitions and/or traumatic dreams such as Alice encountered. The present moment as an opportunity to evolve out of this paralyzing chrysalis does not exist, and past, present, and the future are painfully equivalent.

However, as Anna Freud states, the infantile neurosis may also promote growth under more favorable conditions so that more "sophisticated reaction patterns" emerge. A growth-promoting infantile neurosis, it would seem, is one characterized by flexibility and serves a stabilizing function in development by organizing into a narrative the ongoing anxieties and conflicts to foster incremental growth unhampered by the dangers of catastrophic change (Bion, 1970). In this situation, the *present moment* is the crucible in which the past is retrospectively reworked through and the future is re-anticipated as linked, but not chained, to the past. This kind of growth-enhancing present moment depends on the capacity for the kind of life-promoting dream that Bion has described, which, even though it occurs intrapsychically, is an intersubjective event based upon the dreamer's access to the internalized dreaming couple. And when access is impossible, as in Alice's case, the patient needs to join with the analyst's capacity to dream in order for this analytic pair to become a dreaming couple suitable for the patient to assimilate internally. The person is thus equipped to "dream himself into existence" (Ogden, 2003b) from moment to moment, especially at times when confronted with painful experiences emanating from within the self, from others through projective identification, or from previous generations.

*   ★   *

Eight years after Alice's child analysis ended successfully I received a voicemail from her asking to speak. She was now a freshman at a prestigious university, was having some difficulty with depression, and

229

found herself wondering lately whether she had been sexually abused as a child. Alice did not have any specific memories of abuse, but she had a "sense" that something may have happened and wanted to know if I could shed any light on her suspicion. I said that the question of sexual abuse never arose during the course of her analysis, but I added that a central part of our work together had to do with working through Claudia's cruel treatment of her. I said that it might be possible that she was reinterpreting these earlier experiences through the lens of sexuality, and I offered to review my notes for a follow-up conversation. She was eager to arrange another telephone appointment.

When we spoke a few weeks later, I asked her more about what she had been thinking regarding this possible sexual abuse. She said that she noticed in 7th grade that she became afraid of boys and that she had "created a false memory" about some abuse from a boy in summer camp. She didn't elaborate on this "false memory" but said that her current therapist thinks it was something she might have constructed as she entered adolescence and her sexual feelings matured, that this comes from her history of violating experiences with her sister, feeling unprotected by her parents, and having been bullied at her school. In addition, she recently lost a lot of weight which freed her to accept a date with a boy in which there was an (unspecified) "interaction," and since then she has been having scary dreams of sexual assault. However, she still has a feeling that something sexual happened when she was a smaller child. I asked if she could tell me, and she felt that there might have been some inappropriate touching, though was unsure by whom.

I said that I had reviewed my notes and could offer her some thoughts about this question from the perspective of what she played out in treatment. I described the intensity of the attacks on her play character by the older sister, the mutilations, etc. She only vaguely remembered this play but was very interested. Then I mentioned that prior to this play she told me a dream in confidence, and she quickly said she remembered the dream and still has it from time to time. I was curious about whether it had changed from what she told me years ago; I asked if she would like me to read the childhood version of it, and she wanted to hear it. She said that she remembers the dream pretty much as I recounted, but with a couple of details differently. The current dream had changed the scanner into an electronic scale and, instead of a stove, the children were placed in a laundry washing machine and she could see them/her tumbling around in it. In addition, the parents ate the children, and, finally, it was she who was going up the steps and was wearing her mother's skirt.

As we continued to talk, she picked up on my mentioning the failure of the school administration to protect the little girl (and its connection to her feeling neglected by her parents in the play as well as in the dream), and she grew a bit accusatory of me. In a challenging tone she asked, "Didn't you talk to my parents about that?" I said that I met regularly with them and did bring up her feeling of not being adequately protected. I felt on the defensive, and she asked if I had spoken with them about her feeling bullied at school. I said I didn't recall if I had or not, but that I do remember meeting with people at her school about this issue. I said that I could see the feelings of being neglected were still with her, and she agreed. In closing, Alice asked whether the dream might have additionally been stimulated by an actual experience of sexual abuse, and I said we could not rule out that possibility and she should continue to explore it in psychotherapy.

Reflecting on the conversation with Alice, I began to question my confidence in asserting that I did not think there had been any sexual abuse in her history. I had this case "figured out": her symptoms of depression and obesity could be explained by the painful, unmentalized experiences of Claudia's cruelty, feeling unprotected by her parents, struggling under the burden of her mother's projections, and unconsciously offering herself through an altruistic identification to transform mother's sadness. Her repetitive nightmares and long play sequence of being sadistically victimized were evidence of Alice's inability to dream, whether awake or asleep, the powerful affects associated with these events and also signaled her need for an analyst who could lend his capacity to dream. But the nightmare had returned, albeit in a slightly revised version, and Alice's feeling of being unprotected quickly surfaced in relation to me.

These reflections led me to consider whether my allegiance to this very satisfying "explanation" for Alice's difficulties was, in fact, a resistance against allowing new information, and perhaps new understanding, to upend my elaborate theory. To hold too firmly to one's speculative narrative is to run the risk of that theory becoming petrified, not unlike the "extensive form" of the infantile neurosis (A. Freud, 1970) that is impervious to change. Instead, one's understanding should always remain fluid, adapting to new developments, like a temporary bridge laid down to reach a river's opposite bank, but quickly reconfigured when facing the next river with its unique currents and terrain. I felt reluctant not to stay the course with my familiar assumptions and also enjoined by Alice's feeling of being unshielded by me to want to buffer her against yet another trauma in her life – thus my reluctance to consider the possible sexual abuse.

My initial conclusion, which agreed with her present therapist's impression, was that Alice's suspicion of sexual abuse was a fantasy that combined adolescent sexual experience reworked under the aegis of the childhood trauma of physical abuse from her sister. Her "sense" that there may have been abuse was a conjecture that had not yet become a conviction, and so our discussion occurred at a particular moment in which the birth of an idea was in process that, if accepted as "truth,"[2] would bring a particular coloration to her future. Alice was again feeling menaced and unprotected by an act of aggression that had reawakened an old nightmare, and now the former ghosts threatened to join forces with current demons to conjure up a new enemy. There was a window of opportunity, which seemed to be slowly closing in the direction of a narrative that she had been sexually abused, in which I might intervene in order to help Alice tolerate the ambiguity necessary to keep her mind open to a future of other possibilities. I felt like I was feverishly stacking bags of sand against an impending flood, a feeling that, in hindsight, must have captured her anxiety as well as reflected my answering the call of her transference wish for protection. However, realizing she was no longer my patient, the best I could offer was to encourage Alice to continue to deal with her therapist and be open to various understandings of her sense of abuse.

I also wondered whether the subtle changes in Alice's ancient nightmare might offer clues as to the possible existence of a trauma that had not come under our purview during the analysis. There were four changes: the supermarket scanner had been changed to an electronic scale; the stove to a laundry washing machine; the parents ate the children; and Alice wore her mother's skirt when she went up the stairs. I thought the scale must be an allusion to her having told me she recently lost a substantial amount of weight, which preceded the recurrence of bad dreams following a date with a young man with whom she had an unnamed "interaction." Rather than being placed on a stove to be cooked she is put in a washing machine, which may express a sense of being dirtied, perhaps by the frightful encounter with her date. Is the dream image of being eaten by her parents a representation of the internalized "combined parental couple" (Klein, 1932, 1945) that commands a harsh superego? If so, then wearing her mother's dress, and the symbolic sexual meaning of going upstairs (Freud, 1900), may reflect her unconscious sense of having trespassed onto territory she is forbidden to enter (the Oedipal realm that was denied in the Harry and Henrietta play). However, my speculations, all of which center on the possible meanings of elements of the dream in the light of a likely sexual encounter, bring us no closer to the question of whether there is any evidence of sexual abuse in childhood.

Alice contacted me at a moment in time that her psyche was, I believe, engaged in unconscious work to bring emotional meaning to her current anxiety by re-narrating her history and, therefore, resetting her course for a new future. She sought me out to see if I possessed some hidden truth about what had happened to her, an essential traumatic truth that had remained an invariant in her psychic life and was now being recycled anew. In discussing the question of whether development transforms supposed invariants, Salomonnson (2007) argues that we can never be sure whether such events actually occurred; however, he states that "What is transformed in the clinical situation is not an invariant infantile essence, but signs denoting the patient's inner reality . . . [and that] we [should] look at transformation as a perpetual semiotic conversion process" (p. 1202). I would say that this "perpetual process" is the ceaseless operation of *après coup*, which is constantly reinterpreting and restructuring the past in the light of the present and which depends on the capacity for dreaming while awake and asleep. These processes help to push development forward, a point emphasized by Birksted-Breen (2003):

> retroactive resignification *is* developmental progression. For there to be progression there also has to be this kind of retroactive resignification. The forward movement necessitates a backward movement at the same time and, equally, the continued incorporation and restructuring of the past in the backward movement necessitates the ability to move forward.
>
> (p. 1509, italics in original)

It is here that our humility must guide us to recall Freud's (1900) statement (cited in Chapter 9):

There is often a passage in the most thoroughly interpreted dream which has to be left obscure. . . . This is the dream's navel, the spot where it reached down into the unknown.

(p. 525)

Probably the more relevant question is not whether there was an actual event of abuse, which may likely remain unknown, but what meaning a given analyst and patient couple thinking together "in the presence of the other" (Schafer, 2000) will construe of the evolving unknown (Bion's "O") emerging before them. If there is a truth to be ascertained, it can only be known through its shadow; however, that which casts the shadow is gradually approximated by an analytic pair dreaming together, slowly imagining a truth that seems to capture an unfolding moment. It is in that moment, when two minds are communicating with each other on multiple channels, most of which are unconscious, that an impression of the truth, anchored in that particular moment, is born. This new arrival, bearing the lineage of both its parents, in the best of circumstances continuously evolves into something unexpected, and it is that surprise that enriches and sustains the couple and gives them the courage to move forward into an unknown future.

Notes

1   What I am calling an *altruistic identification* differs from Anna Freud's (1936) concept of *altruistic surrender*; the latter implies an unconscious denial of a vital component of the self, such as sexuality, and projecting it into another, thereby diminishing the self that desires what appears out of reach. An altruistic identification, in contrast, is born of concern for the other and an identification with their pain in order to ease their burden, but the self is not reduced.
2   In this case, the "truth" would have been a foreclosure of openness to other possible meanings of Alice's experiences. Britton & Steiner (1994) write about the defensive use of interpretation as an "overvalued idea" rather than as offering a "selected fact" that truly brings emotional coherence.

References

Abraham, K. (1916). The first pregenital stage of the libido. In *Selected Papers on Psycho-Analysis*. New York: Brunner/Mazel, pp. 248–279.

Abraham, K. (1924). A short study of the development of the libido, viewed in the light of mental disorders. In *Selected Papers on Psycho-Analysis*. New York: Brunner/Mazel, pp. 418–501.

Aguayo, J. (1997). Historicising the origins of Kleinian psychoanalysis: Klein's analytic and patronal relationships with Ferenczi, Abraham and Jones, 1914–1927. *International Journal of Psychoanalysis*, 78: 1165–1182.

Anzieu, D. (1993). The film of the dream. In: S. Flanders (Ed.), *The Dream Discourse Today*. London: Routledge, pp. 137–150.

Arlow, J. (1969a). Fantasy, memory, and reality testing. *Psychoanalytic Quarterly*, 38: 28–51.

Arlow, J. (1969b). Unconscious fantasy and disturbances of conscious experience. *Psychoanalytic Quarterly*, 38: 1–27.

Aron, L. (1995). The internalized primal scene. *Psychoanalytic Dialogues*, 5: 195–237.

Aron, L. (2006). Analytic impasse and the third. *International Journal of Psychoanalysis*, 87: 349–368.

Aron, L., & Benjamin, J. (1999). "The Development of Intersubjectivity and the Struggle to Think." Paper presented at the Spring Meeting, Division of Psychoanalysis (39), American Psychological Association, New York City, 17 April.

Auerhahn, N., & Laub, D. (1984). Annihilation and restoration: Post-traumatic memory as pathway and obstacle to recovery. *International Review of Psychoanalysis*, 11: 327–344.

Balint, M. (1969). Trauma and object relationship. *International Journal of Psychoanalysis*, 50: 429–435.

Balter, L., Lothane, Z., & Spencer, J. (1980). On the analyzing instrument. *Psychoanalytic Quarterly*, 49: 474–504.

235

Baranger, M. (2005). Field theory. In S. Lewkowicz & S. Flechner (Eds.), *Truth, Reality, and the Psychoanalyst: Latin American Contributions to Psychoanalysis*. London: International Psychoanalytical Association.

Baranger, M., & Baranger, W. (1961–62). The analytic situation as a dynamic field. *International Journal of Psychoanalysis*, 89 (2008, No. 4): 795–826.

Baranger, M., Baranger, W., & Mom, J. (1983). Process and non-process in analytic work. *International Journal of Psychoanalysis*, 64: 1–15. Also in M. Baranger & W. Baranger, *The Work of Confluence*, ed. L. Glocer Fiorini. London: Karnac, 2009, pp. 63–88.

Baranger, M., Baranger, W., & Mom, J. (1988). The infantile psychic trauma from us to Freud: Pure trauma, retroactivity and reconstruction. *International Journal of Psychoanalysis*, 69: 113–128.

Baranger, W. (1979). "Proceso en espiral" y "campo dinamico." *Revista Uruguaya de Psicoanálisis*, 59: 17–32. English translation, "Spiral Process and the Dynamic Field", in M. Baranger & W. Baranger, *The Work of Confluence*, ed. L. Glocer Fiorini. London: Karnac, 2009, pp. 45–61.

Bass, A. (2000). *Difference and Disavowal: The Trauma of Eros*. Stanford, CA: Stanford University Press.

Beebe, B., Knoblauch, S., Rustin, J., & Sorter, D. (2004). *Forms of Intersubjectivity in Infant Research and Adult Treatment*. New York: Other Press.

Benjamin, J. (2002). The rhythm of recognition: Comments on the work of Louis Sander. *Psychoanalytic Dialogues*, 12: 43–53.

Benjamin, J. (2004). Beyond doer and done to: An intersubjective view of thirdness. *Psychoanalytic Quarterly*, 73: 5–46.

Benjamin, J. (2007). "Our Appointment in Thebes: On the Analyst's Fear of Doing Harm." Paper given at the Massachusetts Institute for Psychoanalysis, 27 January.

Benjamin, J. (2009). A relational psychoanalysis perspective on the necessity of acknowledging failure in order to restore the facilitating and containing features of the intersubjective relationship (the shared third). *International Journal of Psychoanalysis*, 90: 441–450.

Berman, E. (2000). Psychoanalytic supervision: The intersubjective development. *International Journal of Psychoanalysis*, 81: 273–290.

Berman, E. (2004). *Impossible Training: A Relational View of Psychoanalytic Education*. Hillsdale, NJ: Analytic Press.

Bernardi, R. (2008). Letter from Uruguay. *International Journal of Psychoanalysis*, 89: 233–240.

Bezoari, M., & Ferro, A. (1992). The oscillation meanings ↔ affects in the analytic couple at work. *Rivista di Psicoanalisi*, 38: 380–402.

Bick, E. (1968). The experience of skin in early object-relations. *International Journal of Psychoanalysis*, 49: 484–486.

Bick, E. (1986). Further considerations on the function of the skin in early object relations. *British Journal of Psychotherapy*, 2: 292–299.

Bion, W. (1952). Group dynamics: A re-view. *International Journal of Psycho-analysis*, 33: 235–247.

Bion, W. (1954). Notes on the theory of schizophrenia. *International Journal of Psychoanalysis*, 35: 113–118. Also in *Second Thoughts*. New York: Jason Aronson, 1967, pp. 23–35.

Bion, W. (1957). Differentiation of the psychotic from the non-psychotic personalities. *International Journal of Psychoanalysis*, 38: 266–275. Also in *Second Thoughts*. New York: Jason Aronson, 1967, pp. 43–63.

Bion, W. (1958). On arrogance. *International Journal of Psychoanalysis*, 39: 144–146. Also in *Second Thoughts*. New York: Jason Aronson, 1967, pp. 86–92.

Bion, W. (1959). Attacks on linking. *International Journal of Psychoanalysis*, 40: 308–315. Also in *Second Thoughts*. New York: Jason Aronson, 1967, pp. 93–109.

Bion, W. (1961). *Experiences in Groups*. London: Routledge.

Bion, W. (1962a). *Learning from Experience*. London: Heinemann.

Bion, W. (1962b). A theory of thinking. *International Journal of Psychoanalysis,* 43: 306–310. Also in *Second Thoughts*. New York: Jason Aronson, 1967, pp. 110–119.

Bion, W. (1963). *Elements of Psycho-Analysis*. London: Heinemann.

Bion, W. (1965). *Transformations*. London: Heinemann.

Bion, W. (1967). Notes on memory and desire. In *Cogitations*. London: Karnac, 1992 (extended version 1994).

Bion, W. (1970). *Attention and Interpretation*. London: Heinemann.

Bion, W. (1977a). Caesura. In *Two Papers: The Grid and Caesura*. London: Karnac, 1989, pp. 35–56.

Bion, W. (1977b). The grid. In *Two Papers: The Grid and Caesura*. London: Karnac, 1989, pp. 1–33.

Bion, W. (1991a). *The Long Week-End*. London: Karnac.

Bion, W. (1991b). *A Memoir of the Future: Books 1–3*. London: Karnac.

Bion, W. (1992). *Cogitations* (extended version). London: Karnac, 1994.

Bion, W. (1994). *Clinical Seminars and Other Works*. London: Karnac.

Bion, W. (1997). *Taming Wild Thoughts*. London: Karnac.

Bion, W. (2005). *The Tavistock Seminars*. London: Karnac.

Bion, W., & Rickman, J. (1943). Intra-group tensions in therapy. *Lancet*, 2: 678–681. Also in W. Bion, *Experiences in Groups*. London: Routledge, 1961, pp. 11–26.

Birksted-Breen, D. (2003). Time and the *après-coup*. *International Journal of Psychoanalysis*, 84: 1501–1515.

Birksted-Breen, D. (2009). "Reverberation time", dreaming and the capacity to dream. *International Journal of Psychoanalysis*, 90: 35–51.

Blum, H. P. (1980). The value of reconstruction in adult psychoanalysis. *International Journal of Psychoanalysis*, 61: 39–52.

Boesky, D. (1990). The psychoanalytic process and its components. *Psychoanalytic Quarterly*, 59: 550–584.

Botella, C., & Botella, S. (2005). *The Work of Psychic Figurability: Mental States without Representation.* New York: Brunner-Routledge.

Brenman Pick, I. B. (1985). Working through in the countertransference. *International Journal of Psychoanalysis*, 66: 157–166.

Brickman, H. (1993). "Between the Devil and the deep blue sea": The dyad and the triad in psychoanalytic thought. *International Journal of Psychoanalysis*, 74: 905–915.

Britton, R. (1989). The missing link: Parental sexuality in the Oedipus complex. In R. Britton, M. Feldman, & E. O'Shaughnessy (Eds.), *The Oedipus Complex Today.* London: Karnac, pp. 83–101.

Britton, R. (1992). The Oedipus situation and the depressive position. In R. Anderson (Ed.), *Clinical Lectures on Klein and Bion.* New York: Routledge.

Britton, R. (1998). *Belief and Imagination: Explorations in Psychoanalysis.* London: Routledge.

Britton, R. (2003). *Sex, Death and the Superego: Experiences in Psychoanalysis.* London: Karnac.

Britton, R. (2004). Subjectivity, objectivity and triangular space. *Psychoanalytic Quarterly*, 73: 47–62.

Britton, R., & Steiner, J. (1994). Interpretation: Selected fact or overvalued idea? *International Journal of Psychoanalysis*, 75: 1069–1078.

Brown, L. J. (1985). On concreteness. *Psychoanalytic Review*, 72: 379–402.

Brown, L. J. (1996). A proposed demography of the representational world. *Melanie Klein & Object Relations*, 14: 21–60.

Brown, L. J. (2002). The early Oedipal situation: Developmental, theoretical and clinical implications. *Psychoanalytic Quarterly*, 71: 273–300.

Brown, L. J. (2004). The point of interaction, mutuality and an aspect of the analyst's Oedipal conflict. *Scandinavian Review of Psychoanalysis*, 27: 34–42.

Brown, L. J. (2005). The cognitive effects of trauma: Reversal of alpha function and the formation of a beta screen. *Psychoanalytic Quarterly*, 74: 397–420.

Brown, L. J. (2006). Julie's museum: The evolution of thinking, dreaming and historicization in the treatment of traumatized patients. *International Journal of Psychoanalysis*, 87: 1569–1585.

Brown, L. J. (2007). On dreaming one's patient: Reflections on an aspect of countertransference dreams. *Psychoanalytic Quarterly*, 76: 835–861.

Brown, L. J. (2008). "Catastrophic Change and Trauma: Damage to the Internalized 'Thinking Couple.'" Paper given at the Bion Rome Conference, January.

Brown, L. J. (2009a). The ego psychology of Wilfred Bion: Implications for an intersubjective view of psychic structure. *Psychoanalytic Quarterly*, 78: 27–55.

Brown, L. J. (2009b). "Discussion of 'The Use of the Alpha Function in Analytical Construction' by Marina Parisi and Lucilla Ruberti." Paper given at the International Psychoanalytical Association Congress, Chicago.

Brown, L. J., & Miller, M. (2002). The triadic intersubjective matrix in supervision: The use of disclosure to work through painful affects. *International Journal of Psychoanalysis*, 83: 811–823.

Busch, F. (1995). *The Ego at the Center of Clinical Technique*. Northvale, NJ: Jason Aronson.

Busch, F. (1999). *Rethinking Clinical Technique*. Northvale, NJ: Jason Aronson.

Busch, F. (2006a). A shadow concept. *International Journal of Psychoanalysis*, 87: 1471–1485.

Busch, F. (2006b). Countertransference in defense enactments. *Journal of the American Psychoanalytic Association*, 54: 67–85.

Caper, R. (1996). Play, experimentation and creativity. *International Journal of Psychoanalysis*, 77: 859–870.

Caper, R. (1997). A mind of one's own. *International Journal of Psychoanalysis*, 78: 265–278.

Caper, R. (2000). *Immaterial Facts*. New York: Jason Aronson.

Carpy, D. V. (1989). Tolerating the countertransference: A mutative process. *International Journal of Psychoanalysis*, 70: 287–294.

Casement, P. (1991). The internal supervisor. In *Learning from the Patient*. New York: Guilford Press, pp. 29–51.

Cassorla, R. (2005). From bastion to enactment: The "non-dream" in the theater of analysis. *International Journal of Psychoanalysis*, 86: 699–719.

Cassorla, R. (2009). "Reflections on Non-Dreams-for-Two, Enactment and the Analyst's Implicit Alpha Function." Paper presented at the Bion in Boston conference, July.

Chodorow, N. (2004). The American independent tradition: Loewald, Erikson, and the (possible) rise of intersubjective ego psychology. *Psychoanalytic Dialogues*, 14: 207–232.

Churcher, J. (2008). Some notes on the English translation of "The Analytic Situation as a Dynamic Field." *International Journal of Psychoanalysis*, 89: 785–793.

Coburn, W. (1997). The vision in supervision: Transference-countertransference dynamics and disclosure in the supervision relationship. *Bulletin of the Menninger Clinic*, 61: 481–494.

Corrao, F. (1987). Il narrative come categoria psicoanalitica. *Orme I*. Milan: Cortina, 1998.

Davoine, F., & Gaudilliere, J.-M., (2004). *History Beyond Trauma*. New York: Other Press.

de León de Bernardi, B. (2000). The countertransference: A Latin American view. *International Journal of Psychoanalysis*, 81: 331–351.

de León de Bernardi, B. (2008). Introduction to the paper by Madeleine and Willy Baranger: "The Analytic Situation as a Dynamic Field." *International Journal of Psychoanalysis*, 89: 773–784.

Doehrman, M. J. G. (1976). Parallel processes in supervision and psychotherapy. *Bulletin of the Menninger Clinic*, 40: 9–104.

Ellman, S. (1998). Enactment, transference, and analytic trust. In S. Ellman & M. Moskowitz (Eds.), *Enactment: Toward a New Approach to the Therapeutic Relationship*. Northvale, NJ: Jason Aronson, pp. 183–203.

Erikson, E. (1954). The dream specimen in psychoanalysis. *Journal of the American Psychoanalytic Association*, 2: 5–56.

Etchegoyen, R. H. (1993). Angel Garma (1904–1993). *International Journal of Psychoanalysis*, 74: 829–834.

Etchegoyen, R. H. (2005). Melanie Klein in Buenos Aires: Beginnings and developments. *International Journal of Psychoanalysis*, 86: 869–894.

Eugenides, J. (2002). *Middlesex: A Novel*. New York: Picador.

Faimberg, H. (2005). *The Telescoping of Generations*. London: Routledge.

Faimberg, H. (2007). A plea for a broader concept of Nachträglichkeit. *Psychoanalytic Quarterly*, 76: 1221–1240.

Favero, M., & Ross, D. (2002). Complementary dreams: A window to the subconscious processes of countertransference and subjectivity. *American Journal of Psychotherapy*, 56: 211–224.

Federn, P. (1926). Some variations in ego-feeling. *International Journal of Psychoanalysis*, 7: 434–444.

Federn, P. (1932). Ego feeling in dreams. *Psychoanalytic Quarterly*, 1: 511–542.

Feldman, M. (1993). The dynamics of reassurance. *International Journal of Psychoanalysis*, 74: 275–285.

Feldman, M. (1997). Projective identification: The analyst's involvement. *International Journal of Psychoanalysis*, 78: 227–241.

Ferenczi, S. (1909). Introjection and transference. In *First Contributions to Psycho-Analysis*. London: Hogarth Press, 1952, pp. 35–93.

Ferenczi, S. (1911). Letter from Sandor Ferenczi to Sigmund Freud, 7 February 1911. In *The Correspondence of Sigmund Freud and Sandor Ferenczi, Volume I: 1908–1914*. Cambridge, MA: Harvard University Press, 1993, p. 253.

Ferenczi, S. (1913). Stages in the development of the sense of reality. In *First Contributions to Psycho-Analysis*. London: Hogarth Press, 1952, pp. 213–239.

Ferenczi, S. (1931). Child analysis in the analysis of adults. In *Final Contributions to the Problems and Methods of Psycho-Analysis*. New York: Brunner/Mazel, 1980, pp. 126–142.

Ferenczi, S. (1952). *Final Contributions to Psycho-Analysis*. New York: Brunner/Mazel, 1980.

Ferro, A. (1992). Two authors in search of characters: The relationship, the field, the story. *Rivista di Psicoanalisi*, 38: 44–90.

Ferro, A. (1993). The impasse within a theory of the analytic field: Possible vertices of observation. *International Journal of Psychoanalysis*, 74: 917–929.

Ferro, A. (2002). *In the Analyst's Consulting Room*. New York: Brunner-Routledge.

Ferro, A. (2005). *Seeds of Illness, Seeds of Recovery*. New York: Brunner-Routledge.

Ferro, A. (2009). *Mind Works: Technique and Creativity in Psychoanalysis*. New York: Routledge.

Fivaz-Depeursinge, E., & Corboz-Warnery, A. (1999). *The Primary Triangle*. New York: Basic Books.

Fleming, J., & Benedek, T. (1966). *Psychoanalytic Supervision*. New York: Grune & Stratton.

Fliess, R. (1942). The metapsychology of the analyst. *Psychoanalytic Quarterly*, 11: 211–227. Reprinted in *Psychoanalytic Quarterly*, 762 (2007): 679–695.

Fonagy, P. (2005). An overview of Joseph Sandler's key contributions to theoretical and clinical psychoanalysis. *Psychoanalytic Inquiry*, 25: 120–147.

Fonagy, P., & Target, M. (2007). Playing with reality: IV. A theory of external reality rooted in intersubjectivity. *International Journal of Psychoanalysis*, 88: 917–937.

Frank, C., & Weiss, H. (1996). The origins of disquieting discoveries by Melanie Klein: The possible significance of the case of "Erna." *International Journal of Psychoanalysis*, 77: 1101–1126.

Freud, A. (1936). *Ego Psychology and the Mechanisms of Defense*. New York: International Universities Press.

Freud, A. (1970). The infantile neurosis: Genetic and dynamic considerations. *The Writings of Anna Freud, Vol. VII*. New York: International Universities Press, pp. 189–203.

Freud, S. (1891). *On Aphasia*. New York: International Universities Press, 1953.

Freud, S. (1894). Draft H. Paranoia. In *The Complete Letters of Sigmund Freud to Wilhelm Fliess, 1887–1904*. Cambridge, MA: Belknap Press/Harvard University Press, 1985, pp. 107–112.

Freud, S. (1900). *The Interpretation of Dreams. Standard Edition*, 4–5.

Freud, S. (1901). On dreams. *Standard Edition*, 5: 629–686.

Freud, S. (1905a). Fragment of an analysis of a case of hysteria. *Standard Edition*, 7.

Freud, S. (1905b). Jokes and their relation to the unconscious. *Standard Edition*, 8: 1–247.

Freud, S. (1910a). The future prospects of psycho-analytic therapy. *Standard Edition*, 11: 139–151.

Freud, S. (1910b). Session of the Vienna Society, 9 March 1910. In H. Nunberg & E. Federn (Eds.), *Minutes of the Vienna Psychoanalytic Society, Volume II: 1908–1910*. New York: International Universities Press, 1967.

Freud, S. (1911). Formulations on the two principles of mental functioning. *Standard Edition*, 12: 215–226.

Freud, S. (1912). Recommendations to physicians practising psycho-analysis. *Standard Edition*, 12: 109–120.

Freud, S. (1914). Remembering, repeating and working-through. *Standard Edition*, 12: 147–156.

Freud, S. (1915a). Observations on transference love. *Standard Edition*, 12: 157–171.

Freud, S. (1915b). Instincts and their vicissitudes. *Standard Edition*, 14: 111–140.

Freud, S. (1915c). The unconscious. *Standard Edition*, 14: 159–215.

Freud, S. (1917). A metapsychological supplement to the theory of dreams. *Standard Edition*, 14: 217–235.

Freud, S. (1918). From the history of an infantile neurosis. *Standard Edition*, 17: 1–124.

Freud, S. (1919). The uncanny. *Standard Edition*, 17: 217–256.

Freud, S. (1920). *Beyond the Pleasure Principle. Standard Edition*, 18, 3–64.

Freud, S. (1922). Dreams and telepathy. *Standard Edition*, 18: 195–220.

Freud, S. (1923a). *The Ego and the Id. Standard Edition*, 19: 3–66.

Freud, S. (1923b). Two encyclopaedia articles. *Standard Edition*, 18: 233–259.

Freud, S. (1925). Negation. *Standard Edition*, 19: 233–240.

Freud, S. (1926). *Inhibitions, Symptoms and Anxiety. Standard Edition*, 20: 77–174.

Freud, S. (1942). Psychopathic characters on the stage. *Psychoanalytic Quarterly*, 11: 459–464.

Frie, R., & Reis, B. (2001). Understanding intersubjectivity: Psychoanalytic formulations and their philosophical underpinnings. *Contemporary Psychoanalysis*, 37: 297–327.

Friedman, H. (2009). Review of Paul Wachtel, *Relational Theory and the Practice of Psychotherapy. Psychoanalytic Quarterly*, 78: 1206–1210.

Friedman, T. (2005). *The World Is Flat.* New York: Farrar, Straus & Giroux.

Garcia Marquez, G. (2005). *Memories of My Melancholy Whores.* New York: Knopf.

Garma, A. (1946). The traumatic situation in the genesis of dreams. *International Journal of Psychoanalysis*, 27: 134–139.

Garma, A. (1955). Vicissitudes of the dream screen and the Isakower phenomenon. *Psychoanalytic Quarterly*, 24: 369–382.

Gediman, H., & Wolkenfeld, F. (1980). The parallelism phenomenon in psychoanalysis and supervision: Its reconsideration as a triadic system. *Psychoanalytic Quarterly*, 49: 234–255.

Gerzi, S. (2005). Trauma, narcissism and the two attractors in trauma. *International Journal of Psychoanalysis*, 86: 1033–1050.

Gibb, E. (1998). Dreaming after a traumatic bereavement: Mourning or its avoidance. In: C. Garland (Ed.), *Understanding Trauma: A Psychoanalytic Approach* (2nd edition). London: Karnac (Tavistock Clinic series), pp. 123–138.

Gooch, J. (2002). The primitive somatopsychic roots of gender formation and intimacy: Sensuality, symbolism, and passion in the development of mind. In: S. Alhanati (Ed.), *Primitive Mental States, Vol. II: Psychobiological and Psychoanalytic Perspectives on Early Trauma and Personality Development*. London: Karnac, pp. 159–173.

Gray, P. (1994). *The Ego and Analysis of Defense.* Northvale, NJ: Jason Aronson.

Green, A. (1974). Surface analysis, deep analysis (the role of the preconscious in psychoanalytical technique). *International Review of Psychoanalysis*, 1: 415–423.

Green, A. (2000). The intrapsychic and intersubjective in psychoanalysis. *Psychoanalytic Quarterly*, 69: 1–39.

Greenberg, J., & Mitchell, S. (2000). *Object Relations in Psychoanalytic Theory*. Cambridge, MA: Harvard University Press.

Grinberg, L. (1962). On a specific aspect of countertransference due to the patient's projective identification. *International Journal of Psychoanalysis*, 43: 436–440.

Grinberg, L. (1990). *The Goals of Psychoanalysis: Identification, Identity and Supervision*. London: Karnac.

Grosskurth, P. (1986). *Melanie Klein: Her Life and Her Work*. New York: Jason Aronson.

Grotstein, J. (1981). *Do I Dare Disturb the Universe? A Memorial to Wilfred R. Bion*. Beverly Hills, CA: Caesura Press.

Grotstein, J. (1997). Integrating one-person and two-person psychologies: Autochthony and alterity in counterpoint. *Psychoanalytic Quarterly*, 66: 403–429.

Grotstein, J. (1999). Projective identification reassessed: Commentary on papers by Stephen Seligman and by Robin C. Silverman and Alicia F. Lieberman. *Psychoanalytic Dialogues*, 9: 187–203.

Grotstein, J. (2000). *Who Is the Dreamer Who Dreams the Dream?* Hillsdale, NJ: Analytic Press.

Grotstein, J. (2004). The seventh servant: The implications of a truth drive in Bion's theory of "O." *International Journal of Psychoanalysis*, 85: 1081–1101.

Grotstein, J. (2005). "Projective transidentification": An extension of the concept of projective identification. *International Journal of Psychoanalysis*, 85: 1051–1069.

Grotstein, J. (2007). *A Beam of Intense Darkness: Wilfred Bion's Legacy to Psychoanalysis*. London: Karnac.

Grotstein, J. (2009a). Dreaming as a "curtain of illusion": Revisiting the "royal road" with Bion as our guide. *International Journal of Psychoanalysis*, 90: 733–752.

Grotstein, J. (2009b). "... *But at the Same Time and on Another Level ...*", Vol. I: *Psychoanalytic Theory and Technique in the Kleinian/Bionian Mode*. London: Karnac.

Grotstein, J. (2009c). "... *But at the Same Time and on Another Level ...*", Vol. II: *Clinical Applications in the Kleinian/Bionian Mode*. London: Karnac.

Grubrich-Simitis, I. (1986). Six letters of Sigmund Freud and Sandor Ferenczi on the interrelationship of psychoanalytic theory and technique. *International Review of Psychoanalysis*, 13: 259–277.

Harrison, T. (2000). *Bion, Rickman, Foulkes and the Northfield Experiments*. London: Jessica Kingsley.

Hartmann, H. (1958). *Ego Psychology and the Problem of Adaptation*. New York: International Universities Press.

Heenen-Wolff, S. (2005). The countertransference dream. *International Journal of Psychoanalysis*, 86: 1543–1558.

Heimann, P. (1950). On counter-transference. *International Journal of Psychoanalysis*, 31: 81–84.

Herzog, J. (1991). "Early Interaction and Representation: The Father's Role in Early and Later Triads, the Father as Expediter from Dyad to Triad." Unpublished paper presented in Basel, Switzerland.

Herzog, J. (2001). *Father Hunger: Explorations with Adults and Children*. Hillsdale, NJ: Analytic Press.

Hoffman, I. (2006). The myths of free association and the potentials of the analytic relationship. *International Journal of Psychoanalysis*, 87: 43–61.

Ingham, G. (1998). Mental work in a trauma patient. In C. Garland (Ed.), *Understanding Trauma: A Psychoanalytic Approach* (2nd edition). London: Karnac (Tavistock Clinic Series), pp. 96–107.

Isaacs, S. (1948). The nature and function of phantasy. *International Journal of Psychoanalysis*, 29: 73–97. Also in P. King & R. Steiner (Eds.), *The Freud–Klein Controversies 1941–45*. New York: Routledge, 1991, pp. 199–243.

Isakower, O. (1938). A contribution to the psycho-pathology of phenomena associated with falling asleep. *International Journal of Psychoanalysis*, 19: 331–345.

Isakower, O. (1957). Chapter two: Preliminary thoughts on the analyzing instrument. *Journal of Clinical Psychoanalysis*, 6 (1992): 184–194.

Isakower, O. (1963a). Chapter three: Preliminary thoughts on the analyzing instrument: A Faculty discussion—October 14th, 1963. *Journal of Clinical Psychoanalysis*, 6 (1992): 195–199.

Isakower, O. (1963b). Chapter four: The analyzing instrument: Further thoughts. *Journal of Clinical Psychoanalysis*, 6 (1992): 200–203.

Isakower, O. (1963c). Chapter five: The analyzing instrument: States of consciousness and the dream psychology of Dr. Bertram Lewis. *Journal of Clinical Psychoanalysis*, 6 (1992): 204–208.

Isakower, O. (1963d). Chapter six: The analyzing instrument: An illustrative example—a student's account of a period of analysis and supervision: "The Mona Lisa Theme." *Journal of Clinical Psychoanalysis*, 6 (1992): 209–215.

Jacobs, T. (1983). The analyst and the patient's object world: Notes on an aspect of countertransference. *Journal of the American Psychoanalytic Association*, 31: 619–642.

Jacobs, T. (1986). On countertransference enactments. *Journal of the American Psychoanalytic Association*, 34: 289–307.

Jacobs, T. (1991). *The Use of the Self: Countertransference and Communication in the Analytic Situation*. New York: International Universities Press.

Jacobs, T. (1992). Isakower's ideas of the analytic instrument and contemporary views of analytic listening. *Journal of Clinical Psychoanalysis*, 1: 237–241.

Jacobs, T. (2007). Review of "The Metapsychology of the Analyst" by Robert Fliess. *Psychoanalytic Quarterly*, 76: 715–724.

Jaques, E. (1979). *The Collected Papers of Roger Money-Kyrle*: Edited by Donald Meltzer [review]. *International Review of Psychoanalysis*, 6: 383–384.

Joseph, B. (1971). A clinical contribution to the analysis of a perversion. *International Journal of Psychoanalysis*, 52: 441–449. Also in M. Feldman & E. Spillius (Eds.), *Psychic Equilibrium and Psychic Change: Selected Papers of Betty Joseph*. New York: Routledge, 1989, pp. 51–66.

Joseph, B. (1975). The patient who is difficult to reach. In M. Feldman & E. Spillius (Eds.), *Psychic Equilibrium and Psychic Change: Selected Papers of Betty Joseph*. New York: Routledge, 1989, pp. 75–87.

Joseph, B. (1985). Transference: The total situation. *International Journal of Psychoanalysis*, 66: 447–454. Also in M. Feldman & E. Spillius (Eds.), *Psychic Equilibrium and Psychic Change: Selected Papers of Betty Joseph*. New York: Routledge, 1989, pp. 156–167.

Joseph, B. (1987). Projective identification: Some clinical aspects. In M. Feldman & E. Spillius (Eds.), *Psychic Equilibrium and Psychic Change: Selected Papers of Betty Joseph*. New York: Routledge, 1989, pp. 168–180.

Kancyper, L. (2005). The confrontation between generations as a dynamic field. In S. Lewkowicz & S. Flechner (Eds.). *Truth, Reality, and the Psychoanalyst: Latin American Contributions to Psychoanalysis*. London: International Psychoanalytical Association, pp. 72–86.

Kantrowitz, J. L. (1993). The uniqueness of the patient–analyst pair: Approaches for elucidating the analyst's role. *International Journal of Psychoanalysis*, 74: 893–904.

Kantrowitz, J. L. (1995). The beneficial aspects of the patient-analyst match. *International Journal of Psychoanalysis*, 76: 299–313.

Kantrowitz, J. L. (1999). The role of the preconscious in psychoanalysis. *Journal of the American Psychoanalytic Association*, 47: 65–89.

Kantrowitz, J. L. (2001). The analysis of preconscious phenomena and its communication. *Psychoanalytic Inquiry*, 21: 24–39.

Kernberg, O. (1967). Borderline personality organization. In *Borderline Conditions and Pathological Narcissism*. New York: Jason Aronson, 1975, pp. 3–47.

Kernberg, O. (2006). The coming changes in psychoanalytic education: Part I. *International Journal of Psychoanalysis*, 87: 1649–1683.

Khan, M. (1963). The concept of cumulative trauma. *Psychoanalytic Study of the Child*, 18: 286–306.

King, P. (2003). The rediscovery of John Rickman and his work. In P. King (Ed.), *No Ordinary Psychoanalyst: The Exceptional Contributions of John Rickman*. London: Karnac, pp. 1–68.

King, P., & Steiner, R. (Eds.) (1991). *The Freud–Klein Controversies 1941–45*. New York: Routledge.

Klein, M. (1924/1925). *Lecture about Erna*. Unpublished manuscript, Melanie Klein Trust Archives, London.

Klein, M. (1926). Infant analysis. *International Journal of Psychoanalysis*, 7: 31–63.

Klein, M. (1928). Early stages of the Oedipus complex. In *Love, Guilt and Reparation*. London: Hogarth Press, 1975, pp. 186–198.

Klein, M. (1930). The importance of symbol-formation in the development of the ego. *International Journal of Psychoanalysis*, 11: 24–39.

Klein, M. (1932). *The Psychoanalysis of Children*. London: Hogarth Press, 1975.

Klein, M. (1935). A contribution to the psychogenesis of manic-depressive states. In *Love, Guilt and Reparation*. London: Hogarth Press, 1975, pp. 262–289.

Klein, M. (1945). The Oedipus complex in the light of early anxieties. In *Love, Guilt and Reparation*. London: Hogarth Press, 1975, pp. 370–419.

Klein, M. (1946). Notes on some schizoid mechanisms. In *Envy and Gratitude*. London: Hogarth Press, 1975, pp. 1–24.

Klein, M. (1961). *Narrative of a Child Analysis*. London: Hogarth Press.

Kohut, H. (1971). *The Analysis of the Self*. New York: International Universities Press.

Kris, E. (1936). The psychology of caricature. *International Journal of Psychoanalysis*, 17: 285–303.

Kris, E. (1950). On preconscious mental processes. *Psychoanalytic Quarterly*, 19: 540–560.

Krohn, A. (1974). Borderline "empathy" and differentiation of object representations. *International Journal of Psychoanalytic Psychotherapy*, 3: 142–165.

Lacan, J. (1977). *Ecrits*, trans. A. Sheridan. New York: W. W. Norton.

Langer, M. (1957). La interpretacion basada en la vivencia contratransferencial de conexion o desconexion con el analizado. *Revista de Psicoanálisis*, 14.

Langer, M., Puget, J., & Teper, E. (1964). A methodological approach to the teaching of psycho-analysis. *International Journal of Psychoanalysis*, 45: 567–574.

Langs, R. (1982). Supervisory crises and dreams from supervisees. *Contemporary Psychoanalysis*, 18: 575–612.

Laub, D. (2006). *Traumatic Psychosis—Narrative Forms of the Muted Witness*. Unpublished manuscript.

Laub, D., & Auerhahn, N. (1993). Knowing and not knowing massive psychic trauma: Forms of traumatic memory. *International Journal of Psychoanalysis*, 74: 287–302.

Laub, D., & Podell D. (1995). Art and trauma. *International Journal of Psychoanalysis*, 76: 991–1005.

Levine, H. (2008). Review of Botella & Botella "The Work of Psychic Figurability: Mental States without Representation." *Psychoanalytic Quarterly*, 77: 639–648.

Levine, H. (2011). The consolation which is drawn from truth: The analysis of a patient unable to suffer experience. In C. Mawson (Ed.), *Bion Today*. Hove: Routledge, pp. 188–211.

Levine, H., & Friedman, R. (2000). Intersubjectivity and interaction in the analytic relationship: A mainstream view. *Psychoanalytic Quarterly*, 9: 63–92.

Lewin, B. D., & Ross, H. (1960). *Psychoanalytic Education in the United States*. New York: W. W. Norton.

Lewin, K. (1935). *A Dynamic Theory of Personality*. New York: McGraw-Hill.

Likierman, M. (1993). Primitive object love in Melanie Klein's thinking: Early theoretical influences. *International Journal of Psychoanalysis*, 74: 241–253.

Little, M. (1951). Counter-transference and the patient's response to it. *International Journal of Psychoanalysis*, 32: 32–40.

Loewald, H. (1960). On the therapeutic action of psychoanalysis. In *Papers on Psychoanalysis*. New Haven, CT: Yale University Press, 1980, pp. 221–256.

Loewald, H. (1980). The waning of the Oedipus complex. In *Papers on Psychoanalysis*. New Haven, CT: Yale University Press, pp. 384–404.

Lothane, Z. (1994). The analyzing instrument and reciprocal free association. *Journal of Clinical Psychoanalysis*, 8: 65–86.

Lothane, Z. (2006). Reciprocal free association: Listening with the third ear as an instrument in psychoanalysis. *Psychoanalytic Psychology*, 23: 711–727.

Mahler, M., Pine, F., & Bergman, A. (1975). *The Psychological Birth of the Human Infant*. New York: Basic Books.

Maldonado, J. L. (1984). Analyst involvement in the psychoanalytical impasse. *International Journal of Psychoanalysis*, 65: 263–271.

Marshall, R. (1997). The interactional triad in supervision. In M. Rock (Ed.), *Psychodynamic Supervision*. Northvale, NJ: Jason Aronson, pp. 77–101.

Matte Blanco, I. (1941). On introjection and the processes of psychic metabolism. *International Journal of Psychoanalysis*, 22: 17–36.

Mitchell, S. (1998). The analyst's knowledge and authority. *Psychoanalytic Quarterly*, 67: 1–31.

Mitrani, J. (2001). "Taking the transference": Some technical implications in three papers by Bion. *International Journal of Psychoanalysis*, 82: 1085–1104.

Modell, A. (1984). *Psychoanalysis in a New Context*. New York: International Universities Press.

Mollon, P. (1989). Anxiety, supervision and a space for thinking: Some narcissistic perils for clinical psychologists in learning psychotherapy. *British Journal of Medical Psychology*, 62: 113–122.

Money-Kyrle, R. (1956). Normal counter-transference and some of its deviations. *International Journal of Psychoanalysis*, 37: 360–366.

Morales, E. (1995). *The Guinea Pig: Healing, Food, and Ritual in the Andes*. Tucson, AZ: University of Arizona Press.

Myers, W. (1987). Work on countertransference facilitated by self-analysis of the analyst's dreams. In A. Rothstein (Ed.), *The Interpretation of Dreams in Clinical*

Work. New York: International Universities Press (American Psychoanalytic Association Workshop Series, Monograph 3), pp. 37–46.

Nicolson, J. (2009). *The Great Silence 1918–1920: Living in the Shadow of the Great War*. London: Murray.

Ogden, T. (1983). The concept of internal object relations. *International Journal of Psychoanalysis*, 64: 227–241.

Ogden, T. (1989). The concept of an autistic–contiguous position. *International Journal of Psychoanalysis*, 70: 127–140.

Ogden, T. (1994a). The analytic third – working with intersubjective analytic facts. *International Journal of Psychoanalysis*, 75: 3–20.

Ogden, T. (1994b). *Subjects of Analysis*. Northvale, NJ: Jason Aronson.

Ogden, T. (1996). Reconsidering three aspects of psychoanalytic technique. *International Journal of Psychoanalysis*, 77: 883–899.

Ogden, T. (1997a). Reverie and metaphor: Some thoughts about how I work as a psychoanalyst. *International Journal of Psychoanalysis*, 78: 719–732.

Ogden, T. (1997b). Reverie and interpretation: Henry James (1884). *Psychoanalytic Quarterly*, 66: 567–595.

Ogden, T. (2001). *Conversations at the Frontier of Dreaming*. Northvale, NJ: Jason Aronson.

Ogden, T. (2003a). What's true and whose idea was it? *International Journal of Psychoanalysis*, 84: 593–606.

Ogden, T. (2003b). On not being able to dream. *International Journal of Psychoanalysis*, 84: 17–30.

Ogden, T. (2004a). An introduction to the reading of Bion. *International Journal of Psychoanalysis*, 85: 285–300.

Ogden, T. (2004b). This art of psychoanalysis: Dreaming undreamt dreams and interrupted cries. *International Journal of Psychoanalysis*, 85: 857–877.

Ogden, T. (2005). On psychoanalytic supervision. *International Journal of Psychoanalysis*, 86: 1265–1280.

Ogden, T. (2007). On talking-as-dreaming. *International Journal of Psychoanalysis*, 88: 575–589.

O'Shaughnessy, E. (1988). The invisible Oedipus complex. In E. Spillius (Ed.). *Melanie Klein Today, Vol. 2: Mainly Practice*. New York: Routledge, pp. 191–205.

O'Shaughnessy, E. (1992). Enclaves and excursions. *International Journal of Psychoanalysis*, 73: 603–611.

O'Shaughnessy, E. (1999). Relating to the superego. *International Journal of Psychoanalysis*, 80: 861–870.

Paniagua, C. (1991). Patient's surface, clinical surface and working surface. *Journal of the American Psychoanalytic Association*, 39: 669–685.

Parisi, M., & Ruberti, L. (2009). "The Use of Alpha Function in Analytical Construction." Paper presented at the International Psychoanalytical Association Congress, Chicago.

Parsons, M. (1999). The logic of play in psychoanalysis. *International Journal of Psychoanalysis*, 80: 871–884.

Pergeron, J. (1996). Supervision as an analytic experience. *Psychoanalytic Quarterly*, 65: 693–710.

Phillips, S. (2006). Paul Gray's narrowing scope: A "developmental lag" in his theory and technique. *Journal of the American Psychoanalytic Association*, 54: 137–170.

Poland, W. (1992). From analytic surface to analytic space. *Journal of the American Psychoanalytic Association*, 40: 381–404.

Poland, W. (2000). The analyst's witnessing and otherness. *Journal of the American Psychoanalytic Association*, 48: 17–34.

Pray, M. (2002). The classical/relational schism and psychic conflict. *Journal of the American Psychoanalytic Association*, 50: 250–280.

Quinodoz, J. (1994). Transference of the transference in supervisions: Transference and countertransference between the candidate-analyst and analysand when acted out in the supervision. *Journal of Clinical Psychoanalysis*, 3: 593–606.

Racker, H. (1953). A contribution to the problem of counter-transference. *International Journal of Psychoanalysis*, 34: 313–324. Also published as "The countertransference neurosis," in *Transference and Countertransference*. New York: International Universities Press, 1968, pp. 105–126.

Racker, H. (1957). The meanings and uses of countertransference. *Psychoanalytic Quarterly*, 26: 303–357. Also in *Transference and Countertransference*. New York: International Universities Press, 1968, pp. 127–173.

Racker, H. (1968). *Transference and Countertransference*. New York: International Universities Press.

Rangell, L. (2002). The theory of psychoanalysis: Vicissitudes of its evolution. *Journal of the American Psychoanalytic Association*, 50: 1109–1137.

Reed, G., & Levine, H. (2004). The politics of exclusion. *Psychoanalytic Inquiry*, 24: 122–138.

Reeder, J. (2004). *Hate and Love in Psychoanalytic Institutes*. New York: Other Press.

Reik, T. (1937). *Surprise and the Psycho-Analyst*. New York: E. P. Dutton.

Reik, T. (1948). *Listening with the Third Ear: The Inner Experiences of a Psycho-analyst*. New York: Grove Press.

Renik, O. (1993). Analytic interaction: Conceptualizing technique in light of the analyst's irreducible subjectivity. *Psychoanalytic Quarterly*, 62: 553–571.

Renik, O. (1995). The ideal of the anonymous analyst and the problem of self-disclosure. *Psychoanalytic Quarterly*, 64: 466–495.

Renik, O. (2004). Intersubjectivity in psychoanalysis. *International Journal of Psychoanalysis*, 85: 1053–1056.

Renik, O. (2007). Intersubjectivity, therapeutic action, and analytic technique. *Psychoanalytic Quarterly*, 76: 1547–1562.

Ricci, W. (1995). Self and intersubjectivity in the supervisory process. *Bulletin of the Menninger Clinic*, 59: 53–68.

Rickman, J. (1945). *Contribution to the Discussion of Dr. W. R. Bion's Paper on "Intra-group Tensions in Therapy: Their Study a Task of the Group," given to the Medical Section of the British Psychological Society, 19 December 1945.* Rickman Papers, Archives of the British Psycho-Analytic Society.

Rickman, J. (1951). Number and the human sciences. In *Selected Contributions to Psycho-Analysis.* London: Hogarth Press (International Psychoanalytical Library, 52), 1957, pp. 218–223.

Robertson, B., & Yack, M. (1993). A candidate dreams of her patient: A report and some observations of the supervisory process. *International Journal of Psychoanalysis*, 74: 993–1003.

Rolnik, E. J. (2008). "Why is it that I see everything differently?" Reading a 1933 letter from Paula Heimann to Theodor Reik. *Journal of the American Psychoanalytic Association*, 56: 409–430.

Rose, G. (1995). *Necessary Illusion: Art as Witness.* Madison, CT: International Universities Press.

Rosenfeld, H. (1987). *Impasse and Interpretation.* London: Routledge.

Rudge, A.-M. (1998). A countertransference dream: An instrument to deal with a difficult transference situation. *International Forum of Psychoanalysis*, 7: 105–111.

Sachs, D. M., & Shapiro, S. H. (1976). On parallel processes in therapy and teaching. *Psychoanalytic Quarterly*, 45: 394–415.

Salomonnson, B. (2007). Semiotic transformations in psychoanalysis with infants and adults. *International Journal of Psychoanalysis*, 88: 1201–1221.

Sandler, J. (1976). Countertransference and role-responsiveness. *International Review of Psychoanalysis*, 3: 43–47.

Sandler, J., & Rosenblatt, B. (1962). The concept of the representational world. *Psychoanalytic Study of the Child*, 17: 128–145.

Sandler, J., & Sandler, A. (1992). Psychoanalytic technique and theory of psychic change. *Bulletin of the Anna Freud Centre*, 15: 35–51.

Sandler, P. (2000). What is thinking – an attempt at an integrated study of W. R. Bion's contributions to the processes of knowing. In P. Bion Talamo, F. Borgogno, & S. Merciai (Eds.), *W. R. Bion: Between Past and Future.* London: Karnac.

Sartre, P. (1964). *Nausea.* New York: New Directions.

Scalzone, F., & Zontini, G. (2001). The dream's navel between chaos and thought. *International Journal of Psychoanalysis*, 82: 263–282.

Schafer, R. (2000). Reflections on "thinking in the presence of the other." *International Journal of Psychoanalysis*, 81: 85–96.

Schafer, R. (2007). On "The metapsychology of the analyst" by Robert Fliess. *Psychoanalytic Quarterly*, 76: 607–714.

Schore A. (2002). Clinical implications of a psychoneurobiological model of projective identification. In: S. Alhanati (Ed.), *Primitive Mental States, Vol. II: Psychobiological and Psychoanalytic Perspectives on Early Trauma and Personality Development.* London: Karnac, pp. 1–65.

Searles, H. (1955). The informational value of the supervisor's emotional experiences. *Psychiatry,* 18: 135–146.

Shapiro, T. (2008). Ubiquitous daydreams and unconscious fantasy: A reassessment of Arlow's "Unconscious Fantasy and Disturbances of Conscious Experience." *Psychoanalytic Quarterly,* 77: 47–59.

Sharpless, E. (1990). The evolution of triadic object relations in the preoedipal phase: Contributions of developmental research. *Psychoanalysis & Contemporary Thought,* 13: 459–483.

Shill, M. (2008). "Intersubjectivity and the Ego." Paper presented at the American Psychoanalytic Association Winter Meeting, New York, 20 January.

Smith, H. (1995). Analytic listening and the experience of surprise. *International Journal of Psychoanalysis,* 76: 67–78.

Smith, H. (1997). Resistance, enactment, and interpretation: A self-analytic study. *Psychoanalytic Inquiry,* 17: 13–30.

Smith, H. (1999). Subjectivity and objectivity in analytic listening. *Journal of the American Psychoanalytic Association,* 47: 465–484.

Spencer, J., Balter, L., & Lothane, Z. (1992). Otto Isakower and the analyzing instrument. *Journal of Clinical Psychoanalysis,* 6: 246–260.

Spillius, E. B. (1989). *Psychic Equilibrium and Psychic Change: Selected Papers of Betty Joseph.* London: Routledge (New Library of Psychoanalysis, 9), pp. 1–222.

Spillius, E. B. (2004). Comments on Owen Renik's "Intersubjectivity in Psychoanalysis." *International Journal of Psychoanalysis,* 85: 1057–1061.

Spillius, E. B. (2007). Melanie Klein revisited: Her unpublished thoughts on technique. In *Encounters with Melanie Klein: Selected Papers of Elizabeth Spillius.* New York: Routledge.

Steiner, J. (1993). *Psychic Retreats.* New York: Routledge.

Sterba, R. (1934). The fate of the ego in analytic therapy. *International Journal of Psychoanalysis,* 15: 117–126.

Stern, Dan. (1985). *The Interpersonal World of the Infant.* New York: Basic Books.

Stern, Dan. (2004). *The Present Moment in Psychotherapy and Everyday Life.* New York: W. W. Norton.

Stern, Dan, Sander, L., Nahum, J., Harrison, A., Lyons-Ruth, K., Morgan, A., et al. (1998). Non-interpretive mechanisms in psychoanalytic therapy. The "something more" than interpretation. *International Journal of Psychoanalysis,* 79: 903–921.

Stimmel, B. (1995). Resistance to awareness of the supervisor's transference with special reference to the parallel process. *International Journal of Psychoanalysis,* 76: 608–618.

Stix, G. (2008). Traces of a distant past. *Scientific American Magazine,* 299: 56–63.

Stolorow, R. (1994b). Subjectivity and self psychology. In R. Stolorow, G. Atwood, & B. Brandchaft (Eds.), *The Intersubjective Perspective*. Northvale, NJ: Jason Aronson, pp. 31–39.

Stolorow, R., Atwood, G., & Ross (1978). The representational world in psychoanalytic therapy. *International Review of Psychoanalysis*, 5: 247–256.

Storch, (1924). *The Primitive and Archaic Forms of Inner Experiences and Thought in Schizophrenics*. Washington, DC: Nervous and Mental Disease Publishing Company.

Symington J., & Symington N. (1996). *The Clinical Thinking of Wilfred Bion*. New York: Routledge.

Tarantelli, C. (2003). Life within death: Towards a metapsychology of catastrophic psychic trauma. *International Journal of Psychoanalysis*, 84: 915–928.

Tronick, E. (2005). Why is connection with others so critical? The formation of dyadic states of consciousness: Coherence governed selection and the co-creation of meaning. In J. Nadel & D. Muir (Eds.), *Emotional Development*. Oxford: Oxford University Press, pp. 293–315.

Tronick, E. (2007). *The Neurobehavioral and Social-Emotional Development of Infants and Children*. New York: W. W. Norton.

Tronick, E., Brushweiller-Stern, N., Harrison, A. M., Lyons-Ruth, K., Morgan, A. C., Nahum, J. P., et al. (1998). Dyadically expanded states of consciousness and the process of therapeutic change. *Infant Mental Health Journal*, 19: 290–299.

Tustin, F. (1980). Autistic objects. *International Review of Psychoanalysis*, 7: 27–39.

Tustin, F. (1991). Revised understandings of psychogenic autism. *International Journal of Psychoanalysis*, 72: 585–591.

Ungar, V., & Ahumada, L. (2001). Supervision: A container-contained approach. *International Journal of Psychoanalysis*, 82: 71–81.

Volkan, V. (1976). *Primitive Internalized Object Relations*. New York: International Universities Press.

Von Klitzing, K., Simoni, H., & Burgin, D. (1999). Child development and early triadic relationships. *International Journal of Psychoanalysis*, 80: 71–89.

Wallerstein, R. (2005). Will psychoanalytic pluralism be an enduring state of our discipline? *International Journal of Psychoanalysis*, 86: 623–626.

Weiss, H. (2002). Reporting a dream accompanying an enactment in the transference situation. *International Journal of Psychoanalysis*, 83: 633–645.

Windholz, E. (1970). The theory of supervision in psychoanalytic education. *International Journal of Psychoanalysis*, 51: 393–406.

Winnicott, D. W. (1949). Hate in the countertransference. *International Journal of Psychoanalysis*, 30: 69–74.

Winnicott, D. W. (1965). *The Maturational Processes and the Facilitating Environment: Studies in the Theory of Emotional Development*. London: Hogarth Press.

Winnicott, D. W. (1953). Transitional objects and transitional phenomena. *International Journal of Psychoanalysis*, 34: 89–97.

Winnicott, D. W. (1974). Fear of breakdown. *International Review of Psychoanalysis*, 1: 103–107.

Wyman, H. M., & Rittenberg, S. M. (1992). The analyzing instrument of Otto Isakower, M. D. Evolution of a concept. *Journal of Clinical Psychoanalysis*, 1: 165–316.

Zwiebel, R. (1985). The dynamics of the countertransference dream. *International Review of Psychoanalysis*, 12: 87–99.

Index

Abraham, K. 11, 23–26, 28, 41, 45, 48–50, 60, 72, 73, 80, 142

"absolute truth", concept of 17

abuse, sexual 185, 230, 231, 232, 233

acting out 63, 163, 187

adolescent analysis, termination phase of 213; clinical illustration 185–194

affect regulation 146, 163

Aguayo, J. 49

alpha (α) element(s) 69, 71, 73, 86, 87, 98, 116–118, 121–123, 133, 151, 164, 170–175; and dream narratives 122; regression to β elements 161, 162

alpha (α) function(s) 11, 12, 72, 73, 82–91, 94–95, 98–108, 116–128, 134–135, 150, 157, 161–165, 169–177, 202, 228; analyst's 136, 156; apparatus of 119, 122, 151; concept of 119, 174; crippling of 163; definition 118–121; and dreaming 120–124; as ego function 117; linked, of analysand and analyst 106; mother's 86, 87, 88, 119, 135; procreative model of 120; transformation, of beta elements into alpha elements 173

altruistic identification 227, 231, 234

altruistic surrender 234

American Psychoanalytic Association 34, 46

American relational school/theories/perspectives 9, 12, 102, 103, 144, 228

anal stage 141

analysis: adolescent, termination phase of 213; faux, collusion in 213; mutual 22, 29, 49, 72; reciprocal 22; third area of experience in 69, 74

analyst: alpha function of 136, 156; authority of 10; capacity of [for reverie 94, 95, 122, 170, 172; to think, attack on 151, 156, 157]; childhood of, reconstruction of 39, 45; conscious work of 91; dreaming [the analysis 123, 176, 208; patient into existence 124, 193, 195–216]; emotional coldness of 179; emotional equilibrium of 6, 39; identification of, with projection 58; introjecting patient's projection 59, 73; levels of awareness in, conscious, preconscious, and unconscious 6; metapsychology of 179; and patient [dreaming together 32, 41, 43, 44, 101, 121; intersubjective connection between 70; unconscious stream of communication between 100]; reverie of 73, 74, 105, 106, 209; self-analysis of 15, 33, 38–40, 45, 52, 184, 198, 200, 203, 206, 207, 208, 209; subjectivity of 11, 12, 15, 34, 37, 55, 63, 64, 179 [patient's awareness of 38]; unconscious of, as instrument of analysis 12 [use of 91, 106, 200];